PITT SERIES IN POLICY AND
INSTITUTIONAL STUDIES

The Promise and Paradox of Civil Service Reform

Patricia W. Ingraham and
David H. Rosenbloom, Editors

University of Pittsburgh Press

Pittsburgh and London

Published by the University of Pittsburgh Press, Pittsburgh, Pa., 15260

Manufactured in the United States of America

LIBRARY OF CONGRESS CATALOGING-IN-PUBLICATION DATA

The promise and paradox of civil service reform / Patricia W. Ingraham
    and David H. Rosenbloom, editors.
        p.   cm. —(Pitt series in policy and institutional studies)
    Based on the Symposium on Ten Years of Civil Service Reform held
at the Maxwell School of Citizenship and Public Affairs, Syracuse
University.
    ISBN 0–8229–3716–6
    1. Civil service reform—United States.   2. Civil service—United
States—Personnel management.   3. Government executives—United
States.   I. Ingraham, Patricia W.   II. Rosenbloom, David H.
III. Series.
JK692.P76   1992
353.006—dc20   92—5668
                                                                   CIP

A CIP catalogue record for this book is available from the British Library.

Eurospan, London

Contents

Introduction

Patricia W. Ingraham and David H. Rosenbloom

In 1988, the Civil Service Reform Act of 1978 (CSRA) marked its tenth anniversary. This landmark legislation was hailed at the time of its passage as the first comprehensive reform of federal personnel systems in one hundred years. Alan Campbell, the chairman of the Civil Service Commission, said that passage of the Civil Service Reform Act demonstrated that federal personnel management "was at the top of the nation's policy agenda" (Campbell 1980). The Civil Service Reform Act has implications beyond personnel reform, however. Both the scope of the reform and the rational and comprehensive design process chosen for its pursuit were unusual for the American public policy arena. For this reason alone, the Civil Service Reform Act and its outcomes provide valuable lessons. Of equal significance, the disparity between the promise of the reform and the reality of its implementation provides important evidence of the conflict between political problem solving and the rational model adopted by the reformers.

The CSRA was intended to redesign a system created by one hundred years of accretion and tinkering. From a set of loosely connected parts the Civil Service Reform Act proposed to create a coherent and productive personnel management system. It was also intended, however, to clarify the relationship of the career bureaucracy—particularly senior career managers—to the president and to political appointees. To achieve its purposes, CSRA relied on academic theory, lessons from other governments and—very heavily—on private sector practices. Participation in the design process was broad based and intense; President Jimmy Carter's interest and consistent attention assured the involvement of policymakers from the White House and the Office of Management and Budget. Other participants included career civil servants, academics, and private sector managers and consultants. From the disparate participants came disparate solutions to a set of very complex problems. The legislative package that emerged from the Personnel Management Project, the Civil Service Commission, and the Office of Management and Budget attempted to reconcile—or, in some cases, merely to combine—differences in both problem definitions and proposed solutions.

As originally proposed, the reform package contained the following provisions:

• The abolition of the Civil Service Commission and the creation of the Office of Personnel Management, the Merit Systems Protection Board, and the Federal Labor Relations Authority.
• New and stronger provisions for the protection of whistleblowers.
• Limitations on veterans' preference.
• Creation of a performance evaluation system to increase productivity and establish a link between performance and pay for federal managers.
• Creation of a merit pay system for midlevel managers that, in conjunction with the new performance evaluation system, would reward excellent performers with financial bonuses.
• Creation of the Senior Executive Service. This component of the reform was intended to create a top level of elite generalist managers, much on the model of the British higher service. Members of the SES would become part of a rank-in-person system, compete for financial awards, be eligible for expanded training and development opportunities, and participate more actively in policy formulation and design activities. Ten percent of the total SES positions governmentwide could be filled by political appointees.
• The act created a new research and development authority that was intended to foster innovation and creativity in federal organizations and personnel.
• Finally, the original package reaffirmed the federal government's commitment to affirmative action and to equal employment opportunity. It did not, however, provide new mechanisms to advance these objectives.

Legislative consideration of the bill was modest but did produce some modifications. Two months after initial submission of CSRA, a murky labor relations title was added to the bill in an effort to reduce union opposition. The limits on veteran's preference were removed after heavy lobbying by veterans organizations. Other components of the legislation emerged virtually intact but also virtually unexplored by members of Congress. Alan Campbell described support for the reform as "a mile wide and an inch deep." Some of that support evaporated as quickly as six months after the bill's passage, when Congress reacted to the first SES bonus payouts by cutting in half the number eligible for them.

The environment in which the reform was implemented was turbulent and intensely political. The election of Ronald Reagan, rounds of budget and personnel cuts in most federal agencies, and a heightened emphasis on political management combined with widespread bureaucrat bashing to create distrust and instability. Some components of the act were never implemented; others proceeded in fits and starts to a kind of reform purgatory. On the other hand, new institutions, such as the Office of Personnel Management, were created, as was the Senior Executive Service. Performance appraisal and merit pay were central parts of the reform package and remain high on the personnel policy agenda. If nothing else, the bureaucratic reforms created by CSRA have proven to be bureaucratic survivors, in that many of the issues they raised or responded to remain with us today.

But, in the first decade of the Civil Service Reform Act's history, what has it achieved? Has it been a success, a failure, or perhaps both? The early years of CSRA were turbulent, and early evaluations reflect that instability. Major components of the act—most notably the SES—were often declared a failure. In later years, at least in part because of major staff and budget reductions at the Office of Personnel Management, formal evaluations were less frequent and were, generally, less negative in their conclusions. The environment of later evaluations was tempered by the new political realities of the Reagan administration and its emphasis on political control of the bureaucracy rather than on other reforms.

Never in its history, however, have all the major components of the act been analyzed with emphasis on their collective, rather than individual, impact. This book presents that analysis. Some of the chapters in the book were originally presented at the Symposium on Ten Years of Civil Service Reform at the Maxwell School of Citizenship and Public Affairs, Syracuse University. Discussion and analysis at that conference was lively, and greatly enhanced by the participation of staff from the House Subcommittee on Civil Service, the U.S. General Accounting Office, the Office of Personnel Management, and the U.S. Merit Systems Protection Board. The chapters in this book incorporate, but move beyond those discussions, to include developments that have occurred since the symposium was held. Chapters from experts who were not able to attend the conference have been added to present a comprehensive range of perspectives and analyses of this major effort to change and reform the federal bureaucracy.

We wish to thank the Maxwell School for its support of the initial conference, the *Policy Studies Journal* 17 (1989) for publishing a symposium that included some of the papers presented at the conference, the authors in this volume for their constant interest and willingness to revise and update chapters as new events and legislation created new issues and problems, and the many public managers who commented on various drafts of the chapters in this book and who are, after all, the heroes and the victims it describes.

SOURCE

Campbell, Alan K. 1980. "Civil Service Reform as a Remedy for Bureaucratic Ills." In *Making Bureaucracies Work*, ed. Carol H. Weiss and Allen H. Barton. Beverly Hills, Calif.: Sage.

Part I DESIGNING CHANGE

1. The Reform Game

Patricia W. Ingraham

> This stuff is really boring!
> —Jimmy Carter, describing his reaction to the briefing package on the
> Civil Service Reform Act of 1978

By most accounts, civil service reform is not a spellbinding issue. It deals with the nuts and bolts of personnel administration, merit systems, labor relations, and improved efficiency and productivity of government agencies. Even an advocate so ardent as Jimmy Carter found his eyes glazing over when the reality of reform was discussed. Only in Carter's presidency was civil service reform a major item on the presidential agenda. Virtually every president in this century, however, has described the civil service system as problematic and troublesome; most have expended substantial amounts of time trying to find ways around the system. So, too, have the bureaucrats who must work within its confines. The common frustrations, coupled with the increasingly complex demands placed upon government bureaucracies, have produced a series of incremental reforms, most with the announced intention of making the operation of government more efficient and more productive. The frequency of reform efforts and the variety of techniques employed resemble a game, or a series of experiments: if one technique doesn't produce the desired objectives, another is tried.

The limited nature of these reforms and their consistently technical content have long masked their fundamental purpose: to create a federal bureaucracy competent to serve its critical purpose in democratic government. Mosher summarized the issue

The accretion of specialization and of technological and social complexity seems to be an irreversible trend, one that leads to increasing dependence upon the protected, appointive public service, thrice removed from direct democracy. Herein lies the central and underlying problem . . . how can a public service so constituted be made to operate in a manner compatible with democracy? (Mosher 1968:3)

At least since the New Deal, the major protagonists in the debate around the issue have been the president and the permanent bureaucracy. The president, Schlesinger notes, occupies "the apex of the pyramid of frustration" (Schlesinger 1978:258). He arrives in Washington expecting to achieve at least some of the changes promised in the campaign. The inability to do so quickly—or, in some cases, at all—engenders frustration, anger, and a search for a scapegoat. Very often, that scapegoat turns out to be the permanent bureaucracy. Reform ensues.

Despite March and Olsen's assertion that the rhetoric advocating administrative reorganization and reform emphasizes two purposes— one technical, one political—the presidential desire to achieve better administrative control is nearly always couched in technical or mechanistic terms (March and Olsen 1983: 281–96). Richard Nixon, for example, supported his efforts at major reorganization with the following claim: "Bad mechanisms can frustrate even the noblest aims . . . the major cause of the ineffectiveness of government is not a matter of men or money. It is principally a matter of machinery" (Nixon 1971). Jimmy Carter observed that there was no merit in the merit system, and advocated technical reforms to remedy the situation. Neither president argued that better political controls on the bureaucracy were necessary for better government, yet that is clearly what both men intended. This is not to suggest that the actual performance of the bureaucracy is of no concern to presidents. Improved performance in pursuit of *presidential* objectives is the point, and the end that the technical improvements are intended to achieve.

For its part, the bureaucracy operates with rules and timetables different from those produced by the political process. As bastions of institutional memory and expertise, public bureaucracies view problems, solutions, and actions in a historical context. Elections are only part of a longer term; politicians come and go. They are one aspect of the life and environment of the organization, but the organization and its members will not die when the politician departs. In this classic conflict between stability and change, bureaucrats are lodged firmly in the corner of stability; politicians are not. Their window of opportunity for policy change is brief, and quick action to achieve it is mandatory. Given the demands on both politician and bureaucrat, it is little wonder that the tension between them produces consistent calls for reform.

In the past fifty years, three fundamental issues have been a part of the reform agenda. The first, the definition of the proper role of bureaucracy in the policy process, is a result of the move away from the simplicity and familiarity of the politics-administration dichotomy. The clear separation of politics and administration is not possible for modern government, but no generally accepted replacement has been found. Of the demise of the dichotomy, Mosher writes, "The ideological crutch which segregated policy and politics from administration can today hardly satisfy any but the blind or those who willfully close their eyes" (Mosher 1968:229). He concludes that finding a replacement for the dichotomy is the leading problem of contemporary public administration. It is also a leading problem for those who would reform the civil service.

The second issue underlying modern civil service reform is the relationship between the president and the permanent bureaucracy. Particularly since the New Deal and the report of Franklin Roosevelt's Brownlow Committee, the move toward improved presidential management and control has been a notable characteristic of virtually all reform efforts. Richard Nixon created the "administrative presidency." Jimmy Carter created the Civil Service Reform Act of 1978. Ronald Reagan's efforts, while administrative rather than legislative, were unrivaled in scope and intensity. All of these efforts have been couched in terms of improved management and efficiency; without any doubt, their intent and effect has been to strengthen the Executive Office of the President at the expense of other key actors in the policy system. Frederik Malek, Nixon's director of personnel, addressed the issue head on:

In our constitutional form of government, the executive branch is, and always will be, a political institution. This is not to say that the application of good management practices, sound policy formulation, and the highest calibre of program implementation are not of vital importance. The best politics is still good government. But you cannot achieve management, policy, or program control unless you have established political control. (Malek 1979:160)

This raises the third issue fundamental to civil service reform: what is the role of Congress in relation to the permanent bureaucracy and to the president, in terms of policy making and control? If the other two issues have been masked by the rhetoric of reform, the role of Congress has been nearly obliterated. With the exception of passage of the Civil Service Reform Act of 1978, the congressional role has most often been to reject presidential initiatives. The proposals emanating from the Brownlow Committee foundered in Congress; Richard Nixon's proposals for major reorganization of the federal bureaucracy were essentially ignored.

When it considers the reform issue at all, Congress appears to rely on its role as guardian of merit; that is, protector of the career service from the partisan intrusion of the president and his appointees. Of course, recent presidencies have provided ample cause for alarm in that regard. Nonetheless, the question at the foundation of the merit system—to what extent does a strong central personnel system violate the constitutional powers of both the president and the Congress over personnel matters?—remains relevant today.

Essentially, Congress has answered this question by default. Ripley observes that "the basic congressional response to the fact of a large expert bureaucracy administering hundreds of programs has been to seek influence by cooperating with the bureaucracy most of the time and challenging it only now and then" (Ripley 1978:270). Congress has rejected many presidential initiatives directed at altering the pattern of bureaucratic control and direction, but it has not devised a positive strategy of its own. The questions, of course, go beyond the relationship between the Congress and the bureaucracy. They are essentially constitutional, and relate to the shared responsibility of the president and the Congress for the effective operation and oversight of the executive branch.

These issues are complex and interrelated. To better understand them and their place in the rhetoric and reality of reform, it is useful to examine each in more detail.

Shaping the Role of Bureaucracy in the Public Policy Process

The creation of the federal classified service in 1883 was a major milestone in federal reform. The move away from the spoils system to a set of procedures that ensured a neutral and competent federal service redefined the nature of the relationship between civil servants and elected officials. Political leaders would direct the public bureaucracy; they would not manipulate or abuse its offices. The bureaucracy, in turn, would be responsive to political direction. In Kaufman's terms, the bureaucracy would be "a hammer or a saw; it would do nothing at all by itself, but it would serve any purpose, wise or unwise, good or bad, to which any user put it" (Kaufman 1954:36). This model of the federal service was supported by scientific management theorists, who argued that politics had to be separated from administration if administration was to be efficient.

The growth and increasing complexity of government, the advent of the New Deal, and Franklin Roosevelt's proclivity for administrators who were not neutral experts but advocates of his policies, signaled the end of both scientific management principles and the politics-administration dichotomy. By 1949, Norton Long argued that

there is no more forlorn spectacle in the administrative world than an agency and a program possessed of statutory life, armed with executive orders, sustained in the courts, yet stricken with paralysis and deprived of power. . . . The lifeblood of administration is power. . . . The bureaucracy under the American political system has a large share of responsibility for the public promotion of policy and even more in organizing the political basis for its survival and growth. (Long 1949:257)

This transformation of the "hammer or saw" posed significant problems for both the theory and the practice of government. Practically, the merit system labored under many years' accumulation of incremental and disjointed changes; its configuration and procedures were shaped more by politics than by conscious design. The result was an unwieldy maze of regulations and controls.[1] Franklin Roosevelt avoided the system whenever possible by creating entire agencies outside its purview. Dwight Eisenhower created the Schedule C appointment authority to permit the placement of larger numbers of political appointees in "policy sensitive" positions; the intent was to achieve better understanding and control. For those operating inside the confusing web of merit system rules and regulations, each addition or bypass effort only exacerbated an already difficult problem. The federal service was expected to undertake new and complex tasks—often at the edge of scientific and technological capabilities—within the confines of an overly standardized, constrained, and severely outdated system.

From a political perspective, the problems were no less severe. The federal bureaucracy is perceived, by many elected officials and others, to lack constitutional legitimacy in public policy formation and advocacy. As Mosher notes, a powerful institution "thrice removed" from popular control must be regarded with some suspicion in a democratic society (Mosher 1968:chap 7). At the same time, the stability and expertise of bureaucratic organizations and their members automatically creates influence for them in a rapidly changing political system. Eisner and Meier note:

The growth of bureaucratic discretion and the consequent reduction of presidential and congressional control are seen as highly problematic in a democratic policy . . . [Yet] some argue that greater political control has been eschewed because the expansion of bureaucratic discretion reinforces the goals of elected officials. By transferring power to administrators, politicians minimize personal responsibility while retaining the ability to claim credit and meet the demands of special constituencies. (Eisner and Meier 1990:270)

Eisner and Meier demonstrate that even when concerted presidential efforts, such as those of the Reagan administration, are made to redirect policy outcomes, the bureaucratic role remains very important. Ingraham reports similar findings from the Reagan administration (Ingraham 1990).

The final element of this mélange is the natural tension between the president and the Congress in many policy areas, including bureaucratic reform. Aberbach and Rockman summarize:

It is as though Congress and the central executive were polar magnets. Their distinctive perspectives on reorganization usually are developed around the pole on which they are situated. Occasionally, Congress can be persuaded to allow more opportunities for control to move to the center when the issue seems to be entirely abstract or one that seems to involve only the harmless matters of process that are the passion of professors of public administration. (Aberbach and Rockman 1988:1)

As noted earlier, however, "harmless matters of process" shape bureaucratic competence and ability; they are the stuff of bureaucratic power. That is one reason why technical reforms are a consistent part of civil service reform efforts.

The President and the Bureaucracy

Franklin Roosevelt's appointment of the President's Committee on Administrative Management (the Brownlow Committee) demonstrated his concern for the management problems the New Deal had created. At the same time, his admonition to the committee that he "wanted no surprises" revealed his conviction that strengthening the office of the president was the solution to those problems. The Brownlow report concurred "Canons of efficiency require the establishment of a responsible and effective chief executive as the center of energy, direction, and administrative management" (in Mosher 1976:113). The report recommended sweeping reorganization of agencies in the executive branch, transfer of the Bureau of the Budget directly to the Office of the President, and a greatly increased presidential staff. Arnold notes that "Brownlow assumed that the interests of good administration and the President's interest were overlapping, if not identical (Arnold 1976:117).

The Brownlow Committee report was an unequivocal statement of positive presidential management and control. Egger has labeled it "probably the most important constitutional document of our time" (in Mosher 1975:71). Despite its historic significance, however, it did not achieve all that President Roosevelt had intended. Roosevelt's imbroglio with the Congress over Supreme Court appointments had soured chances for successful presidential initiatives at the time the Brownlow Report was released. This effort at reform represented one of the few real political confrontations over reorganization and reform issues: more than one hundred Democratic congressmen voted against the reorganization bill, thus handing Roosevelt a defeat from a heavily Democratic Congress. That this level of contention is unique is noted by March and Olsen, who observe that "pitched battles have usually been avoided by conventional political bargaining among the parties involved, and most plans for major reorganizations fail to survive normal political trading. Presidents are reluctant to use the reorganization authority they have in the face of opposition. (March and Olsen 1983:285).

Presidents have not, however, been reluctant to *propose* reorganization and reform. President Truman included it in his list of items for priority action, noting that his mail ran heavily in favor of such activity (ibid.:290). The first Hoover Commission, the most successful in this century in terms of legislative approval of recommendations and proposals, provided Truman with additional clout—and unusual success—in his reorganization efforts.

Presidents Eisenhower, Kennedy, and Johnson all appointed or participated in reorganization and reform commissions, but these efforts and decidedly mixed results. The second Hoover Commission coincided with the Eisenhower presidency; Herbert Hoover did not have the same good working relationship with Eisenhower that he had enjoyed with Truman. There was, in fact, considerable friction between the former and the incumbent presidents, including threats by Hoover to "take the Commission's case to the people."[2] Arnold summarizes the outcome. "The tense dance between the partisans of the Hoover Commission and the [Eisenhower] Administration did not end in a neat climax; over time it simply ran down to a stop" (Arnold 1986:200).

President Kennedy's commission never met. Lyndon Johnson's first commission had very poor access to the president and very little support in Congress. It was doomed to the "what else is new?" syndrome. Johnson's second commission, chaired by private sector executive Ben Heineman, had better access to the president (Ingraham 1992). The report of the Heineman Commission was released in 1967, however, when Johnson's attention was riveted on Southeast Asia. The mantle of reform passed to—and was eagerly accepted by—the next president, Richard Nixon.

Nixon's vision of the presidency included elements of control quite beyond those pursued by previous presidents. When he assumed the office after eight years of Democratic presidents, he was convinced that he inherited a permanent bureaucracy ideologically and program matically opposed to him and his policies. The research of Aberbach and Rockman later proved this assessment to be essentially correct (Aberbach and Rockman 1976). Nixon appointed the President's Advisory Council on Executive Organization (commonly called the Ash Council, after its chairman, Roy Ash) shortly after assuming office. The Ash Council recommended sweeping changes in the organization of the executive branch, and additional changes in the Executive Office of the President. The Office of Management and Budget replaced the old Bureau of the Budget; coordination, planning, and management oversight of executive agencies were to be new and very important tasks. Hart describes the purpose in more political terms. It was, he argues, to ensure "greatly improved executive branch responsiveness to presidential priorities" (Hart 1987:79).

The Nixon strategy was multipronged. In addition to the creation of OMB, the Domestic Council was created in the Executive Office of the President. The purpose of this council was to provide better policy control over the domestic agencies. This objective was also the presidential rationale for the reorganization of domestic agencies into four "super departments" and for the creation of block grants, which would replace many of the categorical programs in operation at that time. In addition, the president relied heavily on the placement of political appointees—carefully screened executives and lower level appointees who would not "go native," in John Erlichman's term—throughout the bureaucracy. The top managers of OMB were, for example, political appointees and not the apolitical budget analysts and accountants of previous administrations. Underlying all of these initiatives was a fundamental—indeed, nearly paranoid—distrust of the career bureaucracy and an absolute commitment to bypass or isolate its members whenever possible. Richard Nathan (1975) describes these activities as the "plot that failed." Nixon himself was somewhat grander. "I shall," he said, "ask to change the framework of government itself . . . to reform the entire structure of American government" (1971:51).

Once again, history (or, in this case, perhaps the president himself) intervened. Watergate cut short the administrative presidency; momentarily, at least, it also raised serious questions about the consistent transfer of additional power and control to the president. But memories are short and bureaucratic reforms are innocuous. The potential of the administrative presidency was not lost on future presidents. In his brief time in office Gerald Ford introduced the President's Management Initiatives. These were scuttled by Jimmy Carter, who had campaigned on the promise of comprehensive civil service reform.

Carter was the first president in history to campaign with civil service reform at the top of his policy agenda. Reform was, said Carter, absolutely necessary to "bring the horrible bureaucratic mess under control" and to improve the overall management of the federal government (March and Olsen 1983:290). (Note that in two years' time, the problem of Watergate had become identified with the bureaucracy rather than the president!) Carter's reforms and the processes by which they were designed and adopted are described in detail in later chapters in this book. In the context of overall reform efforts, however, it is important to note how closely the Carter reforms followed the tradition of improved presidential control.

Without any doubt, Jimmy Carter cared about better management. He believed that he had improved the functioning of the Georgia state government in his term as governor and he believed that he could do the same thing in Washington. Better management techniques and procedures were, therefore, an important part of his reform. The rhetoric surrounding the content of the reform was unfailingly technical—the "boring stuff" of this chapter's opening quotation—and many of the reforms were described simply as technical improvements. On the other hand, the structural changes, notably the creation of the Office of Personnel Management with a director appointed by the president, enhanced the control of the president over federal personnel in general. The creation of the Senior Executive Service placed the most senior and most experienced career managers directly under the direct control of political executives. Pay for performance and the merit pay and bonus systems introduced another source of political control over the career bureaucracy that had not previously existed.

In addition, Carter had learned to use larger numbers of political executives for presidential purposes. In his term, the total number of Schedule C political appointees increased 66 percent (Ingraham 1987:427). Overall, the Carter reforms contained all three components of the earlier administrative presidency strategy: reorganization, increased numbers of political appointees in more places in the bureaucracy, and structural changes that gave the president more direct control over critical resources. Carter believed that the changes he was successful in achieving would be effective no matter who held the office of the presidency. He believed, in other words, that his reforms would serve the institution and not the president himself. That confidence was put to a cruel test with the election of Ronald Reagan.

In one of the pithiest assessments of the Civil Service Reform Act of 1978, Aberbach and Rockman observe that it "enabled Reagan to be a successful Richard Nixon (Aberbach and Rockman 1988:7). Reagan came to Washington proclaiming that government was not the solution to the problem: government *was* the problem. The permanent bureaucracy was an obvious and immediate target. The focus in the early Reagan years was on budget and program reduction; there was little emphasis on management. The turbulence of the budget cuts and the reductions in force that accompanied them overwhelmed many of the reform's components. This was particularly true of the more technical components of the reform. When an agency's budget is reduced by 60 percent (as was the Department of Housing and Urban Development's, for example), delegation of examining authority loses its punch (Ingraham 1990).

The parts of the reform that did not lose their punch in this new environment were those related to improved political direction and control. The Senior Executive Service, with its provisions for improved political control, was quickly recognized as a valuable tool. The ability to place political members of the SES in non-policy-sensitive positions enabled implementation in some agencies of "jigsaw puzzle management" (Sanera 1984). In other agencies, the new management flexibilities of CSRA permitted the movement of career executives into insignificant positions and the creation of shadow staff composed of Schedule C political appointees (Ingraham 1987:430–32). The impact of political control of performance or merit bonuses under the new system was also important.

The implementation of specific components of CSRA and their history in the Reagan administration are discussed in other chapters of this book. It is sufficient to note here that the reform not only fit well with previous presidential management strategies, but permitted new levels of control in the Reagan presidency. The heavy emphasis on idealogical fit between political appointees and Reagan policy initiatives provided a clear blueprint for political direction of bureaucratic activities. Increased reliance on larger numbers of lower level political appointees, coupled with the flexibilities that CSRA gave political executives, permitted exclusion of career bureaucrats from many significant program and policy decisions. As the scandals at the Department of Housing and Urban Development demonstrated, however, the absence of a bureaucratic reality check can have serious consequences.

Recent research demonstrates that the federal bureaucracy is a "rather adaptable civil service and civil service system" and one that responds to "an administration [with] a substantial degree of coherence in its overall program goals and its personnel system, and [an apparently] strong political momentum (Aberbach, Copeland, and Rockman 1987:20). President Nixon and his staff did not believe that; neither did presidents Carter and Reagan. Despite some indications that President Bush views the permanent bureaucracy in more favorable terms, the inexorable demand for more presidential power remains. It is safe to predict that future efforts at reform will also carry a heavy political control load.

The Congress and Civil Service Reform

Where, in all of this debate about control, is Congress? The congressional role has most often been slight and frequently one of naysayer to presidential initiatives. In chapter 4, Newland argues that the Civil Service Reform Act was the natural outcome of longer-term changes in the relationship between the president and the Congress; formally marking the shift from the view that the president was responsible for seeing that laws were faithfully executed, sharing over-sight with Congress, to a policy of political control of the civil service by the president.

The report of the Brownlow Committee, and congressional reaction to it, provides an apt example of the dimensions of the change. The report was released in 1937 when, as noted, President Roosevelt's ef-forts at increased presidential power had alienated even members of his own party in Congress. The report's recommendations were rebuffed. Two years later, however, Roosevelt was successful in obtaining pas-sage of the Reorganization Act of 1939. The powers granted the pres-ident by this act served as a cornerstone for later efforts to strengthen the institution of the presidency (the authority was removed after Wa-tergate, but restored in the Carter administration). The basic compo-nents of Brownlow's recommendations, debated so fiercely in 1937 and 1938, were recast by the first Hoover Commission. March and Olsen observe, "Now, a strong, unified executive was considered to be essential to democratic institutions." They conclude, "Different times. Different meanings" (March and Olsen 1983:288). Different mean-ings perhaps, but the beginning of a consistent pattern. The initiative was the president's; the reaction was left to Congress.

After the second Hoover Commission, even the commissions and groups that formulated the proposals for reform were presidential in-itiatives with little—or, more often, no—congressional participation (Ingraham 1992). Richard Nixon came to view Congress as nearly as immovable as the permanent bureaucracy during his attempts to move his reorganization proposals through the legislature (Nathan 1975). Jimmy Carter had a difficult time finding a legislative sponsor for his reform package. Even after a prominent legislator, Congressman Morris Udall, agreed to manage the administration's efforts in the House, Alan Campbell characterized understanding of and support for the bill as "a mile wide and an inch deep" (Ingraham 1984:5).

Further, congressional debate focused primarily on "external interest-group politics, . . . notably veteran's preference, Hatch Act re-peal, labor-management relations and equal employment opportu-nity" (chap. 4). Except for the presidential appointment of the director of the Office of Personnel Management, little attention was given to the role the reform played in strengthening the office of the president. The presidential politics issue was cast primarily in terms of partisan in-trusion into merit. Ten years after the reform was passed, that essential personnel concern was reemphasized. At hearings on the design of the

CSRA, Senator Ted Stevens, a member of the Senate Governmental Affairs Subcommittee on Federal Services, Post Office and Civil Service, observed:

I remember we felt that this reform act gave tremendous power to a presidential appointee, that the career work force has the right to a different type of nonpartisan professional advice, and that that advice was necessary to see that the Civil Service Laws were administered on an impartial and nonpartisan basis. I've got to confess to you that I've still got the same questions about the Civil Service Reform Act. (U.S. Senate 1988:3)

To a large extent, the congressional focus on the mechanics of merit, rather than the other issues inherent in civil service reform, typifies the success of the presidential strategy of casting questions of power in technical terms. It may also raise questions about the ability of the legislature to address the larger issues of responsibility and control. The proper administration of the civil service laws, while important in preventing abuse of the system, has become a very modest part of the larger issues related to the permanent bureaucracy. A focus on enforcement of existing laws and the status quo precludes or limits consideration of a more fundamental problem: the condition of the merit system itself and the shared responsibility for effective administration of the federal government.[3]

The Context and the Content of Reform

These issues of shared responsibility and the merit system are an important part of the historical context of civil service reform. They have shaped the debate or, in the case of Congress, have been notable for their absence. To a large extent, these issues have also shaped the content of reform. Presidential efforts to control the permanent bureaucracy have been consistently guided by the view that bureaucratic policy making is legitimate only to the extent that it is responding to presidential objectives. The techniques of management necessary to achieve that goal have been an essential part of reform packages. So, too, have been the constant efforts at structural reorganization and reform. The Civil Service Reform Act of 1978 falls squarely into the modern reform tradition in all these respects.

The Civil Service Reform Act is also different, however, and the differences deserve consideration. Jimmy Carter's reform was billed as the "first comprehensive reform of the civil service system in nearly one hundred years." Without any doubt, the act—in combination with Reorganization Plan No. 2—did look at problems of the permanent bureaucracy in a more complete way than most previous efforts. It did dramatically reorganize the federal personnel management function. Those reforms are discussed in detail in part 2 of this book. CSRA emphasized managerial flexibility and, at least in the language of the legislation, those reforms were directed at career, as well as political, managers. That flexibility was a move away from the constraints and rigidity of federal merit laws and regulations. It gave lip service to addressing the role of the permanent bureaucracy in policy making by arguing that the SES would permit policy activity by top career executives.

At the same time, it can be argued that the Civil Service Reform Act reformed only at the fringes of the system. It permitted delegation of testing and examining to the agencies but did not address basic federal entrance requirements and procedures. The courts did that later. The act did not address classification, despite the fact that the Federal Classification Act has not been reexamined since 1949, and narrow and too standardized classification activities have been consistently identified as a serious problem. The act did not address the issue of federal pay, except through bonuses and limited merit pay provisions. These issues too are involved in comprehensive reform. Despite the rhetoric promising a more efficient and productive civil service, therefore, many of the reforms necessary to achieve those objectives were simply not included in the package.

The reform game continues. Technical reforms—even if they work—cannot resolve the controversy surrounding the growth and control of bureaucratic power. As the remaining chapters in this book demonstrate, most of the components of the Civil Service Reform Act made some difference and had some impact, but virtually none turned out as anticipated. The chapters on the Senior Executive Service clearly describe definitions of success and failure; those different definitions are one part of the game. If the president is delighted with the outcomes of a reform, other actors in the system will find ample reason for discontent. Not everyone can win in the reform game, and those who lose, or who perceive that they have lost, will spearhead the next reform effort. At its base, bureaucratic reform is about political power. The stakes for the president, the Congress, members of the permanent bureaucracy, and the citizenry are enormous. The Civil Service Reform Act of 1978 did not achieve its promise. Perhaps it was not possible to do so. The importance of the promise, however, and the fundamental issues of democracy that it represented, ensure that another reform will try.

NOTES

1. See Ingraham and Rosenbloom (1992) for a discussion of the growth and development of the merit system.

2. See Ingraham (1992) for a discussion of the general commission tradition and the historical setting of the Hoover commissions.

3. For a discussion of problems with the system, see Ingraham and Rosenbloom (1992).

SOURCES

Aberbach, Joel D., Robert M. Copeland, and Bert A. Rockman. 1987. "The Shifting, Yet Still Clashing Beliefs of the American Federal Executive." Presented at the annual meeting of the American Political Science Association, Chicago.

Aberbach, Joel D., and Bert A. Rockman. 1988. "Political and Bureaucratic Roles in Public Service Reorganization." In *Organizing Governance: Governing Organizations*, ed. Colin Campbell and B. Guy Peters. Pittsburgh: University of Pittsburgh Press.

Aberbach, Joel D., and Bert A. Rockman. 1976. "Clashing Beliefs Within the Executive Branch: The Nixon Administration Bureaucracy." *American Political Science Review* 70:456–68.

Eisner, Marc A., and Kenneth J. Meier. 1990. "Presidential Control Versus Bureaucratic Power: Explaining the The Reagan Revolution in Antitrust." *American Journal of Political Science* (February):269–87.

Ingraham, Patricia W. 1984. "The Design of the Civil Service Reform Act of 1978." in *Legislating Bureaucratic Change: The Civil Service Reform Act of 1978*, ed. Ingraham and Carolyn Ban. Albany: SUNY Press.

————. 1987. "Building Bridges or Burning Them? The President, the Appointees and the Bureaucracy." *Public Administration Review* (Sept./Oct.):425–35.

————. 1991. "Political Direction and Policy change in Three Federal Agencies." In *The Managerial Presidency*, ed. James P. Pfiffner. Chicago: Dorsey.

————. 1992. "Commissions, Cycles and Change: The Role of Blue Ribbon Commissions in Executive Branch Change." in *An Agenda for Excellence: The American Public Service*, ed. Ingraham and Donald F. Kettl. Chatham, N.J.: Chatham House.

Ingraham, Patricia W., and David H. Rosenbloom. 1992. "The State of Merit in the Federal Government." In *An Agenda for Excellence: The American Public Service*, ed. Ingraham and Kettl. Chatham, N.J.: Chatham House.

Kaufman, Herbert. 1954. "The Growth of the Federal Personnel System." In *The Federal Government Service*, ed. the American Assembly. New York: Columbia University Press.

Long, Norton E. 1949. "Power and Administration." *Public Administration Review* (Autumn):257.

Malek, Frederick (for the White House Personnel Office). 1979. "The Malek Manual." In *Public Personnel Administration*, ed. Frank Thompson. Oak Park, Ill.: Moore Publishing.

March, James G., and Johan P. Olsen. 1983. "Organizing Political Life: What Administrative Reorganization Tells Us About Governing." *American Political Science Review* 77:281–96.

Mosher, Frederick C. 1968. *Democracy and the Public Service*. New York; Oxford University Press.

Nathan, Richard P. 1975. *The Plot That Failed: Nixon and the Administrative Presidency*. New York: Wiley.

Newland, Chester A. 1992. "The Politics of Civil Service Reform." in *The Promise and Paradox of Bureaucratic Reform*, ed. Patricia W. Ingraham and David H. Rosenbloom. Pittsburgh: University of Pittsburgh Press. (Chap. 4, this volume.)

Nixon, Richard M. 1971. "State of the Union Message." In *Public Papers of President Richard Nixon*. Washington, D.C.

President's Committee on Administrative Management (The Brownlow Committee). 1976. *Report*. In *Basic Documents of American Public Administration, 1776–1950*, ed. Frederick C. Mosher, New York: Holmes and Meier.

Ripley, Randall B. 1978. "Congress and the Bureaucracy." In *Bureaucratic Power in National Politics*, 3rd ed., ed. Frances Rourke. Boston: Little, Brown.

Sanera, Michael. 1984. "Implementing the Mandate." In *Mandate for Leadership II: Continuing the Conservative Revolution*, ed. Stuart Butler, Michael Sanera, and W. Bruce Weinrod. Washington, D.C.: Heritage Foundation.

Schlesinger, Arthur M., Jr. 1978. "Roosevelt as Chief Administrator." In *Bureaucratic Power in National Politics*, 3d ed., ed. Rourke.

U.S. Senate. 1988. *Report of the Joint U.S. Government Accounting Office—Senate Subcommittee on Government Operations Hearing on the Design of the Civil Service Reform Act of 1978*, Washington, D.C.

2. The Design of Civil Service Reform
Good Politics or Good Management?

Patricia W. Ingraham

The Civil Service Reform Act of 1978, once proclaimed to "demonstrate that personnel management has rightly taken its place among the top priorities of the federal government" (Campbell 1980:103), is now a prototype of the need for new change and reform. The legislation's brief tenure as a national priority was cut short by the presidential election of 1980. The tools the reform created, however, have endured. The impact of some of those tools is an object lesson in unanticipated consequences of American public policy.

There are many reasons for the outcomes of the Civil Service Reform Act. Some have to do with politics. Budgetary constraints were, and continue to be, important. The incredible complexity and rigidity of the federal merit system also help to explain why the reforms did not work as expected. Still, the meticulous planning approach pursued by the Carter administration and the effort to create the first comprehensive reform in nearly one hundred years held great promise. What happened?

Three factors are fundamental to understanding CSRA's design and outcomes: (1) Despite promises of comprehensive reform, in fact the act reformed at the fringes of a rigid and arcane personnel system and actually increased its complexity. CSRA did not address fundamental issues such as classification, entrance procedures, and pay. (2) The act combined widely accepted (but essentially untested) precepts of professional management with a heavy dose of improved political control. Even had all these precepts been sound, combining them with enhanced political control made the potential effectiveness of the reform unpredictable. (3) Critical components of the reform were based on the assumption that private sector management techniques could be effectively transferred to the public sector. While this is a long-held tenet of American public administration, there is little solid evidence of its validity. Even more important, the assumption that practices such as pay for performance worked well in the private sector was not supported by research and evaluation.[1]

In addition, there was a serious discontinuity between the technical approaches to the design of the reform legislation and the essentially political and democratic nature of the problems being addressed. In the final analysis, improving the efficiency of the bureaucracy will not matter if the legitimacy of the institution is questioned or if the president simply does not trust it. Technical solutions do not solve political problems. Failure to acknowledge the political nature of the problem undermines all potential solutions and essentially ensures that the reforms cannot succeed. All of these problems were present in the efforts to design CSRA. In combination, these issues could—and did—attenuate the careful attention to comprehensive planning for which the reform was initially noted.

Analyzing Policy Design

Since Pressman and Wildavsky's (1973) classic analysis of the problems of implementation, most evaluations of public policy have started with that stage of the policy process. Recently, however, analysts have begun to focus on an earlier level of policy development—policy design. Linder and Peters note in this regard that "the implementation perspective has gone too far in stressing lessons of experience over critical appraisal of first principles" (1987:473). Too much time, in other words, has been spent trying to determine what went wrong *between* point A and point B, when the actual problem may be in the *content* of point A.

In recent analyses, the term *design* is used in two ways. In the first, it refers to "the course of events through which problems are framed and defined, goals or purposes are set, and ideas for action are crafted into fully developed policy alternatives." In the second, designs are "blueprints for action" (Schneider and Ingram 1988:4). The key questions from a design perspective, therefore, do not address implementation activities. Rather, they ask whether the problem has been identified correctly, whether valid causal links have been established, whether correct tools have been provided prior to implementation, whether those provided the tools are likely to use them, and whether use of the tools is likely to lead to the achievement of any of the desired goals. The rigor and rationality of such an approach contrasts sharply with the incremental policy making often noted in American politics.

Politics must, of course, also be a primary consideration in the analysis of design. Though policy analysts and many decision makers find rationality and objectivity attractive attributes, a full understanding of both the process and the outcomes of public policies can be reached only if politics is included in the equation (Ingraham 1987). Politics—partisan and bureaucratic—can influence both design processes and design outcomes in a number of ways. It can constrain problem definition and the range of alternative solutions available for consideration. It can direct the design process to a specific conclusion. It can, in fact, eliminate the process of design altogether. Politics can also shape design activities in positive ways and provide the support and resources necessary for their completion.

In the policy analyzed in this book, the Civil Service Reform Act of 1978, the role of politics was consistent and multidimensional. The interest and attention of President Jimmy Carter and some of his political appointees permitted the rare ascent of personnel issues to the national policy agenda. Presidential interest conveyed a sense of urgency to the design process; it also shaped that process to include political, as well as technical, considerations. Presidential interest did not, however, eliminate other sources of political influence on the process: bureaucratic politics among agencies, and interest group politics, most notably in labor and veterans groups, were very much a part of the formulation of civil service reform.

The Activities of Design

Jimmy Carter's constant call for civil service reform in the 1976 presidential campaign ensured its high priority upon his election. Even before the election, Carter moved to expedite preparation of a reform package.[2] Very shortly after assuming office, he established the President's Reorganization Project and named himself chair of its executive committee. A major component of the reorganization project's activities were delegated to the President's Personnel Management Project (PMP), which was specifically directed to prepare a civil service reform package. In Carter's 1978 State of the Union Message, he declared the reforms to be absolutely vital.

The composition of the reform team was purposefully comprehensive. Though formally housed in the Civil Service Commission, staff of the PMP were told to reach out to all federal agencies in preparing their report. The creation of nine task forces was one approach to comprehensiveness. Others included the creation of the Assistant Secretaries Advisory Group, a series of public meetings, and a number of more informal advising sessions. The composition of the task forces was diverse and included career civil servants, private sector representatives, and academic and other personnel specialists. Despite this comprehensive approach, however, the actual problem analysis and drafting of recommendations was dominated by career civil servants staffing the PMP who believed it was necessary to dramatically change the existing system.

A major institutional actor in the design process was the Office of Management and Budget. The deputy director of the PMP was a political appointee from the Office of Management and Budget; as overseer of the larger Reorganization Project, OMB had a double interest in the project. Further, because problems with the Civil Service Commission had intensified in the years leading up to the reform effort, OMB had assumed some of the personnel management functions that had previously resided with the commission. Those managerial functions were now seen as a legitimate part of OMB's activities by many in that agency. Quite clearly, OMB had a stake in retaining some of those activities. It is not so clear how this interest meshed with the interests of the PMP and its task forces. This aspect of the process has not been well documented, but the potential for conflict was clearly present.

The potentially conflicting roles of the two agencies were offset to some extent by the intense lobbying and networking activities of Alan Campbell, chairman of the Civil Service Commission, and his deputy, Jule Sugarman. Campbell's strong advocacy of the reform also exacerbated the conflict, however; he often noted that it was necessary to take the *M* out of the Office of Management and Budget and put it where it would be properly used. In a 1988 reflection on the Civil Reform Act, Campbell noted, "More personnel management decisions were made in OMB than were being made in the Civil Service Commission. Had civil service reform not been a presidential initiative, the underground (opposition) would have been much more above ground in that agency" (U.S. Senate, 1988:17).

From the moment of its inception in the spring of 1977, the PMP was an intense and concentrated effort. It set about its deliberations in an environment characterized by considerable consensus about the multidimensional nature of the problem. That problem consisted of (at least) the following components:

• The dual and conflicting missions of the Civil Service Commission. Protecting merit while also serving as political advisor to the president was widely perceived to be very difficult, if not illegal.
• The excessively complex nature of the civil service system and its procedural baggage.
• The perceived insularity of career civil servants from political direction.
• The perceived inefficiency of massive and largely unaccountable federal bureaucracies.
• The failure of the civil service to create and reward excellent performance.
• The unrepresentative nature of the career civil service, most notably its top management cadres.
• The inability of top career executives to function effectively as policy advisors to political appointees and to be placed in policy-sensitive positions (Ingraham 1984).

In addition, public perceptions of the civil service in general were very negative. A frequently cited 1978 Roper poll found that only 10 percent of those surveyed believed that the government was free of corruption; only 18 percent believed that the government attracted the best possible people; less than one-fourth believed that government was an exciting place to work. President Carter clearly wanted the reform act to address those concerns as well as the specific problems outlined above. In one speech urging support for the reform he noted, "There is no inherent conflict between careful planning, tight management, and constant reassessment on one hand and compassionate concern for the plight of the deprived and the afflicted on the other. Waste and inefficiency never fed a hungry child, provided a job or a willing worker, or educated a deserving student" (Carter 1978b).

Matching Problem to Solution

The nature of the problems that civil service reform wished to address ensured that the design process would have to deal with potentially conflicting solutions. The need to open up the system but also make it more efficient was one obvious example. The pressures for greater bureaucratic responsiveness to political direction as well as for greater managerial discretion and flexibility was another.

The wide range of people and perspectives involved in the process further increased the likelihood of conflicting solutions. The task force operation alone included over one hundred participants. Dwight Ink, executive director of the PMP, estimated that approximately five thousand people participated in the public hearings. Preliminary findings and recommendations were circulated to as many as one thousand organizations for comment. In testimony before the Senate Subcommittee on Government Operations, Ink noted, "Our task force deliberations were very open. . . . Since our draft reports were available to the press and widely circulated to assistant secretaries and career personnel officers within the agencies as well as large numbers of outside organizations, there should have been no surprises in our principle recommendations." (U.S. Senate 1988:42)

There were, in fact, surprises. Some of them were directly attributable to the inevitable differences generated by the open design process; others are more accurately attributed to the political compromises necessary for consensus. Ink and others, however, have characterized the activity as one devoid of politics. In the 1988 Senate subcommittee hearings on the design of the CSRA, for example, Ink noted, "It is very much to the credit of both the CSC and OMB that they preserved the independence of the whole task force operation and insulated us from any political pressures that might have otherwise influenced our work." (U.S. Senate 1988:45).

Given the strong interest of the President and his staff in the reform act, this is a somewhat unusual view. The process did involve politicians, both elected and appointed; it was clearly not devoid of political influence. Further, it is evident that the analysis of some components of the reform—veterans' preference, for example—proceeded with a clear awareness of the power of the veterans lobbies and of their likely impact on the final outcome (FPMD 1977a). Finally, the simple need to put the reform together and sell it ensured that some political activity would be part of the design process.

Thus, the evolving design of CSRA incorporated different perspectives about the basic problems being addressed, the priorities, and the proposed solutions. Failure to reconcile these conflicting objectives— or, the occasional decision to include all of them—caused some components of the legislation to be rather schizophrenic. As the discussion of the Senior Executive Service in chapter 8 demonstrates, the SES provides an obvious example.

Assumptions About the Problem

The most basic building blocks in policy design are the assumptions that support problem definition. These assumptions should contain implicit theories about why the problem exists and which solutions are most likely to be effective. Although assumptions are rarely clearly stated, their impact throughout the process is significant. Failure to be accurate at this point of design can nullify subsequent activities, no matter how rigorous they might be.

In the case of civil service reform, basic assumptions were shaped by long-held views about the professional civil service and the merit system, as well as by more recent events, such as the Watergate scandals. For the career bureaucrats involved in design, effective government was defined by the presence of a strong and neutral merit system to offset political extremism. President Carter, while abhorring the illegal activities of the Nixon administration, was more impressed by the need for the president to exert greater control over executive agencies than by the need to strengthen merit. His observation that there was no merit in the merit system did not suggest that he would consider strengthening it as a building block of the reform.

Perceptions of the problem also reflected Americans' distaste for bureaucrats and their institutions. Carter's campaign rhetoric about the "giant Washington marshmallow," his emphasis on the need to increase whistleblowing activities, and his promise to clear the dead wood from federal agencies played to an image of a federal bureaucracy that was bloated and inefficient. Promises to hold bureaucrats more accountable to the president and his appointees not only reflected the president's desire for tighter managerial controls, but also affirmed public beliefs that bureaucrats were running rampant in Washington. A major working assumption, in short, was that the federal bureaucracy was almost hopelessly broken, at least partially because it had moved beyond traditional controls.

Other basic assumptions concerned the nature of the federal bureaucracy. Somewhat in keeping with Carter's giant marshmallow theme, the federal bureaucracy was viewed as a homogeneous monolith. The theme of a large, unified, and essentially independent bureaucracy is evident in several of the task force analyses. The nature and intensity of problems were viewed as similar across agencies; skills and abilities—most notably, managerial skills and abilities—were assumed to be transferable across agencies as well. With few exceptions, agency-unique problems and organizational cultures do not appear to have entered the deliberative process. The American tradition of developing agency-specific program specialists, rather than general managers, was not addressed. As a result, reforms such as the Senior Executive Service contained provisions for mobility that assumed that a manager in Agriculture, for example, would do just fine in the Department of Labor.

As noted earlier, the assumption that the public sector needed to adopt private sector techniques to become more efficient was pervasive in design activities. This perspective was firmly grounded in traditional public administration theories such as scientific management and in the more recent public management movement. Though a larger dispute about differences in public and private management techniques and skills could have been incorporated into the reform debate, there is no indication in the records or in subsequent analyses that this occurred.[3] As a result, techniques such as performance evaluation and pay for performance, which became critical parts of the reform package, were considered easily transferable from one sector to another. No testing or demonstration in the public sector was deemed necessary prior to recommending governmentwide adoption. In many respects, CSRA became the experiment that tested the base assumption.

Finally, despite a process that encouraged potentially diverse and conflicting options, there was a continuing assumption of internal cohesion in products of the design activities. The 1988 Senate subcommittee hearings provided recent affirmation of this view:

Question to Alan Campbell: Much of the writing that's been done about the design of the Civil Service Reform Act speaks to the fact that the intent was to create a comprehensive . . . and cohesive system but, in fact, it was merely a series of parts that emerged from various task forces that didn't fit together terribly well. What's your view of that assessment?
Campbell: Nonsense! (U.S. Senate 1988)

Campbell argued that any inconsistencies were a result of legislative compromise and not of design activities. Others, however, have pinpointed the process of design as a primary source of some of the problems in the final reform package. In relation to the Senior Executive

Service, for example, Huddleston notes that the PMP task force "recommended a system that seemingly had something for everyone, rhetorically and substantively. . . . It appears as if the SES's designers and supporters had sat around a table in 1977 and 1978 and, in an effort to satisfy everyone's appetite picked a few dishes from column A, a few from column B and so on." (Huddleston 1988:41–50).

Making Choices in Design

The process of reform design and the assumptions that guided it created a reform package that was, at best, loosely coupled; at worst, replete with internal contradictions. The very comprehensiveness of the reform act ensured that the solutions to some problems would conflict with the solutions to others. For CSRA, this problem was exacerbated because some of the solutions themselves reflected internal contradictions. It was inevitable that, while many participants could consider themselves winners in design activities, implementation would have to choose one solution over another. This is not an unusual phenomenon in American public policy: the "gray solution to gray problem" phenomenon is very common. Unfortunately, it rarely limits expectations for policy outcomes. In the case of CSRA, four examples highlight the nature of this problem.

Centralization or Decentralization

The complexity and insularity of the central personnel system clearly pointed to a need for simplification and decentralization. Because CSRA was the first comprehensive attempt at reform in nearly one hundred years, it was forced to address an enormous accretion of rules and regulations and a merit system that had evolved very haphazardly (Ingraham and Rosenbloom 1992). At the same time, the continuing desire to protect merit principles, coupled with a significant level of distrust of career civil servants, mitigated against abandoning a centralized system completely. Further, for many federal managers, the procedures and requirements of the centralized personnel system provided a familiar and comfortable work environment. Despite the civil service system's many problems, virtually no one was willing to urge its total elimination. By default, discussion of decentralization occurred within the context of the existing central system and all of its procedural baggage. Other critical central elements were not even addressed; classification is the leading example.

The centralization-decentralization debate was further complicated by efforts to sort out the many roles the Civil Service Commission had assumed over its history. Many analysts noted a conflict of interest in the commission's joint ownership of adjudicatory functions to protect merit and advisory functions to the president, most notably those dealing with political appointments. These analysts found little focused attention paid to issues related to human resource management under the old system and advanced strong arguments for moving that function to a new central agency. Alan Campbell put an additional twist on the central management function when he wrote, "It is anticipated that OPM would perform for the President the same role relative to personnel management that OMB does for financial management" (Campbell 1978b:100).

Despite considerable consensus that decentralization and greater authority for individual agencies and managers would be beneficial, the provisions of the act created a strong new central force: the Office of Personnel Management. The benefits to the president of this new agency headed by a political appointee were clear; the fit with the provisions for delegation and decentralization was not.

A somewhat quirky dimension of this controversy was contributed by some federal personnel managers and the rather negative role they played in shaping the debate. Quintessential products of the old civil service system, many members of the group were not comfortable with the proposals for a redefined central management agency and decentralized personnel functions. Alan Campbell recalls one early discussion:

I was never quite sure to what extent the personnel community supported the kinds of initiatives that we were undertaking. . . . When my appointment as Chairman of the Civil Service Commission was first announced, a group of personnel directors in the federal government asked to meet with me. . . . We got together and the thing that they pressed on me was their belief that the reform should take the form of personnel directors in the departments and agencies reporting to the Civil Service Commission and not to their own agency management. (U.S. Senate 1988:37)

The impact this would have had on managerial discretion and flexibility is difficult to imagine.

Thus, there were many elements to the centralization-decentralization debates and discussions. Some of them were concerned with structure, others with function or position. They presented dramatically different views of the purpose and outcome of reform. This disparity, though not perfectly reflected, was certainly evident in the reform design. As in all of the preceding debates on this issue (one of the oldest in American public personnel management) there was no resolution. Implementation reflected that failure.

Central Control or Individual Accountability

Very closely related to the above issue was the debate surrounding centralized control or individual accountability. The entire civil service system was based on the concept of control—or, put more positively, guarantee of merit—through centralized rules and regulations. Adherence to those rules necessarily removed individual prerogative as well as political efforts to intrude. Over time, efforts to ensure merit and prevent abuse separated many federal managers from necessary authority and tools for managing. In 1978, many participants recognized the debilitating effect of these constraints on the effectiveness of federal agencies and career managers. At the same time, the memory of Watergate fueled the fear of additional political abuse. Discretion for career managers could as easily be used by political appointees. The inability (or unwillingness) to separate political from career in this case posed a real dilemma.

There were many advocates for decentralization and delegation of appropriate authority to the opening level in the federal agencies. There were probably an equal number who were fearful of moving from procedural controls to managerial discretion and accountability. The report of the Staffing Task Force reflected these strongly held perspectives. On one page, the report summary notes, "Regardless of whether more flexibility is granted, too great a potential for abuse exists, and therefore increased emphasis must be placed on meaningful steps to safeguard merit principles." One paragraph later, the report notes that a key operating assumption of the task force was that, "instead of creating highly complicated personnel systems to thwart dishonest people, personnel systems must be designed for use by honest people" (FPMP 1977a:24).

The reconciliation of these diverse perspectives was partially achieved through the recommendation to create the Merit Systems Protection Board as the new guardian of merit principles. The *Final Report* of the PMP, however, demonstrates continuing unease about this solution.

The Merit Protection Board will greatly strengthen and increase the independence of the merit oversight and investigatory capacity of the federal government. This is essential. *If the Merit Protection Board Recommendation is not adopted, many of the proposals designed to increase management flexibility will have to be reassessed because of their potential vulnerability to abuse.* (ibid.:24, emphasis added)

The attempt to balance individual accountability with systemic controls was made additionally murky by the debate surrounding whistleblower provisions. A personal favorite of President Carter, whistleblower provisions were seen as a means of fighting abuse of the merit system and other laws but were also viewed as an important way to increase the efficiency of government. Here too, an undercurrent of doubt about individual accountability runs through the discussion and emerges in the final report. In arguing for an ombudsman role for the Merit Systems Protection Board that would provide protection for whistleblowers, the report also notes:

Unfortunately, many frivolous and self-serving charges are also made, alongside those which have merit, and it is often difficult to distinguish the valid charges from the invalid. Further, some employees fail to bring these problems to the attention of management in any meaningful way before going public. . . . This area of employee redress requires the careful and thoughtful weighing of facts which will be afforded by the Board. (ibid.:56)

In the final analysis, the designers of the reform opted for institutional controls and procedures more consistently than they opted for individual accountability and additional managerial authority. The basic sentiment was summed up by one participant at the 1988 Senate hearings in this way: "Let's not get too flexible, because God knows what will happen!" (U.S. Senate 1988:64). This view, of course, coincided nicely with the desire to improve political direction and control, rather than to emphasize individual discretion.

Better Management or Better Responsiveness?

The accountability-control debate was also reflected in the efforts to increase political responsiveness. In much of the political rhetoric surrounding the need for civil service reform, there was a common refrain: the insularity of public bureaucracies permitted them to operate inefficiently and in their own self-interest. Prior to the Carter administration, President Nixon had identified better political responsiveness as a key solution to this problem. President Carter, who had campaigned against the Washington bureaucracy, also focused on lack of bureaucratic responsiveness. This long-term presidential interest in improving hierarchical controls on career civil servants initially led to what Howard Messner, Carter's assistant director for management improvement on OMB, called a focus on "the boxes of government" (U.S. Senate 1988:114). The reorganization project's early emphasis on the boxes and on how to achieve better direction within each box was soon supplemented by a concern for the managerial processes that supported improved political direction. As Messner notes:

Cabinet members and presidential appointees . . . were assigned significant program responsibility, but almost no administrative responsibility. . . . Intuitively, they found the process of government unworkable. . . . It didn't make sense to say you are to carry out our national defense policies, or our housing policies, or our transportation policies, and you have a lot of authority to do that with a lot of dollars attached, but on the other hand, you can't touch the personnel process. (U.S. Senate 1988:116)

It can be argued that interest in the Senior Executive Service flowed from this recognition. Members of the SES would understand the personnel system; their improved responsiveness to political direction would enhance political direction of personnel systems as well. The provisions for members of the SES to participate more fully in policy-making activities, on the other hand, were at direct odds with the emphasis on political control. Career participation in policy suggested the European model of *expert advising*. The political control model suggested very different behavior: simple responsiveness to political direction. The inclusion of both perspectives on the Senior Executive Service in the final reform package represents more than a rhetorical tension; it created expectations for two very different kinds of behavior, one of which was bound not to be realized.

Some effort was made to resolve this problem by building protections into the new executive system: "We are aware that a more flexible system will also be more vulnerable to the kinds of abuses seen recently in other Administrations. To prevent such abuses and at the same time make possible better management, we are proposing strong, new safeguards" (FPMP 1977a:196). The report then recommends caps on the number of political appointees, prohibited reassignment in the first 120 days, and recourse to the Merit Systems Protection Board.

The tension between politics and merit is, of course, a hallmark of the federal personnel system. That the framers of civil service reform did not—or could not—resolve it simply testifies to the central role that politics and political actors must play in bureaucratic reform. The use of the SES provisions to move and bypass career executives during the Reagan administration also demonstrates, however, that efforts to combine personnel and politics have very real, and sometimes unfortunate, consequences. The Department of Housing and Urban Development and the scandals related to political appointees in that agency is a dramatic example.

Reorganization or Revitalization?

Another important aspect of CSRA design was the attempt to specify the relationship between structural reform and fundamental reform of the merit system. Was the creation of new structures the best way to address the problems inherent in the old system? For many of the designers, the answer to this question was clearly yes. Campbell states the penchant for structural reform aptly: "In this imperfect world, our success at changing systems is somewhat greater than our success at changing people" (Campbell 1978a:8). This view was shared by other presidential advisors; Harrison Wofford, who had pushed for reform since before the election, reportedly had very little hope of comprehensive change but believed that modest structural change was possible.[4]

The most obvious example of the belief in structural change was the strong consensus surrounding the splitting of the functions of the Civil Service Commission and the creation of new agencies to assume them. The PMP *Final Report* states the commitment to such change succinctly: "Improving the organization of the government for personnel management requires, in the first instance, sorting out and redistributing [CSC's various] functions and authorities" (FPMP 1977a:233). The first page of the report notes that "the recommendations are a complex and inter-related unit. Many are based on the assumption that other recommendations—particularly the division of the Civil Service Commission into an Office of Personnel Management and Merit Protection Board—will be effected" (ibid.:3).

Underlying this commitment was the conviction that structures so effectively shape process that the new system would function effectively in any circumstance and with any political leadership. Campbell restated that belief in 1988: "We did believe, and I still believe, that what we were trying to do would serve the interest of whoever was in power; and that there would be advantage taken of it in positive ways regardless of what happened on the political side" (U.S. Senate 1988:35).

Further, in the often incomprehensible world of personnel management and civil service law, structural reform was both dramatic and easily understood. The support and involvement of President Carter mandated that there be *evidence* of change. Creating new organizations and abolishing old ones was concrete and identifiable. For the reform designers, however, this simplicity was a siren song. The high level of confidence in structural change resulted in the failure to adequately consider other potential reform tools. Worse, it masked consideration of what would happen if the new institutions didn't work.

In summary, then, the tensions in the design of the Civil Service Reform Act were evident throughout the recommendations of the Personnel Management Project. These recommendations resulted in some solutions competing with others—increasing manager's abilities to fire employees, for example, raised problems when considered with increased protections for whistleblowers. The PMP recommendations resulted in some solutions that contained internal conflicts: the members of the Senior Executive Service were to be more independent and authoritative executives, for example, while being more responsive to political appointees. The PMP placed great confidence in institutions as forces of change but created institutions with internal problems; it is still not clear, for example, how the Office of Special Counsel and the Merit Systems Protection Board were to function as one. These design characteristics are important to the analysis of the implementation and outcomes of civil service reform. They shaped both in important ways.

Conclusion

In the end, the promise of the comprehensive planning and design process, already diluted by the realities of consensus and compromise, was further attenuated by the realities of presidential politics. Jimmy Carter had promised speedy action on this centerpiece of his domestic agenda; he was determined that the legislative package be on the Hill as quickly as possible. As a result, drafting of the legislation began before the planning and recommending process was complete. Sugarman took lead responsibility for drafting the package. "I was pretty sure what was going to be in it [the PMP Report]," he later said. "I had seen drafts."[5] Howard Messner concurred that the final report was not necessary before drafting began: "[The PMP Report] was basically a crutch upon which you could build a law."[6] The politics of passage, described elsewhere in this book, also took their toll on orderly design and internal cohesion.

If policy design is a blueprint for action, the product that emerged from CSRA's blueprint should not be surprising. The rhetoric surrounding the reform was more influential in shaping expectations than was any coldly analytic understanding of design flaws, however. The constant emphasis on the rational and comprehensive process and its ability to solve problems was clearly influential in raising hopes for the reform's success. The commitment of the president to the reform strengthened those hopes.

The disparity between the promise of the design process as an exemplary case of rational planning and the reality of the activity is a useful guide for understanding the outcomes of the reform. The problems addressed by CSRA were complex, interrelated, and intransigent. Their intransigence is made clear by their continued—indeed, heightened—presence a decade after civil service reform. The problems were a peculiar mix of the democratic, the technical, the legal, the managerial, and the political problems associated with the permanent bureaucracies of every major modern nation. CSRA addressed bureaucratic reform in political, technical, and institutional terms but excluded critical components of the personnel system from review. The fundamental democratic issues were, of course, not addressed at all. The reform created solutions that were untested and probably inappropriate for the problem. In retrospect, it is quite clear that CSRA could not meet many of the expectations for its success.

A different perspective for understanding the Civil Service Reform Act of 1978 is provided by Herbert Kaufman (1978), who describes a "cycle of reform." In that cycle, at any given time some of the vast number of reform objectives are on the agenda and others are not. Obviously, only those on the agenda are addressed. If we begin with this view, it becomes clear that the design activities in 1977 and 1978 could only begin the movement away from the centralized, procedure-bound system of the past one hundred years. That system had been rejected, but the values around which a new system could be created had not coalesced. The tensions contained in the design reflected that. Further, the strong push for improved presidential control provided the inevitable context for the reform. Given its dominance on the reform agenda, outcomes become both more predictable and more understandable.

Were a new civil service reform to be designed today, it would look different from that created in 1978. There are no guarantees, however, that it would be more successful. Nor would it be less susceptible to ten-year hindsights. Reforming a public bureaucracy means shaping public values, politics, and priorities. It means, as well, changing individuals inside the bureaucracy. The hardest things to do are the things that must be done well if reform is to be effective.

NOTES

1. Research available to the designers of the reform points out serious problems with both the theory and practice of performance appraisal and pay for performance. Not until a decade after the act's passage, however, as the Office of Personnel Management considered extending pay for performance governmentwide, were the theory and the private sector experience systematically analyzed. See Milkovich and Wigdor, 1991.

2. Jule Sugarman, a primary architect of the reform, was on board very early in the campaign and was drafting position papers for Carter's consideration well before the election. (Personal interview with Sugarman, Washington, D.C., October 1989.)

3. See, for example, the testimony of Alan Campbell (U.S. Senate 1988).

4. This assessment is based on a personal interview with Howard Messner, Washington, D.C., October 1989.

5. Personal interview with Jule Sugarman, Washington, D.C., October 1989.

6. Personal interview with Howard Messner, Washington, D.C., February 1989.

SOURCES

Campbell, Alan K. 1978a. "Can Reorganization Reorganize the Low Prestige of Public Service?" *Public Management* 60:8–10.

——— . 1978b. "Civil Service Reform: A New Commitment." *Public Administration Review* 38:99–103.

——— . 1980. "Civil Service Reform as a Remedy for Bureaucratic Ills." In *Making Bureaucracies Work*, ed. Carol Weiss and Allen Barton. Beverly Hills: Sage: 153–66.

Carter, Jimmy. 1978a. "State of the Union Message." delivered in January. In *Public Papers of President Jimmy Carter*. Washington, D.C.

——— . 1978b. "Remarks to Congress Announcing the Administration's Civil Service Reform Proposal." delivered in March. In *Public Papers of President Jimmy Carter*. Washington, D.C.

FPMP (Federal Personnel Management Project). 1977. *Final Report.* Washington, D.C.

Hogwood, Brian, and B. Guy Peters. 1985. *The Pathology of Policy.* Oxford: Oxford University Press.

Huddleston, Mark. 1988. "To the Threshold of Reform: The SES and America's Search for a Higher Civil Service." Paper Presented at the Annual Meeting of the American Political Science Association. Washington, D.C.

Ingraham, Patricia W. 1984. "The Civil Service Reform Act of 1978: Its Design and Legislative History." In *Legislating Bureaucratic Change: The Civil Service Reform Act of 1978,* ed. Ingraham and Carolyn Ban. Albany: SUNY Press.

———. 1987. "Toward More Systematic Consideration of Policy Design." *Policy Studies Journal* 15:611–28.

Ingraham, Patricia W., and David H. Rosenbloom. 1992. "The State of Merit in the Federal Government." In *An Agenda for Excellence: The American Public Service,* ed. Ingraham and Donald F. Kettl. Chatham, N.J.: Chatham House.

Kaufman, Herbert. 1978. "Reflections on Administrative Reorganization." In *Current Issues in Public Administration,* ed. Frederick S. Lane. New York: St. Martin's.

Linder, Stephen H., and B. Guy Peters. 1987. "A Design Perspective on Policy Implementation: The Fallacies of Misplaced Prescription." *Policy Studies Review* 6:459–75.

Milkovich, George T., and Alexandra Wigdor. 1991. *Pay for Performance: Evaluating Performance Appraisal and Merit Pay.* Washington, D.C.: National Academy Press.

Pressman, Jeffrey, and Aaron Wildavsky. 1973. *Implementation.* Berkeley: University of California Press.

Schneider, Anne, and Helen Ingram. 1988. "Filling Empty Boxes: A Framework for the Comparative Analysis of Policy Design." Presented at the annual meeting of the Western Political Science Association, San Francisco.

U.S. Senate. 1988. *Report of the Joint U.S. Government Accounting Office-Senate Subcommittee on Government Operations Hearing on the Design of the Civil Service Reform Act of 1978.* Washington, D.C.

3. The Search for the M:

Federal Management and Personnel Policy

Beryl A. Radin

At a seminar on civil service reform, former Office of Personnel Management Director Alan Campbell commented, "I would suggest to you that more personnel management decisions were being made in OMB [the Office of Management and Budget] than by the Civil Service Commission. . . . As I said at the time, I was often accused of trying to steal the 'M' out of OMB. My response was I didn't think it a great crime to steal something essentially unused" (U.S. GAO 1988:13). While Campbell's comment may have expressed the perceptions and experience of some designers of the Civil Service Reform Act (CSRA) during its development, since then it has sometimes seemed as if the opposite were true—that the M had been taken out of the Office of Personnel Management.

This search for the M reflects an uneasy relationship between personnel and other federal management agendas. Federal personnel policy, its institutions and—most important—its authority base, are inextricably linked to broader federal management concerns.[1] As other chapters in this volume indicate, the CSRA rhetoric, as well as its political impetus, clearly tied these two elements, personnel and management, together. Indeed, the design and strategy for the reform efforts were located within the President's Reorganization Project in the management side of the Office of Management and Budget.

The relationship between personnel and other management agendas has been an uneasy one for many years. No one agency has been given (or has been able to assume) exclusive ability to define these relationships. Attempts to define boundaries between these agendas most often involved OPM (or its predecessor the Civil Service Commission) and OMB (and its predecessor the Bureau of the Budget). The conflict has been fanned as both sets of actors attempted to respond to an underlying question: What does it mean to improve management in the federal government? This question must be answered before answering two secondary questions: Whose responsibility is it to improve management, and how is the personnel function related to this problem?

This chapter examines the relationship between these two sets of actors both before the development and passage of the Civil Service Reform Act and since its implementation. It does this employing three analytical frames: the *management competence* frame, the *executive control* frame, and the *political bargaining* frame. These three frames represent conflicting yet legitimate, paradigms within the public administration community.[2] As in so many other areas of the public administration field, no single overriding paradigm evokes agreement from knowledgeable individuals within the discipline. Indeed, the successes of various management reform efforts in this nation's history reflect the confluence, at particular times, of arguments and supporters flowing from these three frames.

The management competence frame flows from the perspective that could be described as management qua management, emphasizing the institutional processes that are classically associated with the management function. The basis for this frame is consistent with the scientific management view of the field and is clear in the formulation of the classic functions of administration created POSDCORB by Luther Gulick. This is the concept of POSDCORB—Planning, Organizing, Staffing, Directing, Coordinating, Reporting, and Budgeting.

For Gulick, the elements of the work of a chief executive included staffing: "That is the whole personnel function of bringing in and training the staff and maintaining favorable conditions of work" (1977:13). Gulick noted that the seven elements within POSDCORB may be separately organized as subdivisions of the executive, depending on the size and complexity of the enterprise. "In the largest enterprises, particularly where the chief executive is as a matter of fact unable to do the work that is thrown upon him, it may be presumed that one or more parts of POSDCORB should be suborganized" (ibid.).

Writing in 1937, Gulick emphasized values of economy and efficiency and minimized the boundaries between public and private sector organizations. He commented:

It is interesting to note that this [suborganization] has been recognized in many of our larger governmental units, though there has been until recently no very clear philosophy lying back of the arrangements which have been made. For example, in the federal government, at the present time one may identify the separate institutionalization of:

Planning, under the National Resources Committee, though as yet rudimentary in development;

Staffing, under the Civil Service Commission, though it has missed its constructive role;

Reporting, under the National Emergency Council and the Central Statistics Board, in elementary form;

Budgeting, under the Budget Bureau. (ibid.:14)

Gulick's formulation lays the framework for the argument that personnel is one of a number of elements within the management package that are inextricably interrelated. Thus it is difficult to draw boundaries between personnel and other management issues.

As will be illustrated in this chapter, arguments employing this frame are made by those who value management for its own sake, who have a process (rather than outcome) orientation, and who often share the private sector's emphasis on efficiency values.

The executive control frame focuses on the presidency and the Executive Office of the President as a political institution searching for methods to assure control over the executive branch. In some cases, this control becomes an end in itself with the President attempting to operate much as a chief executive officer does in a private organization. This perspective was expressed by Elmer Staats:

The president as head of the executive branch must take care to see that the laws are faithfully executed. He is the chief executive officer of one of the largest corporate organizations in the world. Among his other responsibilities, the president is the general manager of the executive branch and ultimately responsible for how well it is managed. In exercising this responsibility, he must rely on a workforce of nearly five million employees—military and civilian—whose loyalty efficiency, and motivation will, in the final analysis, determine the success or failure of his administration. (Staats 1987:5)

In other cases, the control urge is related to the president's specific policy agenda. Here, personnel decisions (and other management reform efforts) are an expression of the policy agenda; thus, they become means to other ends, not ends in themselves. Under this formulation, personnel can be either an active or a passive tool of presidential power.[3]

However, presidential control is more directly associated with another management element: the budget function. Thus, the agency with budget responsibility plays a pivotal role, both because of the primacy and power of the budget function and because of its access to the president and presidential advisors. These elements allow it to directly reflect the presidential agenda. In addition, the budget control function permits the budget agency to constrain management operations within other organizations.[4]

Arguments employing this frame are often made by proponents of increased presidential control, those who emphasize budget issues, and individuals with substantive policy agendas that they believe can be advanced by a stronger executive branch.

The political bargaining frame emphasizes the theory of democratic institutions and accountability relationships within the American political system. These relationships have created overlapping functions and interests that serve as countervailing pressures on any single mode or node of decision making. The countervailing pressures operate both between levels of government (Congress, the executive branch, and the judiciary) and within the executive branch itself (for example, as a tug between central control functions such as personnel and budget and the struggle for autonomy of program specialization).

Emmette Redford characterized these relationships in the democratic administrative state: "In the case of any of these classifications, the lines between categories often are blurred in the allocation of duties to organizations. Legislative and executive functions may be comingled in the same organizations, policy making and policy execution fused at a given level of organization, and different types of allocation—area, process, clientele, and purpose—mixed in the same organization (Redford 1969:39). Redford continued: "Some amount of autonomy accrues to every organization, but each will be constantly limited by interactions with other organizations in the same functional complex" (ibid.:44). Because of multiple interests, "the ability of overhead political institutions to prescribe behavior is limited, not only by the complexity of interests pressing for continuous representation through established roles, but also by the complexities of organization itself" (ibid.:48).

Redford described a "web of interrelationships that creates the official universe of political-administrative activity in Washington." This web has many strands—Congress, the White House, agencies, inter- and intradepartmental relationships (ibid.:72–82). Redford analyzed this web of relationships as a macropolitical system. Within it, he said, "an overhead structure will exist for organic, allocative, manning, appellate, crisis, co-ordinative, and review functions. This does not mean either that the overhead structure can assume complete direction and supervision or that it will operate with full unity of purpose" (ibid.:114–15).

The intervention of the overhead function, according to Redford, is selective, varied, and highly political. It includes a personnel function "which requires attention at the highest level," and "it cannot be expected that those who establish programs and allocate resources to them will not be continuously interested in the manning of the programs" (ibid.:112).

Proponents of this frame are often those who do not accept a dichotomy between politics and administration within the federal government. They emphasize the fragmented nature of national policy making and the legitimacy of the congressional role in management decision making.

Management and Personnel Policy: A Historical Account

These three frames—management competence, executive control, and political bargaining—are best illustrated through a brief historical account of developments in federal management. Concern about the appropriate authority base, form, and structure for the management of the federal government (and the role that personnel policy plays in that search) has been an obsession of administrative reformers since the turn of the century. Its roots go back to the founding days of the nation. While responsibilities and definitions may appear to be settled in one period, the presence of conflicting imperatives unsettles the agreement and pulls the debate in a different direction.

The Early Period

Apprehension about management authority within the executive branch can be traced back to the earliest days of the United States. As Fritz Mosher noted, the first Congress in 1789 was not willing to give a clear budget responsibility to the president.

The Act to Establish the Treasury Department was distinctly different from those setting up the State and War departments in a variety of respects, most of which reflected a congressional intent that the Treasury be partly if not principally responsible directly to the Congress rather than the president. The Treasury was labeled simply a "department"; the other two were "executive departments." The secretary of the Treasury was "head of the department"; the heads of the other two were "principal officers." (Mosher 1984:14–15)

As the nineteenth century progressed and the nation grew in both scale and complexity, new institutions were created to respond to this social and economic reality. The imperatives of specialization spawned a growth in the federal service. At the same time, checks and balances were never far from the scene. Paul Van Riper's history of the U.S. Civil Service noted that the Civil Service Commission was the first of the separate commissions devised to remove controversial issues from the usual administrative and political channels and to avoid some of the most bitter presidential-congressional conflicts. "The emergence of a new administrative pattern on the federal scene was undoubtedly related to a perception by Congress—whether consciously verbalized or merely sensed does not matter—that the relatively novel idea of political neutrality in civil service selection methods deserved a relatively novel administrative solution if it was to survive" (Van Riper 1958:10). Despite the independence suggested by the concept of the neutral civil service, Van Riper commented that the Civil Service Commission differs in several important respects from later regulatory boards, such as the Interstate Commerce Commission.

The members of the Civil Service Commission may be removed by the President without restriction. While it is their duty to advise the President on matters of policy affecting the public service, the Pendleton Act specifies that the regulations made by them derive their authority from and will be promulgated by the President. Hence, the Commission cannot properly be classed as an *independent* commission, though it represents a political innovation of some importance. (ibid.:110)

Explicit attention to the management function within the federal government can be traced to President Taft's Commission on Economy and Efficiency which required the Civil Service Commission to establish a system of efficiency ratings for federal employees. A Division of Efficiency was established in the Civil Service Commission in 1912, and during the next few years Congress called for reports from that office. In 1915, Congress made the director of the division a presidential appointee. The next year Congress removed the division from the

Civil Service Commission, making it an independent agency reporting to the president with the same powers and duties it had previously held (Mosher 1984:14–15).

According to Van Riper, the report of the Joint Commission on Re-classification of Salaries in 1920 "ran afoul of the normal congressional opposition to an implicit increase in executive power. The refusal to give the Civil Service Commission the authority necessary to become a central personnel agency and to operate as an integral arm of executive management was typical of Congress's aversion to attempts to interfere with historic legislative prerogatives in personnel matters" (Van Riper 1958:297).

The creation of the Bureau of the Budget by the Budget and Accounting Act of 1921 did, however, indicate a new concern about issues of economy in government and the management processes necessary to achieve those goals. Moving the budget function out of the Treasury Department, the act charged the Bureau of the Budget (BoB) with budget preparation and called on it to study the economy and efficiency of federal agency management. As the BoB authority grew, the Civil Service Commission did not fare so well. The shared authority over personnel matters was clear. Playing an oversight role in the personnel field, the Bureau of Efficiency's Annual Report for 1919–1920 listed studies in four categories. One of them was: "Personnel—inequity and inadequacy of salaries, examining methods in the Civil Service Commission, reclassifications and salary standardization" (Mosher 1984:46–47).

The Classification Act of 1923, "instead of being placed under the unqualified supervision of the Civil Service Commission, was made subject to a specially created Personnel Classification Board. This was to be a tripartite *ex officio* body composed of one representative each from the Bureau of Efficiency, the Bureau of the Budget, and the Civil Service Commission" (Van Riper 1958:298). The battles were between the Bureau of Efficiency and the Civil Service Commission, with the Bureau of the Budget holding the balance of power. Until 1932, the Bureau of Efficiency was the closest thing the government had to a management consulting unit. According to Van Riper,

Some tentative efforts at interdepartmental cooperation were made in the early twenties under the stimulus of the Bureau of the Budget. The Director of the Bureau was instrumental in 1921 in the formation of a Federal Personnel Board composed mainly of the appointment clerks of the various departments and operating under the guidance of the Civil Service Commission. . . . It took the Great Depression and the efforts of President Hoover for economy and efficiency in administration to force consolidation of the major personnel functions of the government of the Civil Service Commission. (ibid.)

Some acknowledgement of the primacy of the CSC role was indicated in 1931 when the Council of Personnel Administration was created by executive order, chaired by the Civil Service Commission president. But some viewed this as an unsatisfactory resolution of the personnel authority issue. A 1931 report prepared by Herman Feldman, professor of industrial relations at Dartmouth's Tuck School, contained recommendations that "were based on the concept of the Civil Service Commission as a central personnel agency, the lack of which he felt was at the bottom of much of the difficulty." He called for the establishment of a Service of Administration, with a secretary of administration coordinating efforts of the BoB, CSC, Bureau of Efficiency, Personnel Classification Board, and the elements that eventually went into the GSA created in 1949 (ibid.:305–08).

Following the passage of the Economy Act of 1932, there was a consolidation of functions, with some formally placed in the Civil Service Commission and others gravitating there due to neglect elsewhere (ibid.:310–11). Mosher described this consolidation: "The day before the inauguration of President Franklin D. Roosevelt, the Bureau of Efficiency was abolished in an appropriation act, on the presumed grounds that the functions would be performed by the BoB. Its records and files were moved to that bureau, but its functions were not picked up for several years. The federal government's first experiment with a permanent central management staff was thus abruptly terminated" (Mosher 1984:46–47).

Up until the New Deal, efforts to move toward a self-conscious federal management strategy (and an active personnel role within it) were dominated by the political bargaining frame—shared authority and a strong congressional role. Management competence frame values of good government were found in the creation of the CSC, and values of efficiency were beginning to move in at the end of this period, but skepticism about a strong executive limited efforts to move ahead.

The Brownlow Proposals of the New Deal Years

As Franklin Roosevelt looked forward to a second term of office, he agreed to the creation of a committee, chaired by Louis Brownlow, to analyze government management and organization. Brownlow "looked to the BOB as a directing and controlling agency" but found that management responsibilities were neglected by BoB (Berman 1979:12). The Brownlow report called for the president to have direct control of the "great management functions of the government"—personnel management, fiscal and organizational management, and planning management. (U.S. GAO 1989:22). In the personnel area, it recommended: "Extend the merit system upward, outward, and downward to cover all non-policy-determining posts; reorganize the civil service system as a part of management under a single responsible administrator, strengthening the Civil Service Commission as a citizen Civil Service Board to serve as a watchdog of the merit system; and increase the salaries of key posts throughout the service so that the government may attract and hold in a career service men and women of the highest ability and character" (Emmerich 1971:53). The report also noted, "The three managerial agencies—the Civil Service Administration (personnel), the Bureau of the Budget (finance), and the National Resources Board (planning)—should be a part and parcel of the Executive Office" (ibid.:54).

According to historian Richard Polenberg, the proposals that emerged were representative of the administrative theories of the Brownlow Commission members (1966:21). Among the most vocal was Luther Gulick, who believed that abandonment of the merit system had been less the fault of President Roosevelt than of the Civil Service Commission itself. He was not persuaded that it would be desirable to extend the civil service unless it could at the same time be imbued with new vigor and flexibility. "Replacing the antiquated system with a highly trained, competent personnel director would revitalize the civil service system and at the same time place it at the disposal of the New Deal" (ibid.:22–23). Van Riper has commented that the Brownlow Commission, after "strongly urging a more 'positive' integration of personnel management with general management . . . recommended once again that the Civil Service Commission be clearly designated the central agency for the supervision of all aspects of federal public personnel management" (Van Riper 1958: 336–37).

The administration deliberately bypassed the civil service because New Deal emergency agencies needed to be organized swiftly and manned by sympathetic, specialized personnel. The Civil Service Commission, swamped with applicants, behind in its work, subject to veteran's preference, and mired in obsolete registers, too often failed to recruit "men" of marked ability. New Dealers preferred not to burden their creations "with the kind of civil service system we now have." The multiheaded CSC would be replaced by a civil service administrator who "should be highly competent, should possess a broad knowledge of personnel administration, and should be a qualified and experienced executive" (Polenberg 1966:22, 27). This position, as well as others spelled out in the Brownlow Commission report, would be held by someone who would be a part of the presidential team.

The report generated a great deal of opposition from Congress as well as from the Civil Service Commission. Then Chairman Harry B. Mitchell presented Roosevelt with a detailed critique of the plan to replace the commission with a single administrator. Even a new Roosevelt appointee opposed it after being named (ibid.:93).

There was an immense amount of bureaucratic lobbying of Congress, and the reorganization bill "became entwined in Roosevelt's attempt to alter the composition of the Supreme Court and did not become law until 1939. But eventually he got just about what he asked for with the exception of transferring the functions of the Civil Service Commission to the White House" (Hess 1976:39). Within a coordination strategy, Roosevelt revitalized the Council of Personnel Administration in 1938, a body that consisted of departmental and agency directors of personnel together with representatives of the Bureau of the Budget and the Civil Service Commission.

On the BoB side, however, new activity was undertaken. John Hart writes, "In 1939, a Division of Administrative Management was established within the bureau that was essentially concerned with the internal management of operating agencies in government. It functioned as a management consultant for the rest of the executive branch, giving advice but unwilling to force its recommendations on any department or agency" (Hart 1987:79). According to Hess, "Actually the reorganization act did not measurably increase the size of Roosevelt's White House staff operations. . . . The Bureau of the Budget, on the other hand, blossomed in the Executive Office, and under the directorship of Harold Smith (1939–1945) rapidly expanded from a staff of about 40 to over 500. The bureau retained its position as the central budget review agency and vastly increased its power in the areas of legislative clearance and administrative management" (Hess 1976:39).

As BoB developed, the director's imprint and role became more important. Harold Smith became director in 1939 and "saw himself as the Director of an institutional career staff, distinct from personal White House aides, but concerned with the problems of the President and the presidency." Neustadt noted that Smith "tried to build and operate his Bureau accordingly, not as a "budget" staff but as a presidential staff which was organized around the budget process for the sake both of convenience and opportunity" (Berman 1979:2).

Wartime encouraged more activity both in BoB and CSC. "Concurrently, the Civil Service Commission and a number of defense and other establishments began to undertake surveys of manpower utilization, and the Bureau of the Budget commenced to interest itself more extensively in the problems of management control within the civil establishment." Commissioner Arthur S. Flemming testified to the House Committee on the Civil Service: "We do not believe that any over-all management controls should be placed in the Civil Service Commission. Whatever additional controls of this character may be needed should, in our judgment, be placed in an agency such as the Bureau of the Budget, subject, of course, to the general direction of the President of the United States" (Van Riper 1958:372, 384).

During wartime the CSC decentralized, turning over large portions of its authority for position classification to its own field establishments and to the developing personnel sections in the departments and agencies. Van Riper characterized this period as one of coordination between federal management agencies.

The liaison with the War Manpower Commission and the Bureau of Personnel Administration, the association with the National Resources Planning Board and its Roster of Scientific and Specialized Personnel, and the effective relationship with the Presidential Liaison Office for Personnel Management, together with the creation of several different types of advisory and coordinating committees, meant that personnel management in the federal government, while centralized in one respect, was also becoming the business of an increasingly interlocking mechanism involving many individuals and organizations besides the Civil Service Commission. (ibid.:389)

The Roosevelt years began with an attempt to marry the arguments found in the management competence frame with those of the executive control frame. "Good management," according to the Brownlow Commission, required a centralized authority within the White House. And this clearly fit with Roosevelt's style and agenda. But the arguments that flowed from the political bargaining frame blocked the personnel piece of the proposals. Congress was unwilling to give the chief executive exclusive control of the growing federal bureaucracy. However, agreement was reached on a coordination strategy and a balance struck between the three perspectives that appeared to last through the war period.

The Postwar Period and Beyond

During Truman's era, the relationship between BoB and the White House was extremely close, largely through an extensive interchange of staff between them. "Only the advent of the Korean war and the usual loss of energy that afflicts an administration whose days in office are numbered caused some diminution of the Budget Bureau's influence" (Hess 1976:52–53). "The Federal Personnel Council remained as an extremely important agency in Commission-departmental cooperation, and its functions were strengthened in the rules revision of 1947. Composed of the directors of personnel of the departments and agencies and of representatives from the Commission and the Bureau of the Budget, the Council provided a continuing interdepartmental advisory body which not only initiated and developed plans but spread throughout the service information about personnel practices" (Van Riper 1958:419).

During the postwar period, joint activity continued. The Classification Act of 1949 resulted in the development of a comprehensive program under the joint supervision of the Bureau of the Budget and the Civil Service Commission (ibid.:441). Some of the same arguments were again voiced. For example, the first Hoover Commission in 1949 recommended that an Office of Personnel be established within the EOP (CRS 1980:25–26). In the Eisenhower era, BoB did not fare as well, although the Second Hoover Commission and the Eisenhower Committee on Government Organization (Nelson Rockefeller, Arthur Flemming, and Milton Eisenhower) did call attention to administrative issues (Hess 1976:76).

Fisher writes that the Budget and Accounting Procedures Act of 1950 directed the president, through the budget director, to evaluate and develop improved plans for the "organization, coordination, and management" of the executive branch. In its 1955 report, the Hoover Commission reiterated the claim that the Budget Bureau's responsibility for preparing the budget had overshadowed its overall management and policy functions (Fisher 1975:47). Hart noted that the Bureau never moved much beyond a narrow interpretation of its management responsibilities, "Schick asserts that it failed to adapt to the new kinds of administrative problems that were reaching the president's desk in the 1950s. These were principally problems of coordinating government programs that cut across departmental jurisdictions. . . . The problem of coordination represented a broader sense of the term *management*" (Hart 1987:79).

President Kennedy "preferred to deal with individuals, not institutions. Moreover, two other forces worked to downplay the traditional role of the bureau as an extension of the presidency. The first was Kennedy's disinterest in questions of management, which was an important element in the bureau's portfolio; the second was the tendency for the legislation that was most important to the President to be designed by Sorensen's office after direct negotiations with the departments and renegotiations on Capitol Hill by O'Brien's men" (Hess 1976:90). By the mid-1960s,

a variety of forces were coming together to promote a more "operational" White House. These included the personality of the President, who was impatient with the pace of government and distrustful of those beyond his immediate reach; the collectivity of new presidential programs that Johnson had pushed through Congress, grander in scale and more complex in executive than the machinery of government was capable of coping with; and the new prevailing view of public administration—nurtured by scholars who had come of age during the New Deal period—that was supportive of centralizing the management of the executive branch in the Office of the President. (ibid.:105)

By the end of the Johnson years, an important role in the management area was played by John Macy, who served both as personnel advisor to the President and the CSC chairman (ibid.:98). One Johnson administration effort on management and administration that came to very little was the Task Force on Government Organization, chaired by industrialist Benjamin Heineman. Although the Heineman task force report was never made public, it stimulated a BoB self study on governmentwide management. This BoB study called for the establishment of a new Office of Executive Management which, "its status provided by its being headed by an assistant director [of BoB], could have responsibilities in five areas: government organization, systems design, operational coordination (with a small staff on an ad hoc basis), financial management and accounting, and special projects (on 'Government-Wide Management Problems')" (Redford and Blissett 1981:212). Johnson was unwilling to give his political support to these proposals but, ironically, much of what Heineman argued resurfaced later in the Nixon Ash Council report.

Nixon and the Ash Council

Stephen Hess has described Nixon as "clearly a management-conscious President; the way the White House would be organized was of serious concern to him" (1976:111). Early in the Nixon administration, a joint GAO, OMB, and Civil Service Commission project recommended that a permanent productivity measurement system be established. However, this effort did not materialize (U.S. GAO 1989:69).

The best expression of Nixon's concern is found in the work of the Advisory Council on Executive Organization, chaired by industrialist Roy L. Ash. The council's original proposal was to replace BoB with a new Office of Executive Management, "envisioned as the President's chief management arm, institutionalizing budget and program evaluation, program coordination, legislative clearance, executive personnel development, and organization and management systems improvement." Such an office would be headed by a presidential appointee and, as Berman quotes Ash, "would create a climate more conducive to managerial effectiveness." The council argued that by including executive personnel within its scope, these programs "would finally receive the attention they deserved" (Berman 1979:107).

There was strong congressional opposition to dropping the term *budget* from the name of the agency, causing a change of the name, first to Office of Management, then to the Office of Management and Budget. And, as one might expect, there was great opposition within BoB to the changes.

The first submission of the plan—Reorganization Plan No. 2—to the House subcommittee was not successful; the subcommittee turned it down. It was noted that "the technical objectives, however, covered more deep-seated suspicion of the White House staff and the fact that the Director of the Domestic Council would not be required to testify before Congress" (ibid:110). After tough lobbying, in May 1970 the plan was finally approved as submitted.

Reorganization Plan No. 2 of 1970 transformed BoB into the Office of Management and Budget. It was developed before George Schultz became director (and Caspar Weinberger became deputy director heading up all the budget activities). An associate director was named with responsibility for everything but budget under the general heading of management. One of the divisions reporting to the management associate director was the Division of Executive Development and Labor Relations (Benda and Levine 1986:383–84). This division focused on the functions that CSC considered central to its mission and tension between OMB and CSC over policy leadership resulted. CSC Chairman Robert Hampton took advantage of the OMB focus on these two fields, however, to maintain liaison in support of substantial CSC growth in executive personnel management and labor-management relations.

Hess has written, "It is hardly accidental that the Bureau of the Budget has become the Office of *Management* and Budget. All major study groups since the Brownlow Committee have recommended giving the President additional tools for management as a means of increasing his control over the executive branch" (Hess 1976:147). But in this case, as in the Brownlow period, the arguments for the new structure reflected a confluence of the good government arguments (the management competence frame) with the presidential agenda (the executive control frame). And, as in Brownlow, the proposal from the White House could be crafted to gain congressional acceptance. Once Watergate was uncovered, however, the agreement collapsed.

The Civil Service Reform Act of 1978

Even before Jimmy Carter assumed the presidency, it was clear that the post-Watergate White House of Gerald Ford would move authority away from OMB; indeed, a task force advised President Ford to curb OMB's policy role, arguing that OMB had become too involved in departmental policy processes. Louis Fisher commented on that period:

The problem with OMB was not its deep involvement in "policy" or its interference with agencies. That is inevitable for any central budget staff. What OMB lacked was political judgment, the kind of judgment that becomes second nature to professionals who have worked with Congress and the agencies, who are capable of the give-and-take, compromise, and good-faith efforts that are required in the policy process. OMB became the captive (temporarily we hope) of abstract theories of organization, doctrinaire views of management, and impractical claims of constitutional power. (Fisher 1975:57–58)

Thus, Jimmy Carter assumed the presidency in an environment of skepticism about grand organizational and management designs. At the same time, his personal predilections to focus on management issues gave rise to the establishment of the Presidential Reorganization

Program (PRP), located in OMB under the direction of a new Executive Associate Director of Reorganization and Management. While the PRP emphasized structural consolidations and the streamlining of governmental units, it also included an effort to develop an administrative management program. According to the design, such a program for the president would "provide guidance for internal management reforms in the agencies and departments" (Radin and Hawley 1988:55).

Howard Messner, a participant in the PRP effort, noted that "in its earlier days, the Presidential Reorganization Program focused on the boxes of government, but they quickly realized that the process of government was at least equally important or perhaps more so." Messner commented that that OMB did, "in that instance, what it was supposed to do, which was to act as catalyst for other management arms of the government to organize and carry out a program of improvement" (U.S. GAO 1988:51, 52). The President's Personnel Management Project, a part of the PRP, was among the most visible and active parts of the Carter effort, bringing together well-respected academicians and practitioners from the public administration community. Working in ten task forces, the project group attempted to identify specific problems in the personnel area and possible solutions to them. Although the participants represented a span of views within the public administration field, the predominant arguments that emerged from the effort represented the management competence frame in approaching personnel issues. In addition, as Patricia Ingraham and Carolyn Ban have noted, "The drafters of the legislation borrowed heavily from private management innovations. . . . The result of these influences was an approach that emphasized the values of management flexibility and efficiency and downplayed the traditional public personnel values of equity and procedural uniformity" (Ingraham and Ban 1984:2).

The proposal to reorganize the personnel management function in the federal government emerged from the PRP less than a year into the new administration. Its movement from an analytic activity to a political proposal modified some of the solutions developed by the project staff. It was crafted to support the Carter belief that "there is no inherent conflict between careful planning, tight management, and constant reassessment on the one hand and compassionate concern for the plight of the deprived and the afflicted on the other. Waste and inefficiency never fed a hungry child, provided a job for a willing worker, or educated a deserving student" (U.S. GAO 1988:12). As then Civil

Service Chairman Alan Campbell saw it, "We were attempting to create a system that would at least contribute to the efficiency and effectiveness of government. . . . [I am] fully aware of the kind of detail and nitty-gritty which is involved in the daily management of the system. It is frequently very difficult to relate the broad generalizations we used in talking about the public service to the details of personnel management. . . . We believed that the human resource function, dictated by its history, had developed into a protective negative system primarily designed to prevent patronage, favoritism, and other personnel abuses" (ibid).

When the proposal for what became the Civil Service Reform Act emerged from OMB, it emphasized the protection of the merit system rather than the relationship between personnel and general management concerns. It stated, "We are proposing a number of reforms which we believe will help restore an appropriate balance between these sometimes competing needs for flexibility and efficiency on the one hand, and adequate safeguards on the other, in order to foster effective, fair management in the federal government" (ibid.:71).

In addition to the Personnel Project, the PRP also called for the reorganization of the Executive Office of the President. Among the changes recommended was the transfer of four functions to other parts of the government. One was the Executive Department/Labor Relations Division in OMB (the management function that had been created in the Ash Council report) from the Executive Office of the President to the Civil Service Commission (PRP 1977:4). According to a paper prepared by the Congressional Research Service, "The stress placed by President Carter on keeping the EOP small has required that certain new units, which originally had been thought to be appropriate units for the EOP, be placed outside the EOP in an independent status. . . . When President Carter recommended that the Civil Service Commission be abolished and replaced by an Office of Personnel Management (OPM) and a Merit System Protection Board (MSPB) (Reorganization Plan No. 2 of 1978), both the OPM and the MSPB were given an 'independent' status rather than being included within the EOP" (CRS 1980:25–26).

Scotty Campbell also took his own administrative action to put the M into OPM. He converted the former Bureau of Training into the Workforce Effectiveness Directorate, which was supposed to facilitate productivity improvement throughout government, particularly through improved managers and enhanced management. He changed the *Civil Service Journal* from a personnel journal into a new publication, *Management,* oriented much more broadly than personnel.

The CSRA contained multiple and often conflicting elements in its design. Ban and Ingraham listed three tensions present in the legislation:

The conflict between the desire for greater political responsiveness and the desire for greater managerial capability and independence. . . . The conflict between the concept of a management cadre with a sense of identity and esprit de corps and the concept of competition to increase productivity. The conflict between the goal of increasing managers' ability to fire problem employees and the goal of protecting whistleblowers. (Ingraham and Ban 1984:2–3)

These tensions were present because of the coalitions and compromises that were required to achieve agreement on management reform. As in the earlier instances, the reform represented an admixture of arguments from the management competence frame (the good government perspective); the executive control frame (Carter's interest in the management issue); and the political bargaining frame (the willingness by Congress to give new authority—or at least new administrative structure—to the personnel function).

The Reagan Years

Even before the Reagan administration assumed office, the blueprint of what it promised to achieve was found in the Heritage Foundation volume, *Mandate for Leadership.* The book suggested that the new administration would not use the management capacity in OMB in the same way as had its predecessors.

On the management side of OMB, the major deficiencies stem from the sheer volume of activities which are attempted. Through a decade-long series of Executive Orders, Presidents have delegated to OMB a substantial portion of Presidential duties. While many of these, such as standardizing statistical terminology and definitions, are clearly housekeeping chores appropriate to OMB, decisions concerning river basin commissions, science and technology policy, etc., are clearly outside the scope of OMB's mandate. These functions should be returned to the appropriate departments. In short, the President should redirect the efforts of the departments to administering the government and leave to the Executive Office of the President the responsibility for setting budget policy priorities. (Rogers 1980:957–58)

During the first Reagan term, under the leadership of OPM Director Donald Devine, the personnel function operated hand in glove with the policies emanating from the White House. During that time, OMB was the "focal point for the development of the administration's budget policy, and, as the architect of drastic reductions in domestic expenditures, OMB, more than ever before, is identified as a political arm of the president it serves rather than a career staff of neutral experts supporting the office of the presidency" (Hart 1987:78). Devine eliminated the Workforce Effective Directorate established by Campbell as the major vehicle for OPM's management role. This action, together with drastic budget and staff reductions, led to a perception that Devine's agenda was to eliminate government, not to improve it.

The second year of the Reagan administration, 1982, saw the establishment of the Cabinet Council on Management Administration and formal inauguration of the President's Management Improvement Program, Reform 88. Reform 88 "was clearly the chief management venture undertaken by OMB during Reagan's first term. It quickly became, and has remained, a centerpiece of the administration's intention to make the federal government more efficient, cost effective, and business-like" (Benda and Levine 1986:386).

Much of the administration's interest in management came directly from the White House, the President's Council on Management Improvement, and the President's Private Sector Survey on Cost Control—the Grace Commission. The Grace Commission was another in the line of outside groups, headed by an industrialist, brought in to advise the president. Newland has been quoted to the effect that "OMB . . . lost much of its management policy leadership to the CCMA," the Cabinet Council on Management and Administration (ibid.:387).

As the second administration took form, again a Heritage Foundation volume helped an observer understand the approach to be used. *Mandate for Leadership II* projected an image of OMB controlling OPM like any other agency. It emphasized the relationship between budget and personnel. It highlighted the importance of the discretion of public servants as they implemented policies. The volume ridiculed the concept of a neutral public service and, instead, warned of sabotage by bureaucrats. In this sense, it (as well as its predecessor volume) directly challenged the management competence frame assumptions of the CSRA and relied almost exclusively on the executive control approach (Butler, Sanera, and Weinrod 1984).

The absence of OPM from the federal management scene was illustrated in one depiction of the Reagan presidential management process. The actors listed included the Office of Cabinet Administration, OMB, the Office of Policy Development, and the Office of Planning and Evaluation. In this picture, OPM was not even viewed as an agency performing a coordinating function (Argyle and Barilleaux 1986:727). The peripheral role played by OPM was also depicted in the *FY 1990 Management Document*—the last report accompanying the budget to be issued by the Reagan administration. Highlighting the effort in "Total Quality Management," the report noted that OPM "reviews current personnel policies and practices, and recommends appropriate changes to facilitate productivity and quality improvement; offers training for Federal employees on productivity and quality-related issues; and assists agencies in job placement and retraining to minimize dislocation of employees" (Executive Office of the President 1990:3/47).

By the end of the Reagan administration, it was hard to find even a trace of the management competence frame arguments that had characterized earlier attempts at federal administrative change. The only arguments came from the executive control frame—positions and strategies designed to maximize the president's control of the executive branch. And, as has been noted elsewhere, this strategy was more effectively achieved through fiscal control methods (and attendant personnel ceilings) than through efforts at other forms of administrative change (Fisher 1981). One commentator painted a dark picture of the situation:

The recent political answer to the responsiveness issue has been an assertion of control specifically and predominantly by the executive branch. The policies of Nixon, Carter, and Reagan alike have been directed to presidential supremacy with a corresponding diminution of congressional control, interest group influence, and the self-directing influence of professional and other employee interests. The attempt to create a presidency that "runs the country" has resulted in a closed, top-down policy system which has neither encouraged nor tolerated the infusion of professional ideas and recommendations in the personnel policy process. (Lane 1987:8)

Proposals for Change: The End of the
Reagan Administration

Before the Reagan administration came to an end, new proposals began to surface for change in the federal management system (and related changes in federal personnel management). In a 1986 article in the *Public Administration Review,* Benda and Levine argued that past reform proposals stemmed from concern that OMB (and BoB) "lacked the institutional capacity necessary to sustain management improvement efforts throughout the executive branch." Four proposals were advanced for the next iteration of reform: (1) leave management with OMB but upgrade the M side by creating two statutory deputy directors, one for management and one for budget, and by expanding the *M* side staff; (2) transfer the *M* side functions of OMB to OPM, thereby creating an Office of Management; (3) create a large and powerful Office of Federal Management that would add GSA and OPM to the current OMB (this was recommended by the Grace Commission); and (4) create two entities, an Office of Federal Management Policy in the EOP and an independent Office of Federal Operations (combining operating functions of OMB, OPM and GSA) (Benda and Levine 1986: 387, 388).

Another proposal was advanced in which an Office of Federal Management might be formed alongside an Office of Federal Budget, an Office of Federal Procurement Policy, an Office of Information and Regulatory Affairs, and an Office of Financial Systems. Such an Office of Federal Management would provide general management improvement and evaluation, human resources management, productivity improvement, and organization and coordination management, as well as assistance in developing the president's legislative program (Gilmour and Sperry 1988:395).

A report by the National Academy of Public Administration for the 1988–89 presidential transition emphasized the role of OPM and other central management agencies.

The Office of Personnel Management (OPM) was created as a central management agency in 1978. Designed to serve as the principal human resource planning agency for the federal government, the potential of this agency has not been fully developed. During President Reagan's first term, OPM became an instrument to advance certain policy goals only tangentially related to the agency's mission. As a direct result, the reputation of OPM suffered, as did human resource planning and management. (NAPA 1988:26)

The report provided examples of major budget and management reform initiatives from 1977 to 1987. The listing (the PRP, ZBB, the Executive Group to Combat Fraud and Waste in Government, the President's Management Improvement Council, the President's Council on Integrity and Efficiency, the Grace Commission, the Cabinet Council on Management and Administration, and Reform 88) indicates that little had been done to address the relationship between management improvement and personnel issues since the passage of the CSRA (ibid.).

The General Accounting Office also focused on OMB's institutional capacity to deal with federal management needs. "As it increased efforts to respond to presidential priorities, OMB's commitment to established administrative management functions eroded. For many years, the pervasive philosophy with BOB was that there should be institutional memory in such classical management areas as financial management, organizational policy, and statistical policy" (U.S. GAO 1989:69).

Almost since BOB was created by the Budget and Accounting Act of 1921, its performance in attempting to improve federal management has been much debated. The act charged BOB with preparing the budget and studying the economy and efficiency of federal agencies' management. Over time, the institution's management responsibilities have broadened in response to the growing size and complexity of the federal environment. However, throughout the agency's history, it has struggled to fulfill these management leadership responsibilities effectively.

Nevertheless, it has been continually criticized for failing to fulfill its management responsibilities, for failing to link its management and budget activities properly, for not adapting to its changing environment, and for being insufficiently responsive to the President. (ibid.:22)

The federal management dilemma was spelled out further:

In contrast to its budget role, OMB's management responsibilities have never been well-defined. Almost since its inception, there has been little agreement over either the approaches it should take toward management improvement or the management functions it should oversee. Since its reorganization in 1970, each administration has directed OMB to undertake a major management improvement effort significantly different from that conducted by the previous administration. These efforts generally lacked direction and dissolved as presidential attention waned. In addition, as OMB became more closely associated with presidential policy interests, Congress legislatively directed OMB to exercise leadership on a variety of administrative management issues. These actions exerted lasting effects on the structure of OMB's management activities. (ibid.:67)

Despite this situation, the public administration community continues to rely on the potential of a management function within OMB. The major focus of the proposals relies on assumptions and arguments that flow from the management competence and executive control frames. The NAPA report on the executive presidency for the 1988–1989 transition noted that

past presidents generally looked to the OMB director to provide leadership on the organization and management matters requiring coordination across government. Starting in 1982, the White House staff became more directly involved through the Cabinet Council on Management and Administration, and its successor, the Domestic Policy Council. Whether it be the OMB director or some other official, the next president will need someone to develop strategy for management matters, coordinate the efforts of the central agencies, and other government organizations, and follow up on implementation throughout government. (NAPA 1988:27)

Where Do We Go Next?

This tale of the search for the *M* in federal management reads like a modern-day version of the myth of Sisyphus. In that story, every time it appeared that Sisyphus had rolled the huge stone to the top of the hill, it rolled back down again. Like Sisyphus, proponents of a one best way to organize the personnel function within the federal management portfolio seemed to be doomed to an eternal search for the opportunity to institutionalize a solution. For much of the public administration community (especially those who approach the issue from the management competence frame), federal personnel policy and its implementing agencies belong in the White House, working at the same level as those charged with budget responsibilities. From this perspective, a neat parallelism should exist between personnel and budget, with overhead agencies operating as bookends to hold up federal management practice.

At the same time, it is obvious that personnel policy must be sensitive to the political responsiveness demands of the president and the broader political environment in which the president operates. As was noted at the beginning of this chapter, one cannot focus on this relationship without acknowledging that management improvement in the federal government is contextual; it emerges at a particular time, with a specific set of actors, and in a unique political, economic and social environment. The policy result of this contingent approach suggests that clear authority lines and boundaries of responsibility are not likely to emerge. Coordination—not control—strategies can be expected to continue in this interdependent and interrelated system.

The three frames that have been used to analyze the conflicting paradigms at play in the quest to achieve federal management reform continue to be relevant to an analysis of future proposals for change. This historical account of reform efforts suggests that change does not occur unless a proposal is supported by arguments from all three approaches. Even when this occurs and agreement is reached on the appropriate authority base, form and structure for federal management, this agreement is temporary. Thus, although Alan Campbell sought to steal the *M* out of OMB to bring it to OPM in 1977, it is not surprising that others have reclaimed it.

NOTES

Aaron Wildavsky, Chester Newland, Patricia Ingraham, David Rosenbloom, Ralph Bledsoe, and Frank Gavin provided extremely useful comments on a draft of this chapter.

1. This chapter deals with issues related to management as a policy issue unto itself. There is an equally important analytic approach that looks at management issues not as ends in themselves but related to substantive policy outcomes.

2. Readers will note the similarity between these three frames and those employed by Herbert Kaufman (1956). Kaufman argues that administrative institutions in the United States have been organized and operated in pursuit of three values: representativeness, neutral competence, and executive leadership. The three frames used here modify the Kaufman typology and also draw on Rosenbloom (1989) and on Wildavsky (1987).

3. I have drawn on Edie N. Goldenberg's (1985) characterization of differing views on the role of the civil service.

4. Louis Fisher (1981:159) discusses the impact of OMB power through personnel ceilings.

SOURCES

Argyle, Nolan J. and Ryan J. Barilleaux. 1986. "Past Failures and Future Prescriptions for Presidential Management Reform," *Presidential Studies Quarterly* 4 (Fall):716–733.

Benda, Peter M., and Charles H. Levine. 1986. "OMB and the Central Management Problem: Is Another Reorganization the Answer?" PAR 46 (September/October):379–91.

Berman, Larry. 1979. *The Office of Management and Budget and the Presidency, 1921–1979.* Princeton, N.J.: Princeton University Press.

Butler, Stuart M., Michael Sanera, and W. Bruce Weinrod, eds. 1984. *Mandate for Leadership II.* Washington, D.C.: Heritage Foundation.

CRS, 1980. *The Federal Executive Establishment: Evolution and Trends.* Prepared for the Senate Committee on Government Affairs. Washington, D.C.: Congressional Research Service, Library of Congress.

Emmerich, Herbert. 1971. *Federal Organization and Administration Management.* University, Ala.: University of Alabama Press.

Executive Office of the President. 1990. *Management of the U.S. Government.* Fiscal Year 1990. Washington, D.C.

Fisher, Louis. 1975. *Presidential Spending Power.* Princeton, N.J.: Princeton University Press.

———. 1981. "Effect of the Budget Act of 1974 on Agency Operations." In *The Congressional Budget Process after Five Years*, ed. Rudolph G. Penner. Washington, D.C.: American Enterprise Institute.

Gilmour, Robert S., and Roger L. Sperry. 1986. "Pushing the String: Moving Central Management Reform from the Senate." PAR 46 (September/October): 392–96.

Goldenberg, Edie N. 1985. "The Permanent Government in an Era of Retrenchment and Redirection." In *The Reagan Presidency and the Governing of America*, ed. Lester M. Salamon and Michael S. Lund. Washington, D.C.: Urban Institute Press.

Gulick, Luther. 1977. "Notes on the Theory of Organization." In *Papers on the Science of Administration*, ed. Luther Gulick and L. Urwick. Rpt. of 1937 edition. Fairfield, Conn.: Augustus M. Kelley.

Hart, John. 1987. *The Presidential Branch.* New York: Pergamon Press.

Hess, Stephen. 1976. *Organizing the Presidency.* Washington, D.C.: Brookings Institution.

Ingraham, Patricia W., and Carolyn Ban, eds. 1984. *Legislating Bureaucratic Change: The Civil Service Reform Act of 1978.* Albany: SUNY University Press.

Kaufman, Herbert. 1956. "Emerging Conflicts in the Doctrines of Public Administration." *American Political Science Review* 50:1057–73.

Lane, Larry M. 1987. "Public Service in Crisis and Transition." *The Bureaucrat.* Fall:5–10.

Mosher, Frederick C. 1984. *A Tale of Two Agencies.* Baton Rouge: Louisiana State University Press.

NAPA. 1988. *The Executive Presidency: Federal Management for the 1990s*, A Report by an Academy Panel for the 1988–89 Presidential Transition. Washington, D.C.: National Academy of Public Administration.

Polenberg, Richard. 1966. *Reorganizing Roosevelt's Government: the Controversy Over Executive Reorganization, 1936–39.* Cambridge, Mass.: Harvard University Press.

PRP. 1977. *Reorganization of the Executive Office of the President.* Washington, D.C.: President's Reorganization Project, OMB.

Radin, Beryl A., and Willis D. Hawley. 1988. *The Politics of Reorganization: Creating the U.S. Department of Education.* New York: Pergamon Press.

Redford, Emmette S. 1969. *Democracy in the Administrative State.* New York: Oxford University Press.

Redford, Emmette S., and Marlan Blissett. 1981. *Organizing the Executive Branch: The Johnson Presidency.* Chicago: The University of Chicago Press.

Rogers, Joe. O. 1980. "Office of Management and Budget." In *Mandate for Leadership*, ed. Charles L. Heatherly. Washington, D.C.: The Heritage Foundation.

Rosenbloom, David. 1989. *Understanding Management, Politics, and Law in the Public Sector*. New York: Random House, McGraw-Hill.

Staats, Elmer B. 1987. *Public Service and the Public Interest: An Occasional Paper*. The James E. Webb Lecture. Washington, D.C.: National Academy of Public Administration.

U.S. GAO. 1988. *Civil Service Reform: Development of 1978 Civil Service Reform Proposals*. Washington, D.C.: General Accounting Office.

————. 1989. *Managing the Government: Revised Approach Could Improve OMB's Effectiveness*. GAO GGD, 89–65. Washington, D.C.: General Accounting Office.

Van Riper, Paul P. 1958. *History of the United States Civil Service*. New York: Greenwood Press.

Wildavsky, Aaron. 1987. "Choosing Preferences by Constructing Institutions: A Cultural Theory of Preference Formation." *American Political Science Review* 81:3–21.

4. The Politics of Civil Service Reform

Chester A. Newland

The politics of civil service reform operated mostly at three interrelated levels in 1977–1978: (1) presidential politics and congressional-executive branch relationships, focusing primarily on presidential reorganization authority and proposed executive flexibilities to manage personnel; (2) external interest group politics, most visible in Congress and most notably focused on veterans' preference, Hatch Act repeal, labor-management relations, and equal employment opportunity; and (3) internal public administration–civil service community politics related to all of the above issues but also focused on additional technical personnel provisions, particularly the Senior Executive Service (SES), performance systems and compensation, flexibilities for managers and their line organizations to manage, and protections of merit and employees' rights. In short, the politics of the Civil Service Reform Act of 1978 were complex.

Overlapping periods of political changes before 1978 accounted for the complexity (Newland 1984). First, presidential politics had changed dramatically in less than two decades, evidenced in John F. Kennedy's nomination through domination of primary elections, altered by fallout from the Civil Rights Act of 1964, and then complicated by the divisions of Vietnam and the disaster of Watergate. Ten years of unprecedented conflict, division, and separation of presidential politics from earlier party institutions became a backdrop for the politics of civil service reform. Second, twenty years of turmoil in public personnel administration preceded CSRA, associated mostly with the rapid expansion of forms of collective bargaining in governments, growing litigiousness over employee rights and equal employment opportunity, and mounting public hostility toward expanding government and its costs. Third, forty years of growing orthodoxy in public

63

administration in favor of presidential aggrandizement and twenty-five years of growing orthodoxy in political science in favor of partisan presidential power provided justifications for the political thrust—the core policy—of the CSRA. That this policy of political control of the civil service by the president was adopted is evidence that the constitutional principle of shared congressional-presidential responsibility and authority over the executive branch had shifted by 1978. It was replaced by a conception of separation of powers in which the president was to dominate the executive branch. That was a great departure from the earlier view of presidential responsibility, which held that the executive branch, in joint oversight with Congress, was to ensure that the laws are faithfully executed.

The politics and political lessons of civil service reform are probed here at the three levels, identified above, at which politics operated in 1977–1978. The lessons are too numerous and complicated for thorough treatment in an initial overview. The principal political lessons highlighted by the CSRA experience, however, are as follows. Aggrandizement of presidential power is increasingly an irresistible force in American politics and government; setbacks to presidential power, as after Watergate, are temporary at the most; and presidents use their ever growing political power to advance partisan self-interests in civil service reform as in other matters. The politics of special interests greatly control both Congress and the presidency in civil service legislation as in other policy; those special interests support major legislative changes in civil service so long as their particular interests are also advanced or at least insulated; and increased fragmentation and complexity, rather than simplification and focused responsibility and authority, are the products of such interest group politics, as in the civil service reforms of 1978. The public administration community generally is overwhelmingly and almost unconsciously dominated by a presidential bias. The narrow civil service community is oriented not only to presidential leadership but also to Congress, but that is due less to devotion to a shared constitutional authority concept than to reliance on Congress to protect and advance the special interests of civil servants and their unions. The professional public administration community is responsive to political officials, particularly the president, but while generally technically informed, it responds largely to what is politically fashionable in civil service change, not necessarily to experience-based or researched alternatives.

Presidential Politics: Separation and Aggrandizement

The *May-Malek Manual* and Watergate were initial political obstacles that had to be put aside in 1977–1978 if civil service reform or other reorganizations by presidential initiative were to be achieved by the Carter administration.[1] As a practical matter, the presidency had been stripped of reorganization authority, and regaining that was the initial political challenge for Carter. But even after winning greatly circumscribed authority in 1977 to propose reorganizations, suspicions of the presidency lingered from the years of Nixon's excesses. When H.R. 11280, the CSRA bill, was debated in 1978, for example, Representative Benjamin Gilman, Republican of New York, noted that Alan May, coauthor of the *May-Malek Manual*, was supporting it. Gilman quoted May as saying: "I congratulate President Carter on his proposed civil service reforms. It was exactly to that kind of result that my manual was written" (Gilman 1978). Gilman and some others remained suspicious to the end about the "executive flexibilities" built into the CSRA, but the Carter administration successfully exercised political skills to regain reorganization authority for the president in 1977 and to secure partisan presidential control over the civil service in 1978.

Politics and Reorganization Authority

Carter campaigned against Washington in 1976 and promised to change it—committing himself to shake up the bureaucracy, including the civil service. He pledged executive branch reorganizations to increase the efficiency and responsiveness of government. Although he entered a presidential office stripped of reorganization authority, he brought to Washington the larger authority of election and he set about regaining power for the president, in part by continuing to campaign against Washington.

Carter won the election by building his own coalition, and he owed little to congressional or other party institutions. That cut both ways. But Carter had won in 1976, and although his coalition was too loose and full of contradictions to sustain a successful presidency for long, it helped him with the politics of regaining limited reorganization authority in 1977 and creating a modestly compromised civil service reform plan.

Most notably, Carter was the first president elected by the New South through politics forever changed by the Civil Rights Act of 1964.

The new politics had delivered the South to the Republicans for the first time in 1968 and then again in 1972, but Carter's coalition managed electoral success in the aftermath of Watergate, in significant measure by campaigning against Washington and big government generally. Some forces that combined to elect Carter were also exercising new electoral power—black votes—in southern congressional districts, including the southeast Texas district of Jack Brooks, chairman of the House Government Operations Committee. Brooks had been a long-time ally of Lyndon Johnson, who had pushed the Civil Rights Act through, proudly (but with political apprehensions for his party), signing it into law on 2 July 1964.

It was Brooks who, in 1977, was crucial to the decision to restore reorganization authority to the president. At first he was opposed. Brooks had earlier supported extensive authority for his friend, President Johnson, including reorganization authority to create cabinet-level departments (the Department of Transportation was created that way under LBJ). But in 1977, Brooks harbored concerns from the Watergate years, and he doubted the constitutionality of delegated reorganization authority that was subject only to congressional veto. He would not consider restoring such authority to include cabinet-level organizations. He also wanted authority at lower levels, if restored at all, to be closely circumscribed. In short, Jack Brooks was increasingly of the New South politically as a result of the workings of the Civil Rights Act of 1964. But after Watergate, even for a president of his own party, he supported the old politics of shared congressional-executive authority. Except for LBJ, whom he understood, Jack Brooks did not favor much aggrandizement of the presidency. Others in Congress, however, were amenable to the proposals of the new president.

Less than three months after entering office, on 6 April 1977, President Carter signed into law the Reorganization Act of 1977 (P.L. 95–17; 5 USC 901). It was the most that he could get from Congress and provided authority to submit reorganizations below the cabinet level, no more than one before Congress at any one time, with time constraints making more than three per year impossible and even two a challenge.

President Carter was politically committed to one other reorganization before he could act on civil service reform. Reorganization Plan No. 1 of 1978 kept a political commitment to Coretta Scott King and other New South supporters. It strengthened the Equal Employment Opportunity Commission (EEOC). One aspect of that was that all dis-

crimination appeals were to be filed directly with the EEOC and processed by it, removing authority of the U.S. Civil Service Commission
(CSC) over such appeals (U.S. Congress 1978b). Bitter disputes between EEOC and CSC had recurred throughout the 1970s, with each
resorting to recriminating audits of the other. Carter had promised to
change that. It was his first action under the Reorganization Act of
1977, and Congress allowed it to go into effect as Reorganization Plan
No. 1 of 1978.

Reorganization Plan No. 2 of 1978

On 23 May 1978, the president transmitted to the Senate and the
House of Representatives his proposed Reorganization Plan No. 2 of
1978 (U.S. Congress 1978a). On 2 March, Carter had sent to Congress
the broad outlines of his civil service reform proposal, but the formal
submission of Plan No. 2 was forced to wait in line behind Plan No. 1.
Even long before 2 March, the main provisions of Carter's proposal
had been widely discussed. That openness was a key feature of the
politics of this civil service reform effort.

Broad participation in deliberations by the press and others, extensive involvement of selected leaders of the public administration and
civil service communities (but general exclusion of the public personnel establishment), consultation with wide-ranging interest groups,
and regular dialogue with congressional leaders and staffs characterized the entire process of development, presentation, modification, and
promotion of the reform proposals. This wide-open approach was in
stark contrast to the secrecy imposed by President Franklin D.
Roosevelt in the Brownlow Commission efforts in 1936. Carter employed a vigorous politics of public and press involvement and continued to 'run against the mess in Washington.' The president's
appointee as chairman of the CSC, Alan (Scotty) Campbell, skillfully
involved and co-opted board elements of the Washington establishment and related groups nationally in the politics of reform design
and adoption.

The principal thrust of the 1978 reorganization plan was to authorize direct political control of civil service operations by the president.
Technically, the CSC was transformed into a small Merit Systems Protection Board (MSPB), with an Office of Special Counsel as a principal administrative apparatus; the Federal Labor Relations Council was
changed into the Federal Labor Relations Authority (FLRA); and a
new organization, the U.S. Office of Personnel Management (OPM),

was created to take over the bulk of former CSC work under direct control of a single presidential appointee. The substantive details of the reorganization are examined in other chapters of this book. But it is essential to recall here that the idea of placing civil service directly under the president dated back to the Brownlow proposals. Such presidential control was soundly defeated in Congress then, even though the Brownlow proposal required appointment of an expert professional.

The politics behind the structural changes in Reorganization Plan No. 2 of 1978 heated up in the 1960s and 1970s, largely as a result of collective bargaining pressures, growing criticism of the CSC, and general dissatisfaction with allegedly unresponsive civil service procedures. In 1975, the Ralph Nader organization published a study, *The Spoiled System* (Vaughn 1975), alleging CSC failure to root out violations of merit and suggesting general malaise in the federal service. Then CSC Chairman Robert Hampden appointed Milton Sharon to investigate alleged problems. Sharon was the retired CSC regional director of the Philadelphia region, and he had a reputation for independence and expertise. *The Sharon Report*, completed in 1976 as an internal CSC document and not published, found some CSC failures. The earlier *May-Malek Manual* completed at the outset of the Nixon administration, followed by Richard Nathan's *The Plot That Failed* (Nathan 1977) after Nixon left office, also gave credence to charges that the merit system had been undermined. When Carter entered office, the Democrats seized the opportunity to investigate alleged CSC wrongdoing. A prominent Democratic party–oriented law firm was named to assist with an inquiry, but little came of it. Improprieties were alleged in various agencies, including the General Services Administration (GSA), with vocal criticisms by former personnel specialists at GSA that the CSC's inspections-evaluation bureau had not been attentive to faults there and elsewhere. The new administration used the Intergovernmental Personnel Act to encourage key civil service executives to take assignments elsewhere, and it later used reorganization as a basis to encourage their early retirements. For the first time ever, key CSC positions previously filled by careerists were shifted to political appointees. The 1976 *Sharon Report*, building on Nader's allegations and on lingering suspicions from Watergate, helped to sustain Carter's anti-Washington campaign. Specifically, critics challenged the integrity of the CSC as an institution, providing impetus to the structural aspects of Reorganization Plan No. 2. The administration argued that the CSC had two irreconcilable functions that had to be split.

Problems of the CSC, the FLRC, and the civil service apparatus were real, and their importance was recognized during the Ford administration, when both Congress and CSC leaders took steps to pave the way for reforms after the 1976 election, whatever the outcome. On 31 December 1976, for example, the House Committee on Post Office and Civil Service issued the *History of Civil Service Merit Systems of the United States and Selected Foreign Countries Together with Executive Reorganization Studies and Personnel Recommendations* (U.S. Congress 1976). It was one of several documents waiting to assist the new administration. Well before the 1976 election, CSC Chairman Robert Hampden met in Charlottesville in the Federal Executive Institute library to consider, with three others, prospects for a statutory basis for federal labor-management relations, including reorganization of the Federal Labor Relations Council. Much earlier, former CSC Executive Director Bernard Rosen had recommended continuation of the independent Civil Service Commission, under close congressional scrutiny. He advised substantial enhancement of positions, authorities, and professional quality of agency personnel directors to assure enforcement of merit standards and energetic personnel performance. He also recommended provision of a statutory basis for labor-management relations. Such recommendations would have formed the basis of civil service reform had Ford continued as President. But the election of 1976 led instead to the drastic restructuring proposed in Reorganization Plan No. 2 of 1978. The extensive civil service studies of 1975 and 1976 quickly served, however, to inform the Carter reformers of alternatives, facilitating a fast track for the new Administration's proposals.

The experienced personnel community, personified by Bernard Rosen and supported by Chairman David Henderson of the House Post Office and Civil Service Committee (who did not seek reelection in 1976), did not support drastic restructuring—partisan presidential domination of the Civil Service—of the sort proposed by the Carter Administration. In the 1977–1978 politics of reform, the personnel community was quickly shunted aside as negative and unresponsive, and the larger public administration (PA) community was given a prominent role in development and promotion of the Carter reforms. That larger PA community was already oriented to presidential control of everything in the executive branch, and many in it had long blamed CSC for restrictions which were mostly faults of legal requirements of labor-management relations, EEO, veterans preference, and

Figure 1. Personnel Management Project Organization Chart

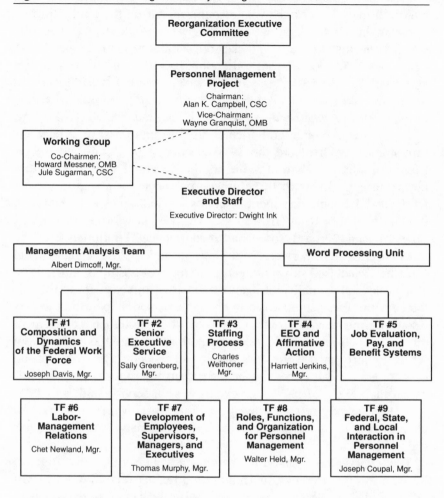

other assorted statutory provisions adopted to satisfy civil service unions and other special interests.

The Personnel Management Project (PMP) was organized as shown in figure 1, with Dwight Ink as Executive Director. Ink was a respected career executive and was the elected President of the American Society for Public Administration in 1978–1979. All but three PMP Task Forces were headed by careerists. The PMP Task Force that related most to the structural proposals in Reorganization Plan No. 2 was managed by Walter Held of the Brookings Institution. That connection was prominently highlighted in congressional testimony in support of proposals to create OPM and MSPB. The Labor-Management Relations Task Force was managed by a university professor with long CSC ties. The FLRA proposal in the Reorganization Plan reinforced statements made to unions during the course of the PMP's work that statutory provisions for labor-management relations would have Administration support if they would go along with the other reorganization proposals. The Job Evaluation, Pay, and Benefit Systems Task Force had no regular manager, although a private-sector executive was briefly involved with it; compensation was clearly too political an issue to tackle in conjunction with all of the other reforms, and, except for bonuses and performance systems, that sensitive subject was deferred for a later time.

The focus in the spring of 1978 was mostly on OPM and MSPB, and those organizations, along with the Senior Executive Service (SES), were the chief concerns of most members of the professional PA community who were enlisted by CSC Chairman Campbell to support the reform. The National Academy of Public Administration (NAPA) made those reorganization proposals and the SES proposal (CSRA, Title IV) the subjects of its Spring 1978 meeting. By then the relevant NAPA panel was willing to endorse the key structural component of the change: "Our Personnel Management Reform Panel agrees that a serious conflict does exist in the Civil Service Commission's responsibilities and that its personnel management and policing roles should be performed by two different organizations" (NAPA, 1978).

Energizing NAPA members in support of the civil service reform was only one small part of a strategically orchestrated effort to win endorsements in the Washington area and nationally. By July, the Civil Service Commission had compiled a roster of 143 newspapers from 43 states, the District of Columbia, and Puerto Rico that had supported the proposals (NAPA, 1978:8). Also lined up in support were 19 professional and civic organizations, 18 business organizations, 17 former Cabinet members of both parties, 8 former officials of presidential commissions, 5 former CSC Chairmen and Commissioners, and 3 labor organizations. Thirty-seven prominent academic and practitioner experts in public administration provided written endorsements which were distributed by the CSC. Public meetings were held by CSC Chairman Campbell at sites around the Washington area to forestall opposition and to generate support. President Carter even led a "Roundtable Discussion with the President" at Fairfax High School in northern Virginia on August 3, 1978.

All of these efforts paid off with decisive support of provisions of Reorganization Plan No. 2 and of many provisions of the CSRA as well. On July 26, 1978, Jack Brooks introduced the report of his committee against the resolution to disapprove the reorganization. Reorganization Plan No. 2 was not rejected. OPM was thus authorized, along with the MSPB and FLRA. Partisan presidential control of the civil service was thus approved with overwhelming support of newspapers, varied interest groups, leaders of the public administration community, and Congress.

By then, strong support also existed for the more detailed proposals of the Civil Service Reform Act, but opposition to key provisions remained strong. The politics of getting that Act adopted disclosed other lessons about civil service reform.

Politics of External Groups and Civil Service Reform

Political reality was that, once the structural changes of Reorganization Plan No. 2 were authorized, Congress had to approve comprehensive civil service legislation to make the system work. That was deliberate strategy and it was effective.

While the proposed CSRA of 1978 was packed with important provisions, four became principal subjects of politics among external interest groups; veterans preference, Hatch Act repeal, labor-management relations (LMR), and equal employment opportunity (EEO). Civil service employees and their special-interest organizations were actively involved in all of these issues, of course, but the politics involved reached well beyond federal employees to energize national veterans groups, organized labor and labor's opponents, and advocates in support of EEO and affirmative action.

The administration's proposed legislation was introduced by request on 3 March 1978, as H.R. 11280. At that point, H.R. 11280 included only sections on merit system principles; civil service functions (OPM, MSPB); performance appraisal and adverse actions; staffing; SES; merit pay; and research, demonstration, intergovernmental, and mobility programs. Conspicuously absent were provisions on labor-management relations, although the PMP *Task Force Report* and other work on that subject had been completed early, building on extensive materials in support of legislation dating from the previous administration. Carter administration reformers decided to defer submission of the LMR proposal to await prior agreement by unions to other CSRA provisions as a condition of administration support of statutory LMR provisions. As a result, the administration briefly lost the initiative on LMR, and it did not secure prior agreement of unions in support of CSRA.

The administration relented and submitted its LMR proposal on 12 May, as a new Title VII to H.R. 11280. That bill then went through committee printings and was altered in varied respects. Members of the House Post Office and Civil Service Committee traded off amendments in committee to satisfy their particular constituencies, which included disproportionately strong groups of civil service employees. Eventually, work on the bill by the Senate Committee on Governmental Affairs became most decisive on Title VII (LMR), but it was H.R. 11280, as reported out on 31 July 1978, by the House Committee on Post Office and Civil Service, that was the focus of most political activities by external special interest groups.

To facilitate debate and the reworking of the bill, the 31 July version was considered by the House functioning as a Committee of the Whole (U.S. Congress 1979a). Committee Vice Chairman Morris K. Udall, Democrat of Arizona, managed the bill for the administration. Ranking Republican Edward J. Derwinski managed for the minority, supporting the administration on the key issues of OPM-MSPB structure and SES and opposing such matters as veterans' preference and varied amendments in committee by Democrats.

Veterans' Preference

Administration proponents of the CSRA—CSC Chairman Campbell and PMP leaders, including the Staffing Task Force—clearly favored major limitations on veterans' preference. They acknowledged needs for limited-term preference for recent veterans, but they wanted to eliminate lifetime and extraordinary preferences in selection and in reductions in force (RIFs) except for those with service-connected disabilities. Such provisions were included in the 3 March version of the bill.

In the House committee, Rep. Patricia Schroeder, Democrat of Colorado, secured amendment to H.R. 11280 to reduce veterans' preference more drastically than the administration's proposal. She charged that veterans' preference results in discrimination against women and minorities, and she succeeded in amending the bill to limit preference to one-time use within fifteen years of discharge. Women's groups were particularly adamant in support of that limit. Congresswoman Schroeder argued that the fifteen-year rule would benefit Vietnam-era veterans, both men and women, including many minorities, who were disadvantaged in competition with more senior veterans. But this effort to split the veterans' lobby did not work. Vietnam veterans were not yet strong in veterans' groups. The veterans' preference issue aroused the earliest and most sustained opposition to CSRA in Congress, and it quickly extended beyond issues of preference. Ed Derwinski made it clear from the outset that he and a majority of committee Republicans would not accept the Schroeder amendment or much other dilution of veterans' preference.

Rep. Ray Roberts, Democrat from Texas and chairman of the House Committee on Veterans Affairs, held separate hearings on CSRA veterans' preference provisions, and his committee compiled a powerful assault on proposed changes. The congressman and staff aides told the manager of the PMP-LMR Task Force, an old associate, that he should inform administration leaders that crucial support for CSRA would be withheld unless veterans' preference provisions were retained and unless SES and compensation provisions preserved rights of personnel employed in veterans' hospitals and related facilities. Congressman Roberts also got that message delivered through close associates from the Johnson administration. It was clear that such opposition would threaten LMR and SES proposals, raising questions of whether altered veterans' preference limits were worth the price of other core elements of H.R. 11280. The final version of CSRA actually strengthened veterans' preference with new noncompetitive appointment provisions for disabled veterans. It also restricted dual pay for retired members of the armed forces subsequently employed in civil service, but that double-dipper provision had some positive political spin to it in newspaper editorials around the nation, whereas limiting veterans' preference raised far more political negatives than positives for Congress.

Hatch Act Repeal

The second most intense political issue involving external interest groups was the proposed repeal of the Hatch Act. President Ford had vetoed Hatch Act repeal legislation upon recommendation of the CSC, public personnel professionals, and various clean-government groups. By deliberate political contrast in return for AFL-CIO support, the 1976 Democratic party platform supported repeal, and Carter campaigned in support of modification. But as a practical political matter, inclusion of Hatch Act repeal in the CSRA would have complicated politics in the House by undermining Republican support for CSRA, and it would have seriously jeopardized the entire bill in the Senate. Consequently, the administration excluded Hatch Act repeal from the CSRA. Carter rationalized that repeal of the Hatch Act was an issue reaching beyond the civil service to postal service employees and that CSRA should deal only with civil service. He promised to give presidential support to separate legislation to modify the Hatch Act.

The House Committee on Post Office and Civil Service added Hatch Act repeal as Title IX to H.R. 11280. Congressman William Clay, Democrat from Missouri, was the chief advocate for the provision, representing the views of postal service unions, federal employee unions, and the AFL-CIO. Separate Hatch Act repeal legislation had already passed the House on 7 June 1977 by a vote of 244 to 164. It remained stalled, however, in the Senate Committee on Governmental Affairs when CSRA reached the House floor on 11 August. It was certain that the separate Hatch Act bill would not clear the Senate that year, and Clay's union clients wanted it tied to CSRA to force stronger administration support. The administration, in turn, was upset by Clay's tactic, because CSRA proponents thought they had a clear agreement to keep the issues separate. Yet Clay commanded sufficient power in the House committee to amend the bill before H.R. 11280 went to floor debate in the Committee of the Whole.

Congressman Derwinski adamantly opposed repealing the Hatch Act and identified it as the most unacceptable provision of CSRA. On the House floor, Derwinski said: "The most damaging addition to the bill is Title IX, which contains the language of H.R. 10, a bill emasculating the Hatch Act and opening the door to politicization of the civil service system. The inclusion of this title is contrary to the concept of reform legislation" (Derwinski 1978:H8468). Derwinski linked Clay's tactic on the Hatch Act to other special interest amendments inserted into the bill by Democratic committee members. He cited Title X, another Clay addition, that provided for reducing the basic workweek of federal fire fighters. Specific legislation to the same effect, supported by the powerful International Association of Fire Fighters, had earlier passed both houses as H.R. 3161, and Carter had vetoed it with a strong rejection message. Derwinski tweaked the Democrats, suggesting that they should avoid "a gratuitous slap at the President" by their injection of special interest provisions into the CSRA.

The Carter administration held firmly to the promise to Derwinski and other House Republicans that Hatch Act repeal would not be supported as a part of the CSRA package. The provision was dropped from the bill, and the separate Hatch Act repeal legislation languished and died in the Senate.

Labor-Management Relations

Unions had pushed the House committee to inject Hatch Act repeal into the CSRA in part because the administration had declined initially to include labor-management relations (LMR) as a part of H.R. 11280. It was a political tactic against an administration that was seen as holding back on support for a statutory framework for LMR to extort support from unions for other CSRA provisions. The unions refused to be forthcoming until after the administration was forthcoming: they proceeded to formulate their own LMR proposals, seizing the initiative from the administration, and they declined to support other CSRA provisions until after the administration added a statutory LMR provision (U.S. Congress 1979b).

Throughout the PMP process of developing CSRA policy alternatives, the LMR Task Force consulted with union leaders as well as agency managers, labor relations officers, and other interest groups. The task force manager, Chet Newland, was usually accompanied in visits to unions only by the deputy manager, David Dickenson, the highly knowledgeable deputy to Anthony F. Ingrassia, the Civil Service Commission's chief LMR expert. It was clear all along that top union officials expected to meet on this issue with higher-level officials. The task force enticed Professor Frank McCulloch of the University of Virginia Law School to assist it. He commanded the respect of AFL-CIO leaders as one of the distinguished elders of the field. Although McCulloch did not participate in visits to unions, his phone calls ensured courteous and candid dialogue on issues.

For the AFL-CIO and its affiliates and for major independent unions as well, the bottom-line issue consistently remained public commitment by the Carter administration to a LMR statutory framework—in advance of union movement on other issues. The unions already had the LMR Task Force reports and related legislative language that, in effect, called for putting existing provisions of Executive Order 11491 into law as a part of CSRA. While they considered that too modest a change, the unions considered it their minimum position, and they could not understand the Carter administration's failure to go at least that far. The unions were discouraged by what they considered a crude political tactic—the attempted extortion of support for other CSRA provisions.

Finally, CSC Chairman Campbell agreed to meet with the principal union leaders as a group. With him on one long side of the CSC conference table were Frank McCulloch, Chet Newland, and David Dickenson representing the PMP, along with Tony Ingrassia and other CSC officials. On the other long side and at both ends were union officials. Only four union presidents participated; others sent subordinates, in part as a deliberate snub of the administration. Initially, the union leaders declined to talk beyond opening courtesies. Following Chairman Campbell's request to hear from the unions, they continued their resistance. Newland and McCulloch talked. Finally, in exasperation, McCulloch pointed his finger to one of his former students across the table and said, "Let me inform you; we are here to talk. Tell the chairman your position." All the union officials spoke essentially the same short line: "We want an LMR statute as a part of the CSRA *before* we can speak on other issues." They did not spell out details at that point, except for insistence on judicial review. They asked only for their bottom line. The meeting was adjourned without a commitment, but LMR language was submitted to Congress by the administration, and it was published on 12 May (over two months after submission of the initial bill) as the administration's version of Title VII. This version of Title VII essentially included provisions of Executive Order 11491, but with provision for the Federal Labor Relations Authority and with refinements of language on rights, consultation, and negotiability. Negotiated grievance processes were given greatly enhanced status.

The language of Title VII that reached the Committee of the Whole in August contained key provisions written by the unions. William Clay, as chair of the Subcommittee on Civil Service, held five days of hearings and then secured committee adoption of the union-oriented provisions as an amended Title VII. The amendments provided for extensive judicial review of FLRA decisions and orders. They also expanded the scope of bargaining to include such management-oriented issues as job classification, promotion standards, and RIF standards and procedures.

Congressman Derwinski rejected the changes. He told the House Committee of the Whole: "I suggest to those who are interested in true reform that it is important to correct title VII so that it essentially conforms with the Executive Order, as originally proposed, and supported by the administration" (Derwinski 1978:H8463).

During deliberations that essentially restored Title VII to the administration's version with the exception of judicial review, labor relations experts from two agencies were always present in the House gallery and active in the lobbies to provide information. They were respected Department of Defense and Civil Service Commission experts. The PMP Task Force staff was also present for that purpose. General Accounting Office experts also monitored the proceedings.

Unions won support in both the House and Senate for their proposal for judicial review of FLRA orders, except those involving arbitration awards and unit determination. Their position was incorporated into the final CSRA, and judicial review became a crucial aspect of implementation of the law.

Equal Employment Opportunity

Equal employment opportunity had strong external support from President Carter's political coalition, and proposals went virtually unchallenged in Congress. Vastly more time was devoted to assuring the exclusion of the FBI from CSRA than was spent on EEO. Equal opportunity was listed as an aspect of both the first and second merit system principles included in CSRA. Discrimination was also listed as a prohibited personnel practice.

Most important, "meeting affirmative action goals and achievement of equal employment opportunity requirements" were listed in CSRA as a required standard in performance appraisals of all senior executives. The Office of Personnel Management identified EEO as a critical element in executives' performance requirements, and sanctions for failure to accomplish such a requirement were such that the provision had a powerful effect—so long as the administration in office supported EEO.

The Politics of the Public Administration and Civil Service Communities

The broad public administration community, typified by the National Academy of Public Administration (NAPA), strongly supported the restructuring of CSC as the MSPB and the creation of OPM to give the president direct political control of the civil service. Leaders of the public personnel community, however, did not support these provisions, and as a result, they were almost totally excluded from deliberations over civil service reform. Civil service unions withheld support of all CSRA provisions until they were assured of the inclusion of statutorily based labor-management relations provisions, including judicial review.

Except for whistleblowing, other issues of importance to the public administration and civil service communities attracted only intermittent or modest attention outside of those groups, Congress, and the Carter administration. But these issues were both crucial and highly political: the senior executive service (SES), performance systems and compensation, flexibility for managers and their agencies, and the protection of merit and employees' rights.

The Senior Executive Service

Substantive SES provisions are dealt with in a separate chapter of this book, and as with other issues, only major aspects of the politics of adoption of Title IV of the CSRA are discussed here.

Except for the issue of partisan political control of the civil service by the president, no civil service reform issue has a longer history than the SES proposals. The idea dated back to the Brownlow Commission, but the proposals of the 1930s contrasted sharply with those of the 1970s. The senior civil service proposed under President Franklin D. Roosevelt was limited to career experts who would have served with career status and protections as high-level administrators. The SES proposals of 1977–1978 had their roots in two failed Nixon administration proposals for a Federal Executive Service (FES) and a subsequent CSC plan developed during the Ford administration. Many career executives in general schedule grades 16, 17, and 18, and others at comparable levels in other systems, recalled Nixon's FES proposals. Those had seemed clearly designed to politicize the system with fixed three-year contracts (Nixon had sought one-year terms initially) and few protections for career executives. Informed civil servants were thus suspicious about the resurrection of a political agenda in the SES provisions.

Politically most troubling to career executives and to congressional members who supported them was the key objective of SES as identified by the Carter administration: executive flexibility for the president. Many thought that the SES, together with the new structural arrangement of OPM, was designed to substitute partisan responsiveness for neutral expertise. Opponents were right about that, some CSRA proponents responded: responsiveness to the president, not neutral expertise, was wanted in the civil service.

Members of Congress from the Washington area, with many careerists as constituents, were sensitive to apprehensions over the SES. Gladys Noon Spellman, Democrat of Maryland, successfully led efforts to amend H.R. 11280 in the House committee. That amendment limited the SES to a two-year experimental program in only three agencies. The administration and representatives Udall and Derwinski held firmly to the view that the SES was the keystone of the CSRA proposal. They eventually won, and Title IV contained the administration's language almost verbatim. Below the concern about the meaning of executive flexibility, the principal political issues over SES were inclusion of political appointees and careerists in the same system, performance standards and tenure protections of careerists from arbitrary or partisanly political adverse actions, and compensation.

Frank Sherwood, the principal expert at the time, outside the federal government, on public executives, favored inclusion of only careerists in the senior executive service. But CSC experts had supported inclusion of both political and career executives in one system since Nixon's first FES proposal. In 1971 and 1973, Seymour Berlin, then director of the bureau of Executive Manpower (later renamed the Bureau of Executive Personnel), argued vigorously in support of a maximum of 25 percent political appointees in the FES, a ratio that CSC said corresponded to the actual number among supergrade (GS 16, 17, 18) personnel at the time. Comptroller General Elmer Staats opposed the 25 percent figure in the Nixon years, citing evidence that supergrade ranks then included no higher than 12.5 percent, a total considered by GAO to be too high. The SES proposals in 1977–1978 called for a maximum of 10 percent political and 5 percent limited-term or emergency appointees. While several members of Congress continued to be apprehensive, this formula won general support.

The professional public administration community, with few exceptions, strongly endorsed the inclusion of political appointees and careerists in one system. Hugh Heclo's book, *A Government of Strangers* (1977), seemed to support some improved arrangement, and that book won accolades and a NAPA award for its perceptive analysis. The chief idea in marketing SES inclusion of careerist and political appointees was that the system would facilitate greater opportunities for careerists to secure presidential appointments and other high-level positions without a loss of career status. The other principal marketing argument was executive flexibility and mobility, which had little attraction and many negatives for careerists.

Concerns over politicization as a result of the SES mix of appointees and careerists resulted in final language requiring that jobs (about 40 percent) that especially require public confidence be reserved for careerists. Everyone agreed that Internal Revenue Service personnel fit that category. Many civil servants also thought that personnel officers and OPM bureau heads should be careerists. Representative Gladys Spellman argued in the Committee of the Whole, "We are talking about attempting to keep from total politicization of the system. If we are going to have political appointees doing the hiring, we can be certain that additional political types are going to be hired" (Spellman 1978: H9362). That issue was raised much earlier in PMP Task Force deliberations and at the spring 1978 NAPA meeting. Only one PMP Task Force manager and two CSC career executives argued strongly that personnel officer positions and CSC-OPM bureau directors' positions should be career reserved. CSC Chairman Campbell forcefully rejected making personnel positions career reserved: the administration perceived of personnel officers as among the major obstacles to responsive bureaucracy, and changing them was a principal purpose of reform. Most participants in the NAPA session on CSRA shared that perception and supported the administration's position. Congress did also, overriding the views of careerists as represented by Spellman and other Washington-area members of Congress.

The protection of SES members and their subordinates from arbitrary or political actions was a persistent issue among careerists. CSRA provisions allowing transfers of executives within agencies with only two weeks' notice and provisions for performance evaluations by political superiors were major political issues among careerists. Among most members of Congress, however, such technical matters raised few questions. The two big employee protection issues for congressional members were whistleblowers and two bites at the apple (negotiated grievance procedures and MSPB appeals) for lower-ranking employees. Whistleblowing was the favorite issue of the media, and thus it became the apple pie political issue for many. Protections for lower-ranking employees were promoted by unions. Executives had no such power bases except among some congressional staffs, and those personnel lacked protection themselves; many embraced politics and expected careerists downtown to do likewise.

SES compensation did not become much of an issue in the politics of CSRA except among executives. Careerists had long been unhappy over the asterisk limit on executive pay. The SES bonus and presidential rank awards were seen as means to circumvent the limit, and, in off-the-record sessions, they were frankly presented that way. But in public politics, the bonuses and financial awards were depicted by the administration as means to reward the worthy while denying increases to the other 50 percent of executives. The politics of the time quickly turned thinking in two directions: (1) financial rewards, not public service or professional satisfactions, are the measure of executive success, and (2) at least 50 percent of executives cannot be recognized by special financial rewards—and thus they are not successful or valued. Following the adoption of CSRA and the initial implementation of bonuses to 50 percent of executives in the National Aeronautics and Space Administration, Congress required a 25 percent limit on eligibles for bonuses, and that was cut to 20 percent by OPM. Because CSRA politics had elevated individual economic rewards to the status of *the* motivation for executives, disillusionment continued among federal executives. During CSRA politics in 1977–1978, skepticism and disillusionment over compensation were already high.

Performance Systems and Compensation

Two fundamental perspectives underlay the substance and politics of 1977–1978 civil service reform: (1) that direct political control of the civil service by the president is essential to responsible government, and (2) that economic incentives are the decisive motivators of performance. Efforts were made to apply the principle of economic man broadly, not just among SES executives. The idea of bonuses for higher-ranking employees sold politically, but the idea that was most easily merchandized was *merit pay:* newspapers and politicians embraced it as their own.

During PMP Task Force deliberations, several long-standing compensation issues were considered. Total compensation comparability—considering pay, fringes, and retirement—had become common in many well-managed governments. The retirement system needed overhauling. Regional pay differentials, as recommended in 1976 by the Rockefeller compensation study, urgently needed consideration. But all of those matters were too big and politically sensitive.

By contrast, merit pay, at least for general schedule supervisors and middle managers, could be made politically attractive. Strong opposition among wage grade (blue-collar) employees and their unions to a proposed end to automatic step increases in pay levels above comparable private sector employees was a greater challenge. Wage grade employees had effective ties to central labor councils all over the country, and those councils could and did exert influence far beyond the numbers of federal employees. But for general schedule supervisors, who had no political influence, the merit pay proposal was easy.

Initially the administration wanted to apply merit pay to all general schedule employees grade 9 and above, but labor relations experts told Jule Sugarman that, politically, this was unthinkable. The administration and Congress finally settled on an unusual provision whereby general managers in grades 13, 14, and 15 would be dependent on bonuses based on performance appraisals. The only source of financing bonuses for some was denial of routine pay increases to all nonsupervisory employees. Linda Smith of the U.S. Office of Management and Budget (OMB) hosted a meeting in her OMB conference room that included O. Glenn Stahl, a personnel expert, and others in an attempt to inject some informed judgment into the process, but by then the details were lost in the fuzz of politics. If it was called *merit pay*, it would sell politically, even if it made no sense; and more important, it would buy support for CSRA generally. This bonus scheme proved unworkable during initial CSRA implementation; it was later changed by Congress.

Research by Professor Edward Lawler of the University of Southern California was cited most often by administration advocates of merit pay. Lawler's research stressed two factors as crucial to make merit pay work: a trusted, valid, reliable performance appraisal system, and bonuses or other merit pay substantial enough to make a marked difference. Those points and others were made in PMP deliberations, noting that neither was likely in the federal government, but leaders of the public administration community ignored the research details. During the politics of CSRA, it was often asserted, incorrectly, that performance appraisal was not practiced in the federal government. Improvements were needed, and considerable effort was devoted by CSC and later by OPM to developing new performance appraisal systems. But while improved government performance was a popular political objective associated with CSRA, such details rarely attracted attention outside the civil service community.

The Authority of Managers to Manage

The political slogan *authority of managers to manage* was popular with operating agencies. It brought powerful support for CSRA from the Department of Defense and other agencies. The slogan represented the administration's promise that OPM would be a facilitator for improved government management, delegating authorities to meet operational needs and not enforcing obstructionist personnel rules.

Some rules to which managers objected were legal requirements that could not be changed by CSC-OPM: veterans' preference, EEO, age discrimination, labor-management contracts, and legal merit standards, for example. But the layering of personnel rules within agencies and at CSC often crippled management, and that could be dealt with. The recognition of legitimate differences in the needs of agencies was required, and when the Carter administration promised that, agency support for OPM was forthcoming.

The administration particularly stressed the need to simplify the process for firing nonperformers. Numerous horror stories about costly and drawn-out employee appeal processes were compiled and distributed to newspapers and groups across the country. Two impressions were encouraged: that the federal government was full of nonperformers, and that the civil service system protected these employees.

Some members of Congress attempted to correct the record. Gladys Spellman observed: "We have heard a great deal of talk about how it takes 18 months to fire an employee. We were at times told it took 27 months, and 3 years, and all that sort of thing. That was nonsense. An employee can be out of the system today in 30 days, and then the appeals process starts" (Spellman 1978). But the record could not be set straight nationally. The Carter administration repeatedly castigated the federal civil service in presidential comments, press releases, and one entire PMP report, giving the impression that the bureaucracy was filled with career loafers and incompetents who could not be fired. The negative image of civil service that resulted was one of the most powerful and enduring products of the politics of CSRA—but it helped to get the reform adopted.

Merit Protection and Employee Rights

Reorganization Plan No. 2 converted the Civil Service Commission into the Merit Systems Protection Board and created the Office of Special Counsel. It was to be a tiny organization compared to OPM and absolutely miniscule compared to most government agencies. But politically this tactic worked to get reform adopted.

At one point in the PMP process, a proposal was considered to combine the MSPB and FLRA into one organization. Muriel Morse, former personnel director for Los Angeles, Arch Pounian, personnel director for Chicago, and others in the International Personnel Management Association recommended one board to secure consistent and better-informed leadership. But that was never seriously contemplated. Politically, two bites at the apple was a more popular formula with unions and employees generally, and MSPB and FLRA were promoted as protecting employee rights—to make feasible the creation of OPM under the president's partisan direction.

Merit principles were spelled out in the CSRA. Except for inclusion of a list of merit principles in the Intergovernmental Personnel Act, put there by Senator Edmund Muskie, no other succinct definition existed. Merit was another "apple pie" (politically popular) feature of the act. The CSRA definition included EEO and affirmative action, adding to its New South political appeal. But the details of merit were rarely discussed in positive terms in the politics of civil service reform. Nonmeritorious bureaucrats were discussed most often.

As noted earlier, details of employee rights attracted little political attention outside of civil service ranks. All the insiders—managers, unions, technical experts—agreed on one enormous detail: negotiated grievance procedures would become a fast, relatively low-cost process for protecting many employee rights. Many such technical matters were resolved quietly. In fact, everyone knew that MSPB would inherit most of the policies, processes, and cases already in the CSC appeals system. Few knew the enormous backlog of neglected cases until after MSPB went to work with its inadequate resources. No one wanted that known amid CSRA politics.

Meanwhile, the great political show was over whistleblower protection. That was a topic on which newspapers and politicians could speak, assuring voters that protections would encourage whistleblowers to root out corruption and incompetence within government. It sold more than newspapers; it delivered a lingering message of widespread incompetence and corruption in government and an absence of systems to prevent or correct it. It also helped to win political support for CSRA.

Political Reflections

Two years after leaving office as OPM Director, Alan K. (Scotty) Campbell commented on the politics of civil service reform. His reflections in the *Public Aministration Review* are candid and insightful, matching his skillful political leadership in winning congressional approval of Reorganization Plan No. 2 of 1978 and the Civil Service Reform Act.

Campbell reflected on the frequent lament of career people "who wanted to know why the president was not saying nicer things about them." He explained: "Interestingly, it was very difficult to get the president to do so. That difficulty was with the political advisors around the president who argued that it was bad politics to do so." Campbell concluded that negative presidential statements were "a reflection of what the politicians believe is public opinion" (Campbell 1982:307). That assessment of why President Carter said so much to damage the civil service and so little to enhance it is consistent with the government-by-polls approach that has characterized the presidency since 1977. Undermining public service was an effective means in 1977 and 1978 to secure congressional adoption of civil service reform. The purpose of that reform was to enhance the political power of the president over the civil service. The costs to the public service and to the long-term effectiveness of government were not a consideration at the time.

Campbell notes that initially, in congressional testimony, he would follow his professorial practice of sharpening distinctions in response to questions. "One day after a hearing, Mo Udall motioned me to follow him to his office. When we got into his office, he pointed to a chair and said, 'Professor, sit down. [Which I did.] I must teach you something. Up here we don't try to sharpen differences, we fuzz them' " (Campbell 1982:306). Campbell learned that lesson, and it clearly helped to secure enactment of the administration's civil service reform package.

Conclusions

The political lessons from civil service reform correspond to those from other legislative experience, but they are clearer and bigger because Reorganization Plan No. 2 of 1978 and the Civil Service Reform

Act constitute a landmark in U.S. history. The politics of 1977–1978 on civil service reform were epochal for fundamental governmental institutions.

The president gained direct political control over the federal civil service. It was the culmination of over forty years of presidential aggrandizement. From the perspective of political science, proponents of the change justified it as essential to partisan political responsiveness. From the perspective of public administration, proponents justified it in terms of hierarchical leadership. From the perspective of history, it marked the culmination of a previously gradual change away from an executive branch under bipartisan and shared authority of Congress and the president, in which the president was chiefly to see that the laws were faithfully executed. Following 1978, the civil service became legally subject to partisan presidential control, and the executive branch became much more a vehicle of partisan presidential politics.

Some old political lessons were relearned in the 1980s as a sequel to the 1970s reforms. Presidents and such partisan appointees as OPM Director Donald Devine use their ever growing power to advance their partisan self-interests. In short, if it was not understood by some in the 1970s, it became clear to nearly all in the 1980s that civil service reform was an exercise in partisan presidential politics. These lessons about special interests and their influence over Congress and the president are the ordinary ones of recent American politics. Veterans groups, unions, and varied EEO interests adamantly opposed reform when their positions were threatened, but so long as their narrow interests were advanced or insulated they would go along with almost anything. Special interests in this instance demonstrated virtually no concerns about the larger needs of government. Congress responded to the powerful groups and largely ignored unorganized civil servants, including career executives. The impacts on government structures in this case were typical of interest group politics: increased fragmentation and complexity, not simplification and focused responsibility (beyond partisan politicization of OPM).

The lessons about the presidential use of opinion polls, the media, and political groups are also ordinary ones, except that the manipulations that have become ordinary were performed with extraordinary strategy and skill in this case. Public opinion was deliberately and brilliantly turned against the public service in the political drive for civil service reform.

The lessons about the public administration and civil service communities are also the expected ones. The public administration community has almost always supported the aggrandizement of executive power at all levels of government. It is in the heritage of public administration, and it has become an almost unconscious bias. In this case, this bias operated effectively in support of Carter's reforms. The public personnel community's heritage has generally differed from the rest of public administration on this matter; and prominent personnel experts dissented. Consequently, experienced personnel administrators were largely excluded from the politics of civil service reform, except for CSC employees in technical specialties.

The federal civil service never did act as a community on the 1977–1978 reforms, and it was only vaguely linked with the positions of the larger public administration community. Unions were active in support of interests of both organized labor and many civil servants. They and unorganized employees looked largely to Congress to protect and advance their special interests, while the public administration community was more closely linked to the Carter administration. Public administration professionals brought technical information to the political process, but they were mostly responsive to whatever political officials wanted. On such technical issues as performance appraisal and merit pay, politically fashionable positions outweighed research and experience. On the core issue of authorizing presidential domination of the civil service, loyalty was to the president.

Ultimately, the principal political lesson from civil service reform of 1977–1978 is found in that focus. The loyalty of government employees is increasingly more to the political boss and less to laws and institutions. The aggrandizement of presidential power is increasingly an irresistible force in American politics and government.

NOTE

1. The *May-Malek Manual* was originally an internal BOB/OMB paper written by Alan May as a guide to incoming Nixon administration officials for the political manipulation of civil service rules. The unpublished paper was commonly referred to as the "Malek Manual," after Fred Malek, but May was the author. Eventually, the paper leaked out and was later published. See "The Malek Manual." *Bureaucrat* 4 (January 1976):429–508.

SOURCES

Campbell, Alan K. 1982. "The Institution and Its Problems." *Public Administration Review* 42:305–08.

Derwinski, Edward. 1978. Remarks on the House Floor. *Congressional Record.* 124:H8460–75.

Gilman, Benjamin. 1978. Remarks on the House Floor. *Congressional Record.* 124:H8460–75.

Heclo, Hugh. 1977. *A Government of Strangers: Executive Politics in Washington.* Washington, D.C.: Brookings.

May, Alan. 1976. *The May-Malek Manual.* Unpublished paper of the Nixon Administration, published as an article, "The Malek Manual." *Bureaucrat* 4 (January):429–508.

National Academy of Public Administration. 1978. NAPA Panel Report. Quoted in U.S. Civil Service Commission, *Commentary on Support for Civil Service Reform.*

Nathan, Richard. 1975. *The Plot That Failed: Nixon and the Administrative Presidency.* New York: Wiley.

Newland, Chester A. 1984. "Crucial Issues for Public Personnel Professionals." *Public Personnel Management* 13:15–16.

Sharon, Milton. 1976. *The Sharon Report.* Washington, D.C. Unpublished internal report to the U.S. Civil Service Commission, commonly referred to by the author's name but never published or officially released.

Spellman, Gladys Noon. 1978. Remarks on the House Floor. *Congressional Record.* 124:H9356–9461.

U.S. Congress. 1975. House Committee on Post Office and Civil Service. *The Merit System in the United States Civil Service.* Committee Print 94–10.

——— . 1976. House Committee on Post Office and Civil Service. *History of Civil Service Merit Systems of the United States and Selected Foreign Countries Together with Executive Reorganization Studies and Personnel Recommendations.* Committee Print 94–29.

——— . 1978. House Committee on Government Operations. *Reorganization Plan No. 2 of 1978.* Report 95–1396.

——— . 1979a. House Committee on Post Office and Civil Service. *Legislative History of the Civil Service Reform Act of 1978.* Committee Print 96–2.

——— . 1979b. House Committee on Post Office and Civil Service. *Legislative History of the Federal Service Labor-Management Relations Statute, Title VII of the Civil Service Reform Act of 1978.* Committee Print 96–7.

Vaughn, Robert G. 1975. *The Spoiled System: A Call for Civil Service Reform.* New York: Charterhouse for the Center for Study of Responsive Law.

Part II THE INSTITUTIONS OF REFORM

Introduction
The Structures of Reform

Patricia W. Ingraham

The decline of what Storing termed the "exquisite symmetry" of the politics-administration dichotomy permitted the rise of structural change and reorganization efforts in the American federal bureaucracy (1978:155). Fueled by an abiding presidential belief in—or hope for—improved hierarchical control of the permanent bureaucracy, structural reforms have been recommended in every presidency since that of Franklin Roosevelt. Congress, too, has initiated reorganization efforts. Their frequent occurrence is testimony to their limited success. Why, then, do proposals for structural change and reorganization continue to appear?

Garnett has observed that the foundation of the federal merit system and career civil service, neutral competence, was "the wrong prescription for the weakness inherent in the separation of powers . . . [the resulting] system of 'diffusion of powers' stimulated a preoccupation with integration and coordination that has since dominated reorganization doctrine" (1987:37).

March and Olsen concur, but note that there are two distinct streams of intent and rhetoric in reorganization efforts:

The history of administrative reorganization in the twentieth century is a history of rhetoric. . . . Two orthodox rhetorics infuse . . . reorganization. . . . The first is that of orthodox administrative theory . . . [which] proclaims that explicit, comprehensive planning of administrative structures is possible and necessary, that piecemeal change produces chaos. . . . The second rhetoric of reorganization is the rhetoric of realpolitik. . . . It speaks of reorganization . . . in terms of a political struggle among contending interests. (1983: 282–83)

These competing interests have produced oddly similar proposals; in the past fifty years, virtually all reorganization and structural change reforms have been directed at—or had the effect of—strengthening the Office of the President. This is so despite the fact that "reorganization threatens prime perquisites of legislative office—access to bureaucratic operations and the linkages between agencies and committees"(ibid.:285). The president, of course, has remarkable incentives to harness the bureaucracy. If campaign promises are to be fulfilled, the federal policy process and machinery must be responsive to the president. The bureaucracy must respond to new direction.

Two theoretical and practical traditions clash here. Politics is the art of the possible; bureaucracy, the reality of routine and precedent. Democracy and electoral politics presume change within the time frame of the political cycle; large public bureaucracies are structured by law and design to work slowly and with a longer-term perspective. Tensions are inevitable. After examining the effects of the 1980 presidential transition on the implementation of the incipient Civil Service Reform Act, for example, the Gaertners concluded that "organizations are ill equipped to deal constructively with the jarring discontinuities of drastic changes in leadership and priorities occasioned by political transition"(1984:219).

From the president's perspective, reorganization is one way to improve bureaucratic response to the new priorities. For the permanent bureaucracy, however, it is but another level of change and turbulence to be added to new policy directives and initiatives. The steadily increasing reliance on larger numbers of political appointees to improve presidential control adds another dimension of change and instability to the public organizations that are the target of reorganization strategies. Jimmy Carter referred to the federal bureaucracy as the giant Washington marshmallow, arguing that prodding or pushing one part only resulted in an uncontrolled bulge in another. That aptly summarizes the president's frustration and partially explains the frequent grand strategies intended to bring the marshmallow under control.

The Carter reforms described in the next three chapters are examples of a fairly rare breed: moderately successful reorganization strategies. They also demonstrate the difficulties inherent in structural reform. Carter promised comprehensive reorganization in his campaign. It was fundamental to his vision of a government that was at once more efficient and more open. Despite the observation of one of his staff, Bert Lance, that "history teaches that efforts to redesign the

Executive branch in a single scheme are not digestible by our political system," Carter did effect the most sweeping change in the history of the American merit system: the abolition of the neutral, bipartisan Civil Service Commission (March and Olsen 1983:287). The creation of the Office of Personnel Management (OPM), the Merit Systems Protection Board (MSPB), the Office of Special Counsel (OSC), and the Federal Labor Relations Authority (FLRA) reflected the duality of purpose that March and Olsen described. The reorganization was rational and comprehensive and could be easily defended in terms of good management. However, it also placed a single presidential appointee at the head of the Office of Personnel Management, thus creating an additional management resource essentially removed from the merit system for the president and his appointees.

The creation of the new agencies also reflected other political realities. Interest group politics played important roles. Title VII of the Civil Service Reform Act, for example, which created the FLRA, was described by one observer as the outcome of a negotiating process that so muddied the content and intent of the new agency that no one knew what it was supposed to do or how it was supposed to do it (Ban 1984:219). Lane's discussion of OPM in Chapter 5 and Rosenbloom's conclusion in chapter 7 that the FLRA is essentially an agency that gets no respect demonstrate the continuing search for an effective identity.

The evaluations of the institutions of reform in this section are important for their commentary on structural reform. The chapters examine the effectiveness of the Office of Personnel Management as a human resources manager, the Merit Systems Protection Board as an adjudicatory body, the Office of Special Counsel as an investigatory and protective body, and the Federal Labor Relations Authority as overseer and adjudicator of labor-management relations in the federal government. The conclusions of the authors clearly demonstrate the enormous difficulties of effective structural change in public bureaucracy. They reflect, too, the reality of administrative reform: whatever their intent, structural reforms are judged and evaluated in broader terms. The issue is not just that new structures were created, but the difference that made. Structural reform outcomes have political implications and political and bureaucratic costs. In public bureaucracy, procedural and technical issues advanced in the name of good management often emerge as events that profoundly shape good government.

SOURCES

Ban, Carolyn. 1984. "Implementing Civil Service Reform." In *Legislating Bureaucratic Change: The Civil Service Reform Act of 1978,* ed. Patricia W. Ingraham and Carolyn Ban. Albany: SUNY Press.

Gaertner, Gregory H., and Karen N. Gaertner. 1984. "Civil Service Reform in the Context of Presidential Transitions." In *Legislating Bureaucratic Change: The Civil Service Reform Act of 1978,* ed. Ingraham and Ban.

Garnett, James L. 1987. "Operationalizing the Constitution via Administrative Reorganization: Oilcans, Trends and Proverbs." *Public Administration Review* 47 (January/February):35–44.

March, James G., and Johan P. Olsen. 1983. "Organizing Political Life: What Administrative Reorganization Tells Us About Government." *American Political Science Review* 81:281–96.

Storing, Herbert J. 1978. "Reforming the Bureaucracy." In *Bureaucratic Power in National Policymaking.* 3d ed., ed. Francis E. Rourke. Boston: Little, Brown.

5. The Office of Personnel Management
Values, Policies, and Consequences

Larry M. Lane

In 1979, the newly created Office of Personnel Management (OPM) assumed its role as the organization principally responsible for the implementation of the Civil Service Reform Act of 1978 (CSRA) and began working toward its initial objectives of improved federal management, stronger executive direction, and modernized personnel management. The history of the first decade of OPM is revealing and instructive regarding the past, present, and future state of the American public service. OPM's organizational record has theoretical and practical as well as normative and operational implications for the American governance process. In the first ten years of CSRA and OPM, the landscape of American public administration was dramatically altered as a result of OPM's policies and their implementation.

The central significance of OPM remains undiminished despite the documented failure of the implementation of CSRA to achieve the objectives of the legislation. The gulf between promise and performance, and the seeming irrelevance of technical success or failure to the political acceptance of the concepts, raise important questions. The explanation of how CSRA and OPM have shaped the current world of the public service, despite technical shortcomings, lies in the significance of the legislation at a higher level of concern. The greatest impact of the act and its implementation—the dominant effect of CSRA's first ten years—has been the radical revision of the values and institutions of the public service.

Ideals and Organizations

In 1958, the U.S. Civil Service Commission celebrated the diamond anniversary of the Pendleton Act by preparing a publication titled *The*

Biography of an Ideal (Cooke 1959). The ideal was the merit system—a fundamentally important expression of a specific set of political and administrative values (U.S. Congress 1975:7). At the time, the merit ideal was embodied in a value-driven government organization, the Civil Service Commission. Only twenty years later, a new civil service reform split the commission into three separate independent organizations, with OPM inheriting the most visible and significant policy and operational functions. If a new biography of ideals were to be written today, it would be very different from the 1958 version. Today's biography would require a narrative of rapid, radical, sequential changes in values and directions.

The Value Shifts, 1978–1988

The organizational history of OPM from the demise of the Civil Service Commission to the present strikingly illustrates and confirms Herbert Kaufman's theory of the cyclical nature and constant realignment of core values pertaining to public administration (1956, 1969). In recent years, other analysts have developed value models that revise or supplement Kaufman's original formulation (Goldenberg 1984; Rosenbloom 1986). Figure 2 provides a matrix of value models that can serve as a road map on which the value-orientation course of OPM may be charted. Each step of this journey reflects some version of the "regime norms and values of the political system" that David Rosenbloom suggests must inevitably attach to public personnel administration (1982:6).

The evolution of the OPM value orientation is charted in some detail in the following pages. As illustrated in figure 3, dominant and secondary value combinations changed from merit/management (pre-1978) to management/politics (1978–1981) to politics/management (1981–1988). Since 1988, yet another significant change has emerged, with the apparent emphasis on the value of the public service and the need to attract and retain more capable individuals in the service. These value realignments and combinations have had significant organizational implications regarding role, mission, effectiveness, clientele, technical operations, morale, and programmatic capacity, not just in OPM but for the public service as a whole.

The Value Role and Significance of Public Organizations

The essential role of public organizations in a political system is to transform ideals and values, as determined through the political pro-

Figure 2. Array of Value Models for Public Service Systems

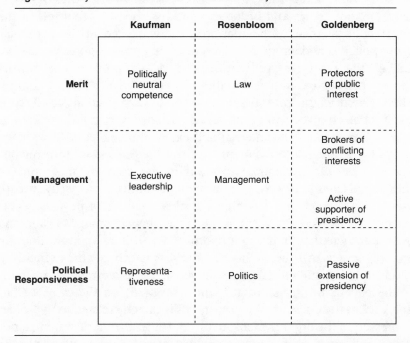

	Kaufman	Rosenbloom	Goldenberg
Merit	Politically neutral competence	Law	Protectors of public interest
Management	Executive leadership	Management	Brokers of conflicting interests Active supporter of presidency
Political Responsiveness	Representativeness	Politics	Passive extension of presidency

cess, into the reality of specific actions, as shaped by the requirements of expertise and competence. This process involves people, organizational arrangements, and technical and administrative technologies. Thus equipped, public organizations become "instruments for the

Figure 3. Institutions, Values, and Organizations

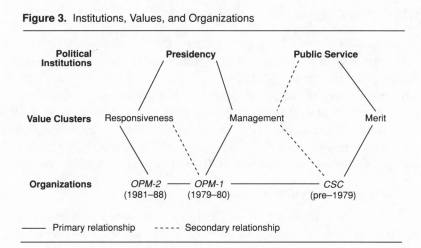

Political Institutions	Presidency		Public Service
Value Clusters	Responsiveness	Management	Merit
Organizations	OPM-2 ——— OPM-1 ——————— CSC
	(1981–88) (1979–80)		(pre–1979)

——— Primary relationship   - - - - - Secondary relationship pursuit of the public interest" (Wamsley et al. 1987:300). Organizations embody ideals and become infused with values that reflect the larger political society and that are directly related to the particular laws, policies, and programs for which they are responsible. Before CSRA, the Civil Service Commission clearly possessed a distinct agency perspective and a specific, powerful organizational culture. The creation of the commission's successor organizations resulted in substantial changes in organizational perspectives, cultures, knowledge requirements, and internal and external relationships.

Public organizations also represent specific interests within the political society. Organizational and system changes of the magnitude of those associated with CSRA implementation must necessarily disrupt and revise clientele relationships and alter balances of power and influence. In reviewing reform as a generic phenomenon, Miewald and Steinman note that "particular reforms have utilities and inutilities for various people. All the traditional goals of reform such as efficiency, accountability, and effectiveness now have to be reevaluated in terms of the payoffs to diverse participants" (1984:8). In the case of OPM and CSRA, the question of who benefits is directly related to the values expressed in the organizations involved. Under the merit system, a policing and enforcement system emphasized the rights of employees and protection against political influence, with only a secondary emphasis on effective management practices. In the 1970s, this formula lost its effectiveness as public program managers insisted on flexibility and political leaders demanded responsiveness.

OPM: The Original Intention

The inadequacies of the Civil Service Commission, in terms of its value preferences and the political conditions of the time, led to the new civil service reform in 1978. Twenty years earlier, the *Biography of an Ideal* had issued what proved to be a prophetic warning: "Institutions built on a high promise of public service, as the merit system was built, must fulfill that promise—or they will surely be discarded and replaced by something else" (Cooke 1959:123). The "something else" turned out to be, in large measure, the Office of Personnel Management.

Origins of the OPM Concept

The roles and missions envisioned for the Office of Personnel Management were not fundamentally revolutionary. The proposed reform had roots in American political and administrative management traditions (Nigro and Clayton 1984:154). The challenge for the builders of the new organization was to give force and effect to a new mix of old doctrines. While the 1978 reform was expressive in some ways of a break with reform tradition (Caiden 1984:251–53), it was more clearly an example of Kaufman's shifting and realigning values. The only marked departure from historical precedent, albeit a very significant change, was the thorough subordination within OPM of the traditional civil service concept—of a merit system of legal and regulatory restrictions, elaborate centralized personnel administration, and protections against politics. And outside of OPM, vestiges of these values continued to live in the language of CSRA and to some extent in the Merit Systems Protection Board (Office of the Special Counsel 1985).

A model of administrative management orthodoxy was the first, most heavily emphasized conceptual origin of OPM (Beam 1978). This traditional public management philosophy centers on the president as chief executive officer and is predicated on hierarchy, control, and accountability. The first deputy director of OPM, Jule M. Sugarman, noted that the old civil service system had "erected a pretty firm wall against effective managerial action" (Beam 1978:74). OPM clearly was intended to be the organizational mechanism for improving management at all levels of federal operations, but the principal emphasis was at the executive level. As David Rosenbloom observed shortly after OPM began operations, "The fundamental values expressed most clearly in the Carter reforms are executive leadership and accountability" (1979:172).

In the public sector context, accountability means *political* accountability. The old Civil Service Commission had preached management, but political leaders felt continually frustrated by the personnel system, which, at heart, was designed to protect against political influence. Early in the Carter administration, cabinet officers demanded that the public service be made more responsive to political direction. Again, this was not a new demand; it has reverberated through American history since the founding of the republic. Accountability of the career service to political officials is a principal tenet of democratic politics and administration (Thompson 1986:329). Thus, OPM became an instrumental expression of the responsiveness of the career public service to the political outcomes of the democratic process as manifested not just in laws but also in the persons of political appointees in the executive branch.

The inception of the Office of Personnel Management was also heavily influenced by the resurgence in the 1960s and 1970s of the American tradition of castigating the public service. Although this was not a new phenomenon, bureaucrat bashing had become a successful theme in the electoral campaigns of Governor George Wallace and presidents Richard Nixon and Jimmy Carter. The selling of the Civil Service Reform Act of 1978 was accompanied by a vigorous public relations effort that featured horror stories and worst-case scenarios about the difficulty of removing incompetent federal employees. The campaign was successful, but the burden of a negative and adversarial image became firmly attached to OPM (Ingraham 1984:21).

Clearly, the new reformers sought a break with almost a hundred years of the evolutionary direction of public personnel administration (Ershkowitz 1984:77). But the break with historical development was to be achieved through another American tradition—an orthodoxy of reform—which would be employed once again to attempt reconciliation of "the tensions of democracy and bureaucracy" (O'Toole 1984:238–39). The conventional wisdom of legislation and reorganization was embraced in the creation of OPM, and as always, this orthodox theory of reorganization was expected to result in economy, efficiency, better management, and enhanced presidential capability to run the country (Seidman and Gilmour 1986:3–36).

The specific concepts of CSRA and OPM were originally proposed in the personnel-related sections of the Brownlow Committee report in 1937 and in the first and second Hoover Commission reports in 1949 and 1955 (Moe 1982). The Brownlow report created the formula for a presidential personnel policy and program office in lieu of the bipartisan Civil Service Commission. The first Hoover Commission advocated a clear line of presidential control and a greater decentralization of the personnel function. The second Hoover Commission sought a better balance between the roles and responsibilities of political and career officials, proposing the creation of a senior civil service and recommending improved processes for the appointment, compensation, promotion, and removal of members of the public service.

The Brownlow Committee and the Hoover commissions were dedicated to the principle of management improvement; however, they operated in the value framework of merit and neutral competence. The prototype of OPM in the Brownlow report was not intended to be a political office. The proposal placed heavy emphasis on the need for the technical competence and professional credentials of the director.

When the proposal became a reality forty-two years later, the political world was altered—management was divorced from the merit concept and remarried to political responsiveness.

The final specific origin of OPM lay in the academic critique of the manner in which public personnel management operated under the merit system (e.g. see Shafritz 1974; Chandler 1986; Vaughn 1975). In its negative function of protection against politicization, the civil service system had become encrusted with laws, regulations, procedures, and administrative inflexibilities that made it appear to many observers to be unresponsive to either political or managerial values (Newland 1984:26—29). The academic critique provided important intellectual respectability and the support of learned analysis to proposals for reform. The chief architect of CSRA and the first director of OPM, Alan K. Campbell, was an academician himself, and he had the support of many of his professional colleagues when he noted the "conspiracy, sycophancy, ideological conformity, caution, and class solidarity" at the expense of "innovation, originality, and the work ethic" that Campbell believed to be endemic to civil service systems (Caiden 1984:252). Clearly, it seemed to many academics that the time had come to modernize public personnel practices (ibid.:262).

All of these influences were brought into focus in 1977—1978 by the Personnel Management Project (PMP), which was established by President Carter to review the federal personnel system and make appropriate recommendations. Under the direction of Dwight Ink, the PMP made a rapid and comprehensive review of past proposals. The project performed no independent research, instead relying on existing information from previous studies (Knudsen et al. 1979:175). The PMP created a comprehensive package of recommendations that formed the basis for a legislative proposal. Perhaps its most significant role, however, was to represent agency and management interests, to build a constituency for reform, and to create the appearance that the reform proposals were the product of the career service.

Legislative Intent

Some reasonably clear intentions regarding OPM emerged from the legislative process in 1978. The legislative history of CSRA, as cited by the Merit Systems Protection Board, specifically identified objectives for OPM: "Taken within the larger context of the other provisions of CSRA, it is clear that Congress intended OPM to be a pro-active central personnel management agency which would provide to the Federal civil service system aggressive leadership, guidance, and oversight" (U.S. MSPB 1989:1). These objectives included decentralization and delegation of personnel authorities to agencies, vigorous oversight to assure compliance with merit principles, and the conduct or facilitation of research and demonstration projects.

During hearings on the reform legislation in 1978, the issue of potential politicization of the civil service was prominently considered and discussed. Supporters of the bill were careful to point out the safeguards and protections that deliberately were placed in the legislation to prevent undue political influence. As CSRA was enacted, there can be little doubt that the legislative intent of Congress was to guard against politicization and to affirm merit principles. As the principal operating agency of CSRA, OPM was expected to operate within the spirit of merit. Upon passage of the reform legislation, the National Academy of Public Administration summarized the situation in this way: "With this reaffirmation of America's commitment to merit as an integral feature of government, the new and existing agencies set about to meet their responsibilities under the Act" (NAPA 1981:10).

Initial Goals and Objectives of OPM

The initial objectives of CSRA and OPM, as enunciated by the Carter administration, fell into three major categories: managerial, political, and technical. The primary goal was identified by Alan Campbell as improved management in federal agencies (1980:157). OPM was intended to "serve as the President's principal agent for managing the federal work force," and Campbell anticipated "that OPM would perform for the President the same role relative to personnel management that OMB does for financial management" (1978:100). The managerial objective sought "to maximize the values of efficiency, economy, and administrative effectiveness" through personnel mechanisms and programs (Rosenbloom and Goldman 1986:194).

In the political arena, the initial objective of OPM was to support President Carter's interest in controlling the bureaucracy. This was essential to maintain the credibility and viability of OPM's management objectives. The focus of the political objective caused OPM to move away from the principle of the separation of personnel administration from politics that had been a central concern of merit system policies and procedures (Sylvia 1983:115). In terms of values "the political approach to public personnel stresses radically different values than the managerial approach. . . . Perhaps its underlying value is to maximize the responsiveness of the public sector work force to political officials and to the public at large" (Rosenbloom and Goldman 1986:209). Within the federal governmental establishment, OPM's political objective was to assume policy leadership and to establish its influence (Campbell 1978:103).

The overall technical objective of OPM was the eventual "transformation of public personnel management into modern-day human resource management" (Cayer 1987:330). Initially, this meant simply the adoption in the public sector of specific private sector techniques of performance appraisal, merit pay, and employee discipline, as well as the implementation of the Senior Executive Service. These technical mechanisms were intended to unite political and managerial values by being useful to line program managers and by enhancing authority of the political executive (Rosenbloom and Goldman 1986:190; Sylvia 1983:116). In its technical personnel administration role, OPM set out to be a policy maker, innovator, and technical leader, with the intention of fundamentally revising the public personnel system.

OPM: The Developing Reality

The initial passage of the CSRA and the creation of OPM had required conceptual and political bargaining skills, resulting in the legislation that legitimated policies and actions reflecting a new combination of values. By 1979, the task changed to one of implementation—the transformation of the organization of the old Civil Service Commission and its ideals into the new mechanism of OPM and its institutional values. This transformation required the inculcation of values, the mobilization of resources, and the development of organizational capacity to translate ideals into administrative action.

Creation of the New Organization

For two brief years, the leadership of Alan Campbell and Jule Sugarman successfully began to move the organization and its people in new directions. Although there was some predictable internal discomfort, the priorities of the organization were clearly established (Ban 1984:49). The staff responded positively to the changes, as Campbell later noted:

It was really a very difficult environment, but the amazing thing to me was once they became convinced that we were serious about making changes, and once I convinced them that it was in the interest of the career civil servants themselves, they very quickly accepted that I was there with good intentions. They rallied around, some more than others. Over time, I had put together a team made up almost exclusively of career people. It was, I felt, as good a group of people as one could find. (Ershkowitz 1984:76)

The pursuit of improved management required the cultivation of a different clientele in place of the personnel community that had been the principal customer of the Civil Service Commission. OPM's managerial approach was directed at line managers, who were actively sought out and included in the development and implementation of CSRA. This approach was implemented through the brilliant innovation of creating an Assistant Directorate for Agency Relations that was responsible for service to agency management and coordination of OPM responses. Initially, this approach de-emphasized the importance of staff personnel functions at the agency level. OPM's objective was the direct encouragement and assistance of line managers in the utilization of personnel tools for enhanced performance and productivity.

The vigorous exercise of leadership and the inculcation of critical values provided the key to making the new organization function effectively. The critical values to be promoted and acted upon were the values of the management and political responsiveness model, to be applied initially within OPM and then throughout the federal government. Unquestionably, the former core value of the merit system became a casualty in this process, virtually disappearing from OPM. In its first review of the significant actions of OPM, the Merit Systems Protection Board found that OPM "has not established a credible presence as a firm and effective monitor of the adherence of agencies to the merit mandates in their personnel management activities" (U.S. MSPB 1981:8). In fact, the MSPB could find no single specific example of how merit considerations "had affected any particular program or policy" (ibid.:22).

Contradictions and Dilemmas

Fundamentally, CSRA fragmented the major responsibilities for federal personnel management by creating OPM, MSPB, and the Federal Labor Relations Authority out of the Civil Service Commission (Rosenbloom 1986). Even within its own sphere of responsibility, OPM contained a basic contradiction. Its management doctrine was dedicated to control and accountability while its operational methodology was committed to decentralization and delegation. As a management agency, OPM had little that it could directly control. The meaningful action in implementing CSRA was at the agency level. The agencies quickly took the initiative to implement their own versions of civil service reform, and OPM found itself in the position of having to catch up with technical personnel program developments. When certain agency actions began to create political problems (primarily in the area of Senior Executive Service pay levels and bonuses), OPM found it necessary to attempt to assert control over agency implementation activities; however, OPM's attempts to exercise program control were universally regarded as too late, too inconsistent, and not sufficiently informed by an adequate level of technical expertise (Ban 1984:51–52).

Confronted with the weakness of administrative control mechanisms in a highly decentralized operational setting, OPM made an extraordinary decision. As Bernard Rosen reports, OPM decided "to reduce significantly the number and scope of evaluations in an already austere inspection program" (1982:44). Inspection and evaluation are primary tools of central management control, but they were apparently too reminiscent of the regulating and policing functions of the old merit system. The problem was further compounded by the organizational association of the inspection and compliance function with the agency relations directorate, which was principally dedicated to management assistance and program coordination. As a consequence, the compliance function was de-emphasized to the point of disappearance.

OPM's neglect of its oversight function, the inadequacy of other management control mechanisms, and the interests of its own political appointees led the organization to rely on a political control process. The formal mechanism for this was the establishment and utilization by OPM of the assistant secretaries group, composed predominantly of political appointees, which became the forum for discussion and promulgation of personnel management initiatives. In effect, OPM's utilization of this group represented the embryonic stage of what was to become the politicization of the administrative process. According to many personnel directors interviewed at the time, "OPM's most senior executives clearly preferred to communicate directly with agency Assistant Secretaries for Administration (or equivalent), rather than through personnel officers (as had been done in the past). In fact, many contended, it appeared that OPM desired to freeze personnel officers out of the line of communications" (U.S. MSPB 1981:51).

One of the most puzzling aspects of OPM in its first ten years was its consistent pattern of excluding the federal personnel community from deliberations on policy and program development. In the Campbell years, despite the eventual efforts of the agency relations staff to establish links with responsible departmental and bureau personnel specialists, the primary OPM commitment of effort was at the political level of federal organizations. A related commitment was made to the equal employment opportunity interests. OPM also invested heavily in the academic and consulting communities for a good-faith effort in research, development, innovation, and evaluation of CSRA implementation (Goldenberg 1985:83).

In OPM's managerial emphasis, the vestiges of the old civil service system and the existing federal personnel community were caught and neutralized between career line managers and political leadership. The encapsulation of the personnel establishment was a brilliant tactic to achieve the objective of breaking past patterns; however, it had the decidedly negative effect of vitiating the governmentwide resources that were required for building new personnel programs at the agency level. This was particularly problematic in view of OPM's value and policy commitments to decentralization, deregulation, and delegation of personnel authorities to agencies.

During these critical formative years at OPM, Campbell clearly regarded the personnel officers of government as part of the problem rather than as possible contributors to its solution. This was undoubtedly due in part to the traditional association of the federal personnel community with the regulations, procedures, and inflexibilities of the civil service system. It was also in part due to the candid expressions by some agency personnel people of the difficulty involved in implementation and the weakness of the theoretical assumptions behind technical features of CSRA (Godwin and Needham 1981). In the first two years of CSRA, OPM leaders were prepared to be influenced by theory and research, but in the implementation process they wanted true believers and team players.

The Dominance of Partisan Politics

Establishing the organizational form and direction of OPM had barely begun when Alan Campbell left the government in December 1980 and a new administration took office in January 1981. New and fragile patterns of organizational behavior, administrative action, and value constructs were disrupted. For OPM, Campbell's departure increased the uncertainty of the presidential transition. In 1981, the MSPB reported turbulence for the merit system and for OPM: "Events of the year may be likened to those that might occur after drastic change in the management of a diversified industrial concern, where the new management sets about radically changing the product line, discontinuing some operations and building up others" (U.S. MSPB 1982:4). The effect on organizational values was equally turbulent.

The new director of OPM, Donald Devine, appeared eager to undo the previous administration's emphasis on the innovations of civil service reform. He called for a recentralization of some authorities, a renewed emphasis on "traditional responsibilities of OPM," and a "back to basics" movement in public personnel administration (ibid.:9). It soon became evident that this did not mean a return to the values of the merit system, even though the specific agenda included an emphasis on upholding civil service rules and regulations. Nor did this mean a continuation of the Carter administration's predominant emphasis on management techniques, although the new agenda included references to upgrading performance and making merit pay and bonus systems available as effective management tools. Rather, the new agenda seemed to be fashioned as a rationale for staff cutbacks in OPM and elsewhere in government and for reductions in personnel program and benefit costs throughout the federal sector (ibid.:9–15).

The major focus of Devine's agenda was to replace OPM's traditional management orientation with an unswerving emphasis on responsiveness of the public service solely to political direction from within the executive branch. Devine sought to have OPM assert ideological leadership and to establish a system of "political administration" throughout the federal sector. The theoretical basis of this system was an interpretation of Weberian bureaucracy in its starkest Prussian manifestation, which, in Devine's words, meant: "The skill and technical expertise of the career service must be utilized, but it must be utilized under the direct authority and personal supervision of the political leader who has the moral authority flowing from the people through an election" (1987:129). Or, as Michael Sanera, a onetime OPM political appointee, states, "success in public-sector management is not dependent on good business management of existing government operations, but rather on managing the President's political philosophy and values" (1987:177). This approach placed OPM in a bitter adversarial relationship with Congress, labor unions, and other representatives of public service interests.

Within OPM, the organizational implications of the shift to "political administration" required the confinement of the policy-making process to an inner circle of political appointees (Devine 1987:131). Under Devine's tutelage, OPM continued to ignore the agency personnel community in the development and implementation of policies and in the communication process, preferring instead to deal substantively with a Personnel Policy Group composed of agency assistant secretaries and other political appointees (U.S. GAO 1984). The most effective and widely accepted aspect of the original OPM, the agency relations function, was abolished, thus turning OPM away from management assistance and program coordination.

OPM itself was subjected to deep cuts in career staffing levels. The outflow of competent career employees began in the Campbell years when OPM approved an early-out retirement offer for its own employees during the initial creation of the organization. Under Donald Devine, staffing levels were driven down significantly. An employment total of 8,280 in 1980 declined to 5,929 in 1986—a significant overall reduction of 28.4 percent. At the same time, key positions in OPM were increasingly filled by political appointees at program director levels and even in the regional offices. The number of political employees increased from fifteen in 1980 (itself a great increase over such appointments in the Civil Service Commission) to a high point in 1983 of thirty-six, then declined somewhat to a total of twenty-seven in 1986 (U.S. GAO 1987:52). The career workforce at OPM was subjected to frequent reorganizations, forced transfers, and assignments of individuals away from areas of their expertise.

During the Reagan administration, OPM also turned away from its initial commitment to experimentation, research, and analysis of CSRA implementation (Goldenberg 1985:83–84). Ultimately, Goldenberg concludes that "Director Devine has politicized the research and evaluation processes in OPM so completely that outsiders no longer accept OPM reports as professional research products" (1985:85). The erosion of staff competence led to the drastic technical decline of OPM as an institution of human resource management. In a major administration-sponsored study, the Grace Commission commented critically on OPM's loss of technical specialists and the deterioration of staffing services (Goldenberg 1985:80). Clearly, OPM began to reflect Thompson's observation that "political responsiveness run rampant can mean administration by amateurs where expertise and competence receive short shrift and public agencies fail to achieve efficiency and effectiveness in their operations" (1988:2).

The immediate successor to Devine as director of OPM, Constance Horner, did not change the value and institutional orientation of the organization, but OPM did begin to address the competence and leadership issues. Capable, career-oriented people were assigned to lead critical program areas such as SES management, training and executive development, and staffing. Soundly conceived policy initiatives began to emerge from OPM in some areas. However, the new initiatives were impeded by the overall lack of resources and competence within the organization. Ten years of value changes, organizational instability, politicization of administrative processes, decline of resources, and hemorrhaging of talent brought OPM to the point of institutional incapacity. In 1989, a comprehensive study of OPM by the U.S. General Accounting Office documented what had become a common assumption in Washington—OPM lacked the institutional capacity to exercise leadership and carry out initiatives in public human resource management.

A Summary Assessment of OPM's First Ten Years

By any measure of performance against legislative intent or against its own goals in both the Carter and Reagan administrations, OPM failed to achieve its objectives. It did not assert effective leadership, maintain aggressive oversight, or facilitate research and development. It did not further merit principles. It did not become the primary management office for the president. Public personnel management at the federal level was not transformed into modern human resource management. In 1988, the regulatory and procedural barriers of the federal personnel system still inhibited managerial action. The technical innovations of CSRA seemed to have made no significantly positive contribution to the overall efficiency or effectiveness of government. Despite clearly established objectives of controlling costs and reducing governmental employment, the employment total, payroll and benefits cost, and average grade and salary of the federal public service all increased significantly (Causey 1988:D2). The most striking results of OPM action were negative—making the public service "increasingly marginal to the activities of government" (Ingraham and Peters 1988:3).

After 1979, the institutional impact of OPM within the government steadily weakened. As OPM's programmatic initiatives failed and its technical competence eroded, its credibility with the operating agencies of government virtually disappeared. OPM lost control of the governmental personnel agenda. Even the Grace Commission, sponsored by the Reagan administration, noted OPM's inadequate leadership on major issues (McGregor 1985:47). The most meaningful personnel program initiatives began to originate and be developed in the Congress, the General Accounting Office, individual governmental agencies (e.g., EPA and the Department of the Army), and outside groups (e.g., the Volcker Commission and the National Academy of Public Administration).

OPM's only apparent success in its first ten years was its contribution to increasing the political responsiveness of the public service to the chief executive; however, responsiveness was a hollow concept because of the erosion of the capacity of the executive branch to carry out political directives. In the case of OPM, responsiveness was purchased at the exorbitant price of passivity, lowered commitment and competence, and a spreading sense of malaise and crisis in the public service (Levine and Kleeman 1986; Clark and Wachtel 1988). The brief history of OPM dramatically demonstrates the point so forcefully made by Gaertner and Gaertner in their discussion of the contradictions between organizational and democratic theory: "In a basic sense, these contradictions suggest that the conditions for an effective democratic regime that responds quickly to shifting electoral mandates are not the conditions that support effective operations of the large organizations designed to implement that mandate" (1984:221).

OPM's Response to the Quiet Crisis

By 1989, a quiet crisis of the public service was being documented, and the need for a new approach to federal human resource management was abundantly evident. The inauguration of George Bush as president was accompanied by a new attitude and a new director of OPM, Constance Newman. For his part, President Bush openly reached out to the public service. Within a week of his inauguration, he convened a meeting in Constitution Hall of some three thousand federal career senior executives. This was a significant occasion—the first group to be addressed by President Bush outside the White House—and his words provided assurance of a new appreciation of the public service. In his address, Bush touched on the importance of the public service as "a noble calling and a public trust." He advised that he was "urging all my appointees to build a spirit of teamwork between the political and career officials" (Bush 1989:3–4). The audience of career executives gave the president a two-minute standing ovation.

The signals of presidential interest and support have been carried forward by Constance Newman as director of OPM. She has attempted to champion the cause of the employees of government in regard to their public image, compensation, and benefits. She has been receptive to the recommendations of the National Commission on the Public Service (Volcker Commission) and the National Academy of Public Administration on issues of recruitment and retention of competent federal employees. OPM has actively sponsored a research agenda for public sector human resource management. Since 1989, OPM has also reached out to the members of the federal human resource community and has used the ideas and suggestions of agency personnel directors in developing program plans and policies. All of these initiatives indicate a fundamental change in OPM's orientation to values and political institutions. The question remains whether the consequences of these initiatives will be adequate to the challenges faced by public sector human resource management, particularly in a time of continuing budgetary crises.

Policy Choices and Consequences

In a framework of values and institutions, OPM's succession of policy choices (and their consequences) illustrates the continuing power of Norton Long's formulation of a basic problem of public administration as "that of organizational identification and point of view. To whom is one loyal—unit, section, branch, division, bureau, department, administration, government, country, people, world history, or what?" (1949:261). Organizational allegiance determines policies. Prior to the Civil Service Reform Act of 1978, the Civil Service Commission continually expressed its commitment to law, rule, and the public service. After 1978, OPM first tied its loyalty to managers and their prerogatives, then to the president's ideology and the imperatives of political administration. Most recently, new OPM policies indicate a loyalty to larger issues of the public service and its viability in democratic governance.

The historical experience of OPM demonstrates that choices regarding values to be maximized and policies to be followed have consequences for organizations, programs, and the public interest. The specific consequences of the Civil Service Reform Act of 1978 and its subsequent implementation by OPM have contributed to a condition of crisis in the public service. In its first ten years, OPM failed to create the capacity, either internally or throughout the federal personnel sector, to deal with the serious demographic and labor-market conditions that confront the government as an employer.

In terms of values, the major impact of OPM's disproportionate emphasis on political responsiveness and partisan ideology was to ignore the historical construct of merit, to reduce the concept of management to an unsubstantiated faith in largely ineffective techniques, and to diminish the ethic of professional and technical competence. For ten years, OPM made no attempt to maintain the balance of competing values that is fundamental to the American political system of separation of powers and representation of multiple interests. In its first decade, the principal organization of civil service reform became an instrument of political persuasion. In the process, it lost its technical capacity—its reason for being.

The evolutionary development of OPM demonstrated clearly that the narrow management values of accountability and control are inadequate for the achievement of modern human resource management objectives. Further, the elevation of political responsiveness and partisan ideology to a position of ultimate value did not lead and cannot lead to the creation and maintenance of institutional capacity for effective governance in a democratic republic. This is an old lesson, but one that has been insufficiently learned in American politics. In democratic governance, executive direction and political responsiveness are essential; they are good and proper values to be embraced and realized. However, it is vital that other values also be represented and given life through implementing policies in order for administrative institutions to operate with any reasonable diligence and effectiveness in the execution of laws, the operation of programs, and delivery of services in the public interest.

The expression of value preferences, the quality of policy choices, and the nature of policy outcomes determine the relative success or failure of specific aspects of democratic governance. In OPM's first ten years, the choices and consequences of its policy decisions and enactments clearly did not result in administrative competence and programmatic effectiveness; however, the question of political success or failure remains. What was the nature of OPM's contribution in its political role as an organization of democratic governance?

Guidance in answering this question is provided by Richard Hofferbert: "The deep structure of political science seems to hold that one determines the worth of a people by the quality of their political life. . . . Political life is not to be scaled by what it *produces* but by what it *is*" (1986:234). As an organization of democratic governance, OPM was intended to facilitate control of the government by the people through the narrow concept of bonding the public service in servitude to the president, and only to the president, in his capacity as representative of all the people. This "administrative presidency" theory (Nathan 1983) provided a limited and incomplete formulation for organizational action within American politics and constitutional structure. The inadequacies of this perspective led inevitably not only to operational problems but also to the failure of OPM as a functioning part of democratic governance as it became isolated from all political influences except the ideology of the administration in power.

Early in the history of CSRA, David Nachmias identified an important concern: "One critical measure of the reorganization success would be whether the end result of the formation stages would be an open system. That is, a system with close and constant contacts with its political, social and economic environments, with input and output across system boundaries" (1979:183). In its development as an organization dominated by partisan and ideological political considerations, OPM became a closed policy system that resisted professional and technical concerns as well as political influences from outside the executive office of the president. By 1988, OPM had forfeited the qualities of democratic political life—openness of process, constructive conflict resolution, and effective representation and participation of all relevant interests. OPM's arbitrary and closed policy system had an influence beyond its internal organizational character, establishing the tone of the relationship of public employees to their agencies and to critical administrative issues.

In the public sector, the choices and consequences of an organization must be judged both by what the organization *is* and what it *produces*. Accordingly, in the measurement scale of political theory (particularly *democratic* political theory), OPM failed in its first ten years because the quality of its existential political life was not in conformance with democratic norms. Similarly, in the scale of administrative performance, OPM was not successful because it did not produce in quantity or quality the human resource management policies and delivery mechanisms that are essential for effective governmental operations.

When political theory and administrative science are joined, the result is a normative structure of public administration that requires attention simultaneously to democratic norms of political theory and to effective instrumental techniques of administrative management. Public administration demands the difficult reconciliation of politics and administration in a democratic polity. When OPM was converted into an instrument of ideological persuasion, it lost its administrative capacity as well as its political morality in the context of democratic governance. OPM's first ten years, therefore, represent a failure by the normative standards of political theory and of administrative management, and thus of the complex ideational structure of public administration.

Since 1988, the new version of OPM, under the direction of Constance Newman, has demonstrated sensitivity to many of the complex issues confronting human resource management in the public sector. It remains uncertain whether this new value and institutional orientation will be supported long enough to reconstitute the nature of the organization and reestablish the validity and usefulness of what it produces. This is a critical endeavor requiring careful policy choices that reflect appropriate political and administrative values. In this context, OPM still has the potential to overcome its history and to make a substantive contribution to the strength of the American public service and, by extension, to the quality of American democratic governance.

SOURCES

Ban, Carolyn. 1984. "Implementing Civil Service Reform: Structure and Strategy." In *Legislating Bureaucratic Change: The Civil Service Reform Act of 1978,* ed. Patricia W. Ingraham and Carolyn Ban, 42–62. Albany: SUNY Press.

Beam, David R. 1978. "Public Administration Is Alive and Well—and Living in the White House." *Public Administration Review* 38 (January/February): 72–77.

Bush, George H. W. 1989. "To Some of America's Finest: Remarks by the President to Senior Executive Service Employees in Constitution Hall, January 26, 1989." *Bureaucrat* 18 (Spring): 3–4.

Caiden, Gerald. 1984. "Reform and Revitalization in American Bureaucracy." In *Problems in Administrative Reform,* ed. Robert Miewald and Michael Steinman, 249–65. Chicago: Nelson-Hall.

Campbell, Alan K. 1978. "Civil Service Reform: A New Commitment." *Public Administration Review* 38 (March/April): 99–103.

——— . 1980. "Civil Service Reform as a Remedy for Bureaucratic Ills." In *Making Bureaucracies Work,* ed. Carol H. Weiss and Allen H. Barton, 153–66. Beverly Hills: Sage.

Cau.   iere to Stay." *Washington Post* (August 21).

Cayer, .   . .   naging Human Resources." In *A Centennial History of the   ierican .   ...ustrative State,* ed. Ralph Clark Chandler, 321–43. New York: Free Press.

Chandler, Ralph Clark. 1986. "The Myth of Private Sector Superiority in Personnel Administration." *Policy Studies Review* 5 (February): 643–53.

Clark, Timothy B., and Marjorie Wachtel. 1988. "The Quiet Crisis Goes Public." *Government Executive* 20 (June): 14–28.

Cooke, Charles. 1959. *Biography of an Ideal: The Diamond Anniversary History of the Federal Civil Service.* Washington, D.C.: U.S. Civil Service Commission.

Devine, Donald J. 1987. "Political Administration: The Right Way." In *Steering the Elephant: How Washington Works,* ed. Robert Rector and Michael Sanera, 125–35. New York: Universe Books.

Ershkowitz, Miriam. 1984. "The Passage of the Civil Service Reform Act of 1978: A Dialogue with Alan K. Campbell." In *Making and Managing Policy: Formulation, Analysis, Evaluation,* ed. G. Ronald Gilbert, 67–83. New York: Marcel Dekker.

Gaertner, Gregory H., and Karen N. Gaertner. 1984. "Civil Service Reform in the Context of Presidential Transitions." In *Legislating Bureaucratic Change: The Civil Service Reform Act of 1978,* ed. Patricia W. Ingraham and Carolyn Ban, 218–44. Albany: SUNY Press.

Godwin, Phil, and Jack Needham. 1981. "Reforming Reform—Challenging the Assumptions for Improving Public Employees' Performance." *Public Personnel Management* 10 (Summer): 233–43.

Goldenberg, Edie N. 1984. "The Permanent Government in an Era of Retrenchment and Redirection." In *The Reagan Presidency and the Governing of America,* ed. Lester M. Salamon and Michael S. Lund, 381–404. Washington, D.C.: Urban Institute.

———. 1985. "The Grace Commission and Civil Service Reform: Seeking a Common Understanding." In *The Unfinished Agenda for Civil Service Reform,* ed. Charles H. Levine, 69–94. Washington, D.C.: Brookings.

Hofferbert, Richard I. 1986. "Policy Analysis and Political Morality: A Rejoinder to Anne E. Schneider's Critique of My Prescription for a Scholarly Division of Labor." *Policy Studies Review* 6 (November): 233–35.

Ingraham, Patricia W. 1984. "The Civil Service Reform Act of 1978: Its Design and Legislative History." In *Legislating Bureaucratic Change: The Civil Service Reform Act of 1978,* ed. Patricia W. Ingraham and Carolyn Ban, 13–28. Albany: SUNY Press.

Ingraham, Patricia W., and B. Guy Peters. 1988. "The Conundrum of Reform: A Comparative Analysis." *Review of Public Personnel Administration* 8 (Summer): 3–16.

Kaufman, Herbert. 1956. "Emerging Conflicts in the Doctrine of Public Administration." *American Political Science Review* 50 (December): 1057–73.

———. 1969. "Administrative Decentralization and Political Power." *Public Administration Review* 29 (January/February): 3–15.

Knudsen, Steven, Larry Jakus, and Maida Metz. 1979. "The Civil Service Reform Act of 1978." *Public Personnel Management* 8 (May/June): 170–81.

118   Larry M. Lane

Levine, Charles H., and Rosslyn S. Kleeman. 1986. *   Quiet Crisis of the Civil Service: The Federal Personnel System at the Crossroads*. Washington, D.C.: National Academy of Public Administration.

Long, Norton E. 1949. "Power and Administration." *Public Administration Review* 9 (Autumn): 257–64.

McGregor, Eugene B., Jr. 1985. "The Grace Commission's Challenge to Public Personnel Administration." In *The Unfinished Agenda for Civil Service Reform*, ed. Charles H. Levine, 43–59. Washington: Brookings.

Miewald, Robert, and Michael Steinman, eds. 1984. *Problems in Administrative Reform*. Chicago: Nelson-Hall.

Moe, Ronald C. 1982. *The Hoover Commissions Revisited*. Boulder, Colo.: Westview.

Nachmias, David. 1979. "The Research Agenda of the 1978 Civil Service Reform Act." *Midwest Review of Public Administration* 13 (September): 182–84.

NAPA. 1981. *Civil Service Reform, 1978–1981: A Progress Report*. Washington, D.C.

Nathan, Richard P. 1983. *The Administrative Presidency*. New York: John Wiley.

Newland, Chester A. 1984. "Crucial Issues for Public Personnel Professionals." *Public Personnel Management* 13 (Spring): 15–46.

Nigro, Lloyd G., and Ross Clayton. 1984. "An Experiment in Federal Personnel Management: The Naval Laboratories Demonstration Project." In *Making and Managing Policy: Formulation, Analysis, Evaluation*, ed. G. Ronald Gilbert, 153–72. New York: Marcel Dekker.

Office of the Special Counsel. 1985. *Protecting the Integrity of the Merit System*. Washington, D.C.: U.S. Merit Systems Protection Board.

O'Toole, Laurence J. 1984. "American Public Administration and the Idea of Reform." In *Problems in Administrative Reform*, ed. Robert Miewald and Michael Steinman, 235–48. Chicago: Nelson-Hall.

Rosen, Bernard. 1982. *Holding Government Bureaucracies Accountable*. New York: Praeger.

Rosenbloom, David H. 1979. "Civil Service Reform, 1978: Some Issues." *Midwest Review of Public Administration* 13 (September): 171–75.

———. 1982. "Politics and Public Personnel Administration: The Legacy of 1883." In *Centenary Issues of the Pendleton Act of 1883: The Problematic Legacy of Civil Service Reform*, ed. Rosenbloom, 1–10. New York: Marcel Dekker.

———. 1986. "A Theory of Public Personnel Reforms." In *Current Issues in Public Administration*, ed. Frederick S. Lane, 361–74. New York: St. Martin's Press.

Rosenbloom, David H., and Deborah D. Goldman. 1986. *Public Administration: Understanding Management, Politics, and Law in the Public Sector*. New York: Random House.

Sanera, Michael. 1987. "Paradoxical Lessons from 'In Search of Excellence.' " In *Steering the Elephant: How Washington Works*, ed. Robert Rector and Michael Sanera, 163–179. New York: Universe Books.

Seidman, Harold, and Robert Gilmour. 1986. *Politics, Position, and Power: From the Positive to the Regulatory State*. 4th ed. New York: Oxford University Press.

Shafritz, Jay M. 1974. "The Cancer Eroding Public Personnel Professionalism." *Public Personnel Management* 3 (November/December): 486–92.

Sylvia, Ronald. 1983. "Merit Reform as an Instrument of Executive Power." *American Review of Public Administration* 17 (Summer/Fall): 115–20.

Thompson, Frank J. 1988. "Political Responsiveness and Merit Systems: An Overview." *Review of Public Personnel Administration* 8 (Spring): 1–6.

U.S. Congress. 1975. House Committee on Post Office and Civil Service, Committee Print 94-10. *The Merit System in the United States Civil Service.* Washington, D.C.

U.S. GAO. 1984. Letter from Rosslyn Kleeman to Patrick S. Korten, July 13.

————. 1987. *Federal Employees: Trends in Career and Noncareer Employee Appointments in the Executive Branch.* GAO/GGD-87-96FS. Washington, D.C.

————. 1989. *Managing Human Resources: Greater OPM Leadership Needed to Address Critical Challenges.* GAO/GGD-89-19. Washington, D.C.

U.S. MSPB. 1981. *Report on the Significant Actions of the Office of Personnel Management during 1980.* Washington, D.C.

————. 1982. *Report on the Significant Actions of the Office of Personnel Management during 1981.* Washington, D.C.

————. 1989. *U.S. Office of Personnel Management: The First Decade—A Report Concerning Significant Actions of the Office of Personnel Management.* Washington, D.C.

Vaughn, Robert G. 1975. *The Spoiled System: A Call for Civil Service Reform.* New York: Charterhouse for the Center of Study of Responsive Law.

Wamsley, Gary L., Charles T. Goodsell, John A. Rohr, Camilla M. Stivers, Orion F. White, and James F. Wolf. 1987. "The Public Administration and the Governance Process: Refocusing the American Dialogue." In *A Centennial History of the American Administrative State,* ed. Ralph Clark Chandler, 291–317. New York: Free Press.

6. The U.S. Merit Systems Protection Board and the Office of Special Counsel

Robert G. Vaughn

The United States Merit Systems Protection Board consists of two institutions, fundamentally separate but mutually dependent. One, the board, functions principally as an adjudicator of personnel action appeals brought by federal employees and by the Office of Special Counsel. The other institution, the special counsel, acts as an investigator of allegations of the commission of prohibited personnel practices, with powers to seek to protect injured employees and discipline managers involved in these practices.

During consideration of Reorganization Plan No. 2, creating the board and the special counsel, and of the Civil Service Reform Act of 1978 (CSRA), defining their powers and procedures, Carter administration officials argued that the board and special counsel would protect the merit system from any abuse resulting from the flexibility created in provisions regarding pay, discipline, and the senior civil service.[1] Indeed, the protections to be provided by the board and special counsel were seen as necessary to the fair application of the managerial discretion granted in other provisions. Because the two institutions together were often referred to as "the Board," congressional debate sometimes failed to distinguish or confused the roles of the board and of the special counsel. These references grouping the board and special counsel suggest the important link between them. From the perspective of history and practice, an evaluation of the performance of the board should include an examination of the special counsel as well.

The CSRA, as demonstrated both in its provisions and in congressional deliberations, establishes the board's quasi-judicial character. For example, the legislation prescribes a judicial model for the board, including granting subpoena power, requiring a trial-type hearing, establishing standards of proof, allowing the recovery of attorney fees, mandating the maintenance of a transcript, and describing trial and appellate functions within the Board. Also, the legislative history repeatedly referred to the adjudicatory functions of the board. The CSRA, however, gives the board additional responsibilities. The board is to conduct studies of the civil service and to comment more generally on the state of the merit system and upon the performance of the Office of Personnel Management (OPM).

The CSRA defines the special counsel as an aggressive protector of merit system principles and of employees harmed by prohibited personnel practices. The CSRA grants the special counsel considerable independence and authority. For example, the legislation gives the special counsel tenure in office; establishes some independence from the board; and grants authority to conduct investigations, seek stays and reversals of improper personnel actions, and request discipline of federal managers for the commission of prohibited personnel practices. Moreover, the legislative history emphasized both the importance of the special counsel in preventing abuse of the increased managerial discretion central to other portions of the act and the aggressive approach that the special counsel should take to its duties. For example, the Senate report stated, "The Special Counsel should not passively await employee complaints, but rather, vigorously pursue merit system abuses on a systematic basis" (U.S. Congress 1978:32).

Various analyses of the CSRA, immediately following its enactment, also commented upon the central role of the board and of the special counsel in protecting merit principles. For example, Alan Campbell stated, "It is my hope that the Merit Systems Protection Board and the Special Counsel, having the kind of independence they do, will capture and hold the support of federal employees on the basis that they believe these new institutions are fairer and more just" (Campbell 1979:36).

Subsequent comments, some years after enactment, tended to be critical. Critics asserted that intended protections had not materialized and that the board had been ineffective (Kirschten 1983; Stahl and McGurrin 1986). These criticisms in part focused on the board's lack of rule-making authority for the civil service and its removal from day-to-day operations as preventing it from becoming an effective counterweight to agency management and to OPM (Huddleston 1982). At least one commentator, however, suggested that the problems lay more with the operation of OPM than with the powers of the board (Huddleston 1982). Moreover, the board's performance in merit system review was faulted (Thayer 1984). In addition, critics argued that the special counsel had failed to establish an institutional identity (Ban 1984; Stanley 1984). The failure of the special counsel jeopardized the protection of employees, specifically whistleblowers, that formed an important component of the reform (Udall 1982).

Against this background, this chapter evaluates the performance of the board as an adjudicatory agency. The evaluation includes those elements used in judging adjudicatory agencies: efficiency, fairness, and professional competence. The chapter also discusses the board's relationships to OPM, to the Equal Employment Opportunity Commission (EEOC), and to federal sector labor relations. The chapter concludes that the board has successfully established itself as an adjudicatory agency but continues to be plagued by perceptions that its decisions are biased in favor of management.

On the other hand, the special counsel has yet to establish itself as an aggressive protector of merit principles, and it labors under the suspicions of employee groups and important congressional committees that it lacks the will to be the guardian often described in the legislative history of the CSRA.

The board has secured an adjudicatory role and fulfilled the expectations that personnel administration would benefit from a judicial treatment of employee appeals. The board and the special counsel, however, have not provided the broader oversight envisioned by many proponents of the CSRA.

In its first years, the board faced formidable obstacles in establishing itself as a credible adjudicatory institution. The first board confronted a substantial backlog of cases left by the Civil Service Commission (Stanley 1984) and lacked sufficient resources to carry out the responsibilities that it had been assigned (Ban 1984; Ingraham 1984). In addition, the board interpreted both a body of law that had often lacked coherence and new statutory provisions that were complex and frequently ambiguous. Perhaps most significantly, the participants in the adjudicatory process that the board was required to establish viewed the board with suspicion and misgiving (Vaughn 1982). Agencies were concerned about insensitive interference with management authority and employee groups doubted if the board could become an independent adjudicator.

Despite these obstacles, the board accomplished a great deal in a short period of time. These early accomplishments identified the board as an adjudicatory agency and helped provide an institutional identity, including a series of restraints on the exercise of discretion that remain the strengths of the board. The board established and adopted adjudicatory procedures patterned after a judicial model, emphasized the role of precedent in its decisions, encouraged participants to approach the board as an adjudicatory body, improved the qualifications of trial-level officials, and introduced many of the restraints that limit trial and appellate courts in their deliberations. An examination of the early opinions of the board demonstrated that the board performed the task of statutory interpretation with the same competence and skill that would mark the efforts of the United States circuit courts of appeal (Vaughn 1982).

In 1981 an event occurred that would not only challenge the nation's air traffic system but influence the performance of the board and perceptions of it for several years. That event, the strike by air traffic controllers, led to the dismissal of nearly 11,000 controllers and flooded the board with an unanticipated and potentially disabling number of appeals.[2] These appeals absorbed the resources and attention of the board during a critical phase in its development.

At the time that the board adjudicated most of these appeals, two of the original members of the board, appointed by President Carter, had resigned and been replaced by new members appointed by President Reagan. Some of the appeals were decided by a board consisting entirely of President Reagan's appointees. The first transition of the board was very important in establishing its reputation as an adjudicatory agency. Although any change in the personnel of an adjudicatory body, including the courts, is likely to lead to modifications in precedent and changes in decision-making, the board was particularly susceptible to charges that its decisions simply reflected the political desires of the administration in power.

The air traffic controller cases presented questions of considerable general interest, the resolution of which had highly important political implications for the Reagan administration and for President Reagan personally. Even so, no credible evidence has ever been presented that any member of the board responded to direct political pressures or followed any explicit instructions in reaching decisions in these cases. In terms of political intervention in specific decisions or groups of related decisions, no fair reading of the evidence permits a conclusion of bias. Indeed, federal courts, particularly the United States Court of Appeals for the Federal Circuit, almost uniformly supported the board's resolution of the legal issues regarding the strike (Murphy 1986). Still, the board received considerable criticism, particularly from the attorneys for the fired controllers, and this criticism coming in the context of changes in the membership of the board undoubtedly has influenced perceptions of the board. A fair reading of the opinions of the board, however, would permit the conclusion that, within the parameters provided by the statutes and by precedent, the board exercised its discretion to adopt, among permissible positions, those that were more favorable to the government's position than to that of the controllers.[3] Therefore, in terms of patterns of policy choices some basis for a claim of bias exists.

A 1987 study by the General Accounting Office concluded that most of the participants in the board's adjudicatory procedures were satisfied with the objectivity, independence, and fairness of the process, believing that the board's decisions were consistent with their supporting rationales (U.S. GAO 1987). Positive evaluations by agency representatives and general counsels may reflect the advantages that agencies acquire in personnel management through the application of clear standards by a third party. The study, however, notes that groups representing employee interests viewed the board less favorably and that two of these groups—private attorneys, who represented employees before the board, and union presidents—were much more likely to hold negative views of the board's independence and fairness (ibid.:4, 39–47). Indeed, a majority of these two groups negatively assessed the board's independence and fairness.

These negative assessments can be explained in a number of ways. The chairman of the board opined that these assessments could reflect the response bias of persons who lost cases before the board (ibid.:52–53), an explanation like that of the first chairwoman of the board to similar criticisms.[4] In addition, these assessments varied little from ones of the adjudication of cases by the Civil Service Commission (Vaughn 1982) and therefore may simply demonstrate that the board has failed to overcome prejudgments by these groups of the adjudicatory process. The board's failure may rest upon historical circumstances, such as the air traffic controllers' strike, beyond the board's control. Therefore, according to these arguments, negative assessments do not reflect the character of adjudication occuring before the board.

Another explanation admits that the board's decisions do reflect policy choices that favor agency management. A thorough discussion of this proposition would require a detailed analysis of substantive decisions beyond the scope of this chapter. A brief presentation of the outline of this analysis, however, permits some evaluation of the methodology and possible conclusions. The argument that the board's decisions are biased in favor of management would rely upon an examination of the permissible choices that the board was allowed by the CSRA and by precedent on a number of important issues. Depending on the sample chosen and the weight given to various issues, a respectable argument might be made that the board's decisions favor management. An example of the methodology and the conclusion is the body of air traffic controller decisions noted above.

Even if the decisions of the board do favor management, one response asserts that the CSRA is itself promanagement in its policy judgments and that most of the range of choices available to the board would be unacceptable to employee groups. For example, the harmful error standard of the CSRA makes procedural reversals difficult to obtain, and the reduced standard of proof in Chapter 43 actions eases the burdens of agencies. This response is weakened if boards with different memberships, appointed by different administrations and holding varying philosophical positions, have resolved similar questions inconsistently. To conclude that this type of change has occurred with a frequency and to a degree to suggest bias would require finding that Reagan-appointed board members had overruled precedents favorable to employees or had construed existing standards in a manner inconsistent with those standards. While some cases can be found in which Reagan appointees have overruled precedent or have more narrowly interpreted existing standards protecting employees, neither the number of cases nor the character of the modifications seems sufficient to support the proposition of bias.

Moreover, in a number of decisions, the board, with members appointed by President Reagan, has adopted standards that reinforce some aspects of the CSRA most challenging to management prerogative. For example, the CSRA authorizes the special counsel to commence disciplinary actions against federal managers who have committed prohibited personnel practices. The CSRA permits the use of disciplinary authority outside of the management structure of a particular agency and is therefore a significant challenge to the concepts of hierarchy and agency control of discipline. In two important groups of decisions, the board broadly interpreted the authority of the special counsel. In one group, the board determined that the special counsel needed to meet a less demanding standard of proof when seeking discipline than when seeking correction of an agency personnel action.[5] In another, the board decided that the special counsel had authority to commence disciplinary actions not only for the commission of prohibited personnel practices but also for the violation of any civil service law or regulation.[6] These decisions reflect articulated policy choices against management prerogative and in favor of forms of employee accountability outside of the structure of an agency. The courts, rather than the board, have restricted the authority of the special counsel in these instances.[7]

One group of board decisions, those dealing with the right of federal employees to disobey illegal or unconstitutional orders, contradicts the analysis above.[8] In this group of decisions, the board adopted the most limiting of three standards for determining the right to disobey.[9] In these decisions, the board emphasized management prerogative rather than individual responsibility.

Another set of decisions could support an argument that the board may exhibit some partisan bias. Following the 1984 presidential election, the Office of Special Counsel commenced disciplinary action against several officials of federal employee unions, charging them with violation of the Hatch Act, an act that restricts certain political activities of federal employees. The charges rested on comments made by union presidents in union publications criticizing President Reagan and urging members to vote for Walter Mondale. Because of the context of the charges, important First Amendment considerations, and the novelty of prosecution of union officials who were federal employees on leave (sometimes for decades), some perceived the prosecution by the special counsel as a partisan response to the support of those union officials for President Reagan's opponent.

The board found violations of the Hatch Act and expressed concern that sanctions might not be effective.[10] Two United States circuit courts of appeal reversed these decisions in opinions suggesting the weaknesses of the government's case, particularly on some charges upheld by the board, the board's deviation from some of its own precedent, and the failure of the board to interpret correctly what the courts believed to be the clear meaning of the statute and regulations.[11] Therefore, an analysis emphasizing the political context and the courts' treatment of the board's decisions would permit the argument that these decisions exhibited some partisan bias. The argument, however, would be weakened somewhat by the unanimity of the board and the support of its Democratic member, although that member was appointed by President Reagan.

Generally, the United States Court of Appeals for the Federal Circuit, the court that reviews almost all of the decisions of the board, has supported the board in an overwhelming number of decisions. Although the exact percentage varies by year, that court has affirmed, from 1983 through 1987, between 91 and 95 percent of the board's decisions appealed to the court.[12]

In part, the affirmation rates result from limited judicial review of the Board's factual determinations; and, uniformly, the participants in adjudication before the board have not viewed the affirmation rates as an appropriate measure for the objectivity of board decisions (U.S. GAO 1987:40). An examination, however, of the federal circuit's decisions demonstrates that the court has credited the board's judgments regarding statutory interpretation as well (Vaughn 1984). The court has consistently supported the board's procedures based upon a judicial model and has acted to protect the board's adjudicatory structure. In addition, in a number of areas, such as Chapter 43 actions, the court has adopted board decisions, sometimes citing at length the board's analysis.[13] In those instances where the court has disagreed with the board on major issues, the board's interpretations of the CSRA may have been superior.[14] Recently, the United States Supreme Court reversed the federal circuit, adopting the position advocated by the board rather than that developed by the federal circuit.[15]

Board decisions may also influence both public and private employment law. Some states have adopted provisions establishing adjudication of personnel claims through a merit board, and board decisions are likely to be persuasive on relevant topics. In addition, some board standards can be used in situations that arise in private employment.[16]

Although delay in the resolution of cases continues to be a problem with those decisions of administrative judges that are reviewed by the board, the board has demonstrated the will and management skill to resolve its decisions in a timely manner (GAO 1987:24–26). The board has managed a substantial caseload in addition to resolving the exceptional number of air traffic controller cases. For example, the

General Accounting Office reported that trial-level offices of the board processed the following percentages of appeals within a 120-day time period: 1982: 82 percent, 1983: 17 percent, 1984: 77 percent, 1985: 95 percent, 1986: 99 percent (ibid.:20). The board's 1987 *Annual Report* stated that 99.8 percent of the trial-level decisions for that fiscal year were made within 120 days (U.S. MSPB 1987:7); the 1988 percentage was 99.6 (U.S. MSPB 1988:30) and 1989, 99.7 (U.S. MSPB 1989:32). The 1983 percentages reflect, according to the board, significant budget cuts and the increased work load created by air traffic controller appeals (U.S. GAO 1987:21).[17]

Indeed, the board's handling of its caseload may be too timely. According to a report prepared for the Administrative Conference of the United States, some private practitioners believe that some cases require more effort than others and that strict application of time limits impairs preparation of these cases (Luneberg 1988:82–83). In addition, meeting the 120-day time limit forms a part of the performance standards for presiding officials thereby emphasizing rapid adjudication. The report concludes, "Current criticisms should . . . spur the Board to a sober look at its focus on the 120 day limit" (ibid.:111).

Expedition, however, remains an important value for an adjudicatory body. Expedition by the board particularly serves the interests of employees. Almost all employees appeal personnel actions to the board after those actions have been taken. Delay harms employees because employees with meritorous cases must await action by the board to overturn unsupported or improper actions. Also, adjudication before the board continues to suffer because in many cases the process is not an adversary one. Many employees are not represented, and the obligations of the board toward these unrepresented employees remains unclear.

Still, the board has established itself as an effective adjudicatory body. Although the changes in membership in the board may have influenced its policy choices, the modifications in board precedent appear within the bounds permitted in adjudicatory bodies, including the courts. The board continues to by plagued by perceptions held by some groups that it is management oriented, and although some evidence supports this view, many of the board's decisions, including important ones concerning the disciplinary powers of the special counsel, cannot be reconciled with it. The board has effectively managed its caseload, and its interpretations of the CSRA have generally fared well in the courts.

The participation of OPM and the EEOC in adjudications of the board has complicated that process but has given those agencies an influence over board decisions. Of the two, OPM has been particularly effective in using its participation to shape the law.

The CSRA permits OPM to intervene in board proceedings to seek review by the board of the decisions of the board's administrative judges. The board seems to have had little difficulty in accommodating this role of OPM. In addition, OPM may, in limited circumstances, seek judicial review of board decisions in which OPM was not a party. OPM has obtained review of a number of board decisions and of the decisions of arbitrators, leading to some significant judicial interpretations of the CSRA.

The CSRA establishes complicated procedures to govern *mixed cases*, those cases involving both a civil service claim and a claim of prohibited discrimination. These procedures reflect a detailed compromise between civil rights groups and others regarding the roles of the board and the EEOC. A few conflicts between the board and the EEOC have required the use of a special panel provided for in the CSRA.[18] These decisions have affirmed the primacy of the EEOC in interpreting discrimination law and limited the role of these panels in reviewing EEOC interpretations of discrimination law. Because the procedures leading to a special panel can be time-consuming and complicated, one board member has called on Congress to modify them.[19]

The board's decisions also relate the board to federal sector labor relations. Although the CSRA gives the Federal Labor Relations Authority (FLRA) jurisdiction to adjudicate disputes regarding collective bargaining, the board has decided issues directly relating to labor relations. For example, the board has defined a strike against the government and the proof necessary to discipline an employee for violating the strike prohibition,[20] has construed the scope of collective bargaining,[21] has determined the propriety of restrictions on rehiring fired controllers,[22] and has interpreted the official time provision of the labor relations title of the CSRA.[23]

On the other hand, the board has often looked to FLRA decisions in interpreting labor relations portions of the CSRA and, by analogy, in interpreting personnel law. In fact, the board has incorporated protections contained in collective bargaining agreements as part of the standards and procedures that the board will apply in reviewing agency personnel actions.[24]

The board's decisions have done much to define the relationship between the statutory appeals and grievance arbitration. First, the board's decisions have determined when statutory appeals can be excluded from board review by a collective bargaining agreement.[25] Second, the board's decisions have emphasized that an employee is bound by the choice to pursue grievance arbitration.[26] Most important, the board's decisions influence the choice between the arbitration and statutory appeals by defining the character of board proceedings.

The courts have required arbitrators to follow certain decisions of the board and have held that the same standards of judicial review apply to the board and to arbitrators.[27] In limited circumstances the board may review the decisions of arbitrators. In these instances, the board has deferred to the decisions of arbitrators unless an employee can show that the arbitrator erred in interpreting civil service law, rules, or regulations.[28] Therefore, board decisions have become important guides for federal sector arbitrators.

Functions of the board other than adjudication have been less significant. These functions include the board's authority to conduct studies and investigations of the civil service and its power to review regulations issued by OPM and to void rules that violate merit system principles.

During the first ten years, the board conducted a number of studies of the civil service. Some of these studies, such as the study of sexual harassment in the federal government (including the recently released follow-up study) and the study of the attitudes of employees toward whistleblowing and the protections against prohibited personnel practices, have informed public and congressional assessments of the civil service. One commentator has suggested that the board had not effectively used its authority to conduct studies (Thayer 1984), and the General Accounting Office has criticized the methodology of one major study (U.S. GAO 1982).

The board has, on occasion, found OPM regulations to violate merit system principles, but these decisions are unusual; the most notable was an early decision of the board regarding discipline under performance appraisal systems.[29] The board may review regulations by request of the special counsel, by a petition of an interested party, or on its own motion. The board has considerable discretion in determining whether to grant a petition for review of a regulation.[30] The annual reports of the board suggest that the use of this jurisdiction is limited and the majority of regulation review has occurred upon petition rather than on the board's own motion.[31]

Other functions of the board have remained subordinate to its adjudicatory role. The primacy of its adjudicatory function agrees with the bulk of the legislative history, although broader views of the role of the board occasionally appeared in the legislative record. However, these subordinate functions of the board include ones that some commentators believe the most likely to influence the operations of the civil service (Huddleston 1982; Stahl and McGurrin 1986).

The Office of the Special Counsel also faced substantial obstacles in establishing itself as an aggressive protector of merit principles. The office was initially underfunded and understaffed (Ban 1984; Ingraham 1984). Leadership in the office changed rapidly, and early conflicts between the special counsel and the board regarding their relationship contributed to the instability of leadership (Ban 1984). Federal agencies remained suspicious, if not hostile, and employee groups and supporters of whistleblowers doubted the commitment of the executive to an effective watchdog institution.

Early decisions by the board and by the courts concluded, properly, it appears from the legislative history of the CSRA, that the powers of the special counsel were more limited than the special counsel urged.[32] Weaknesses in the enforcement provisions regarding prohibited personnel practices, particularly retaliation against whistleblowers, became apparent, and the special counsel argued that Congress had failed to provide it with a number of important powers, including the power to represent itself in court and to appeal decisions of the board adverse to it.[33]

The combination of these factors led to the early alienation of Congress and of employee advocacy groups, groups important to the political strength of the special counsel within the executive. Increasingly, important congressional committees, particularly the Civil Service Subcommittee of the House Post Office and Civil Service Committee,[34] and employee associations and public interest groups (Devine and Aplin 1986, 1988) have perceived the special counsel as ineffective, if not, in fact, hostile to the interests that the special counsel is pledged to defend. Legislation, recently enacted, permits employees to bypass the special counsel and to commence actions for correction of personnel actions taken in retaliation against whistleblowers directly before the board.

The special counsel has successfully prosecuted several actions before the board but has encountered difficulty in proving its allegations in other cases.[35] The limited number of court decisions also presents doubts regarding the role of the special counsel (see Office of Special Counsel 1987). The level of activity by the special counsel before the board also seems unusually low. For example, in fiscal year 1987 the special counsel brought before the board only four disciplinary actions (other than Hatch Act cases), only one request for a stay, and no requests for corrective action (U.S. MSPB 1987:13).[36] Even assuming the resolution of a substantial number of cases informally, the level of prosecutorial activity appears low.

One of the more important, and controversial, functions of the special counsel is to refer to an agency any whistleblower allegations that raise a substantial likelihood that officials of an agency have committed wrongdoing that is the subject of the whistleblower provision.[37] In serious matters, the special counsel may formally request the head of an agency to investigate the allegations and report the results to the special counsel in writing and personally signed by the agency head.[38] In less serious matters, the special counsel may refer the matter to the agency for appropriate action, and the head of the agency is to report what action was taken.[39] The annual reports of the special counsel suggest that a relatively small number of serious matters have been referred to agencies.[40] While the board has established its role as an adjudicator, the role of the special counsel remains less clear. Without an effective special counsel to investigate and prosecute the abuse of personnel authority, the board, as an adjudicatory body, is unable to provide all of the oversight functions envisioned by the proponents of the CSRA.

The passage of the Whistleblower Protection Act of 1989 reflects congressional concern with the effectiveness of protections and with the performance of the Office of Special Counsel. Among other changes, the Whistleblower Protection Act modifies the definition of reprisal and changes the standard of proof for government agencies in cases in which they claim that action would have been taken against the employee without regard to the employee's protected whistleblowing.[41] The change in the standard of proof should make it considerably more difficult for the government to prevail on such a claim. Moreover, the Whistleblower Protection Act limits the role of the special counsel in several ways: its powers to intervene in actions are curtailed, as is the authority of the special counsel to disclose the names of whistleblowers. Most important, whistleblowers are given a right of action to bring their cases directly to the board for relief including stays of personnel actions.[42]

Even if the board has failed to meet all the expectations of the advocates of civil service reform, its performance as an adjudicatory agency in its first ten years opens options for civil service law. One example: recent violations of federal ethics laws combined with constitutional challenges (though now resolved) to the special prosecutor provisions of the Ethics in Government Act of 1978 argue for an improved enforcement mechanism, preferably one relying on administrative adjudication. Without an established adjudicatory body with experience in personnel law, the option of administrative enforcement would become less attractive. However, with the board as an established adjudicatory agency, administrative enforcement becomes a much simpler and arguably more effective alternative. Not surprisingly, one proposal now before Congress provides for administrative enforcement of ethics laws by permitting the Office of Government Ethics to commence disciplinary actions before the board against employees and former employees of the federal government.

A second example, less clear because it also suggests the importance of the role of the special counsel, also illustrates the importance of the board as a credible adjudicatory agency. Public interest and civil rights groups, as well as the Department of Justice, have long been dissatisfied with a tort action as the principal remedy against federal officials who are alleged to have violated the constitutional rights of third parties. One alternative rests on an administrative scheme that permits the receipt and evaluation as well as the adjudication of complaints by institutions other than the agency whose employees are charged with wrongdoing. The board clearly offers such an adjudicatory institution. The effectiveness of the special counsel is less clear, but together these two institutions already provide the foundation for a compromise, turning to administrative adjudication of violations of individual rights now redressed through constitutional tort actions.

Of the Merit Systems Protection Board's two institutions, the board and the special counsel, the board has established the adjudicatory role envisioned for it, but the special counsel still faces significant challenges in creating an institutional identity. The two institutions, functioning together, have not provided the oversight and protection that many of the advocates of the CSRA predicted. Concerns about the effectiveness of the special counsel and the board as protectors against abuse can discourage experimentation and modifications in the civil service. For example, experiments that increase the likelihood of abuse, or modifications, such as proposed changes in the Hatch Act, that require an effective enforcement mechanism, may become more difficult and less advisable. The two institutions, however, have created a structure for future congressional regulation of the civil service. This regulation will rely on adjudication of standards and rules outside of the management structure of individual agencies and will likely subject individual government officials to discipline for violations of standards articulated by Congress.

NOTES

1. Hearings on Reorganization Plan No. 2 of 1978 before a subcommittee of the Committee on Government Operations, House of Representatives, 95th Cong., 2d. sess. 14–15 (testimony, director of Office of Management and Budget), 37–38 (chairman of Civil Service Commission) (1978); Hearings on H.R. 11280 before the Committee on Post Office and Civil Service, House of Representatives, 95th Cong., 2d. sess. 12–13 (testimony, director of Office of Management and Budget), 18 (testimony, chairman of Civil Service Commission).

2. A chronology of the strike and subsequent adjudication is described in Schapansky v. Department of Transportation, 735 F.2d 477 (Fed. Cir.), cert. denied, 105 S.Ct. 432 (1984) and PATCO v. FLRA, 685 F.2d 547 (Fed. Cir. 1982).

3. Schapansky v. Department of Transportation, 12 M.S.P.R. 141 (1984) approved prima facie proof of strike participation through unauthorized absence during a widespread strike rather than requiring proof of actual involvement in the strike, declared that a specific intent to strike was not required, and rejected the claim that the president's announcement on the first day of the strike denied an opportunity to respond; DiMasso v. Dept. of Transportation, 725 F.2d 526 (Fed. Cir. 1984) discussing the board position, rejected the claim that FAA managers improperly directed dismissal of controllers; Johnson v. Department of Transportation, 12 M.S.P.R. 187 (1984), rejected subjective standard for coercion and adopted well-founded fear of death or serious bodily harm; Noa v. Dept. of Transportation, 15 M.S.P.R. 126 (1983), concluded that continuation of the strike beyond 6 August, 1981 could be proven without showing a certain number of co-workers on strike; Brown v. Dept. of Transportation, 15 M.S.P.R. 221 (1983), interpreted the First Amendment to deny protection to the FAA supervisor and found that speech had a limited relationship to this matter of public interest and concern; Dorrance v. Dept. of Transportation, 735 F.2d 516 (Fed. Cir. 1984), discussing board position, sustained the use of documents despite evidence suggesting unreliability.

4. Statement of Ruth Prokop, chairwoman, MSPB, during hearings on Civil Service Reform Oversight, 1980-Whistleblowing before the Subcommittee on Civil Service of the House Committee on Post Office and Civil Service, 96th Cong., 2d sess. 209 (1980).

5. Special Counsel v. Harvey, 25 M.S.P.R. 514 (1984); Special Counsel v. Brown, 28 M.S.P.R. 133 (1985).

6. Special Counsel v. Williams, 27 M.S.P.R. 97 (1985); Special Counsel v. Russell, 28 M.S.P.R. 162 (1985).

7. In Horner v. MSPB, 815 F.2d 668 (Fed. Cir. 1987) the court reversed the board and held that the special counsel's authority was limited to specific grants of authority concerning prohibited personnel practices, the Hatch Act, enforcement of board orders, and the sanctions provision of the Freedom of Information Act; other circuit courts of appeal have expressed doubt as to whether the board's adoption of lesser standards for showing retaliation in disciplinary actions was appropriate. Starrett v. Special Counsel, 729 F.2d 1246, 1253, n. 12 (4th Cir. 1986); Harvey v. MSPB, 802 F.2d 537, 548, n.5 (D.C. Cir. 1986).

8. E.g., Gragg v. United States Air Force, 13 M.S.P.R. 296 (1982); Mode v. TVA, 20 M.S.P.R. 92 (1984); Blevins v. Department of the Army, 26 M.S.P.R. 101 (1985).

9. The board's view permits the employee to disobey only if the order has previously been declared invalid by an appropriate authority. Other views protect the employee if the order is found subsequently to be illegal or if the employee disobeyed with a reasonable belief and in good faith.

10. For example, Special Counsel v. Blaylock, 32 M.S.P.R. 110 (1987); Special Counsel v. Biller, 32 M.S.P.R. 110 (1987).

11. See, Biller v. M.S.P.B., 863 F.2d 1079 (2d Cir. 1988); Blaylock v. M.S.P.B., 851 F.2d 1348 (11th Cir. 1988).

12. Information provided by the clerk's office of the United States Court of Appeals for the Federal Circuit. 1983, 92 percent; 1984, 94 percent; 1985, 95 percent; 1986, 94 percent; 1987, 91 percent.

13. For example, Chennault v. Dept. of the Navy, 796 F.2d 465 (Fed. Cir. 1986), citing Griffin v. Dept. of the Army, 23 M.S.P.R. 657, 663 (1984); Baker v. Defense Logistics Agency, 782 F.2d 1579, 1583 (Fed. Cir. 1986): "We agree with the Board's decision for the reasons set forth in its opinion"; Adkins v. Dept. of Housing and Urban Development, 781 F.2d 891, 895–896 (Fed. Cir. 1986), applying standards set out in the board's decision in Schuman v. Department of the Treasury, 23 M.S.P.R. 620 (1984).

14. For example, Horner v. M.S.P.B., 815 F.2d 668 (Fed. Cir. 1987); Lovshin v. Dept. of the Navy, 767 F.2d 826 (Fed. Cir. 1985).

15. Dept. of the Navy v. Egan, 108 S.Ct. 818 (1988).

16. An example is the board's articulation of factors to be considered in mitigating a penalty. Board administrative judges report that some corporations now specifically use the board's articulation. See, Douglas v. Veteran's Administration, 5 M.S.P.R. 313 (1981).

17. In fiscal year 1982 the board sustained budget cuts of approximately 16 percent.

18. Ignacio v. U.S. Postal Service, 30 M.S.P.R. 47 (Spec. Panel 1986); Shoemaker v. Dept. of the Army, 34 M.S.P.R. 597 (Spec. Panel 1987).

19. Ignacio v. U.S. Postal Service, 28 M.S.P.R. 337 (1985) (comments of Dennis Devaney, then member of the board).

20. Schapansky v. Dept. of Transportation, 12 M.S.P.R. 141 (1984).

21. Fitzgerald v. Dept. of Transportation, 798 F.2d 461 (Fed. Cir. 1986), discussed the board's position and reversed it.

22. Meyer v. OPM, 767 F.2d 868 (Fed. Cir. 1984); disqualification from a Dept. of Defense Controller position; Wagner v. OPM, 783 F.2d 1042 (Fed. Cir. 1986): disqualification from position with FAA; Korte v. OPM, 797 F.2d 967 (Fed. Cir. 1986), rejected constitutional challenges. These decisions indicate the authority of the board in suitability appeals.

23. Fitzgerald v. Dept. of Transportation, 798 F.2d 461 (Fed. Cir. 1986), discussed the board's position and reversed it.

24. Giesler v. Dept. of Transportation, 3 M.S.P.R. 367 (1980).

25. Espenschied v. MSPB, 804 F.2d 1233 (Fed. Cir. 1986), *cert. denied*, 107 S.Ct. 1896 (1987).

26. E.g., Greer v. Dept. of Housing and Urban Development, 19 M.S.P.R. 90 (1984).

27. Cornelius v. Nutt, 472 U.S. 648, 105 S.Ct. 2882, 86 L.Ed.2d 515 (1985); Devine v. Levin, 739 F.2d 1567 (Fed. Cir. 1984); Horner v. Lucas, 832 F.2d 596 (Fed. Cir. 1987).

28. Robinson v. Dept. of Health and Human Services, 30 M.S.P.R. 389 (1986).

29. Wells v. Harris, 1 M.S.P.B. 199 (1979).

30. NTEU v. Sugarman, 5 M.S.P.B. 41 (1981).

31. U.S. MSPB 1989 *Annual Report*, p. 44 (no regulation review cases); 1988 *Annual Report*, p. 37 (no regulation review cases); 1987 *Annual Report*, p. 12 (one regulation review case); 1986 *Annual Report*, p. 11 (three regulation review cases); 1985 *Annual Report*, p. 23 (number not indicated, one significant case discussed); 1984 *Annual Report*, p. 26 (one case discussed); 1983 *Annual Report*, p. 25 (two cases discussed, both review on request of a party); *Fourth Annual Report*, p. 26 (three cases discussed in which review was granted, requests denied in two other cases); *Third Annual Report*, pp. 12–13 (no cases discussed or noted); *Second Annual Report*, pp. 45–46 (six cases of regulation review, three on board's own motion, requests for review denied in three cases); *First Annual Report*, pp. 25–26 (*Wells* case noted).

32. Robert J. Frazier, 1 M.S.P.B. 159 (1979); Frazier v. M.S.P.B., 672 F.2d 150 (D.C. Cir. 1982).

33. Particularly, Office of the Special Counsel (1979) and (1980).

34. Hearings on H.R. 25 before the Subcommittee on Civil Service of the Committee on Post Office and Civil Service, House of Representatives, 100th Cong., 1st sess. (1987); Hearings on Whistleblower Protection before the Subcommittee on Civil Service of the Committee on Post Office and Civil Service, House of Representatives, 99th Cong., 1st sess. 11 (1985) (Chairwoman of Committee, "this guy [Special Counsel] sounds more like a lapdog than a watch dog.") A

study by the General Accounting Office supported the special counsel's refusal to proceed with cases. GAO 1985.

35. Between 1979 and October 1984, the special counsel lost six prohibited personnel practice cases before the board (GAO 1985).

36. The following table is based on one contained in Hearings on H.R. 25 before the Subcommittee on Civil Service of the Committee on Post Office and Civil Service, House of Representatives, 100th Cong., 1st sess. 226 (1987); it shows actions for years previous to 1987.

Fiscal Year	Formal Corrective actions	Informal Corrective actions	Individual Cases or matters	Disciplinary actions
1983	8	14	5	11
1984	3	—	2	8
1985	2	4	0	9
1986 (to 9/5/86)	2	7	2	7

37. 5 U.S.C. §1206(b)(1). The Department of Justice has stated that the special counsel may not use this authority to refer complaints received from private citizens or from anonymous whistleblowers. See Office of the Special Counsel (1981).

38. 5 U.S.C. §§ 1206(b)(3)(4); called (b)(3) referrals.

39. 5 U.S.C. §§ 1206(b)(2)(7); called (b)(2) referrals.

40. Office of the Special Counsel (1980) pp. 20—21: thirteen (b)(3) referrals; Office of the Special Counsel (1981) pp. 4—6: twelve (b)(3) referrals, forty-seven (b)(2) referrals; 1982 *Report to Congress,* pp. 9—10 sixty-eight referrals, not differentiated; 1983 *Report to Congress,* p. 13: seven (b)(3) referrals, twenty (b)(2) referrals; 1984 *Report to Congress,* pp. 17—19: eight (b)(3) referrals, thirty-three (b)(2) referrals; 1985 *Report to Congress,* pp. 15—16: seventeen (b)(3) referrals, thirty-three (b)(2) referrals; 1986 *Report to Congress,* pp. 9—11: fourteen (b)(3) referrals, thirty-eight (b)(2) referrals; 1987 *Report to Congress,* p. 27: fifteen (b)(3) referrals, thirty-nine (b)(2) referrals; 1988 *Report to Congress,* at 11: twelve (b)(3) referrals, thirty-two (b)(2) referrals.

41. A whistleblower need only show that whistleblowing was a contributing factor to the agency's action, not that it was a significant or predominate factor. 5 U.S.C. sections 1221(e)(1), 1214(b)(4), 1221(e)(1). The agency must prove its case by clear and convincing evidence rather than a preponderance of the evidence.

42. 5 U.S.C. sections 1212(c)(2); 1213(h); and 1221.

SOURCES

Ban, Carolyn. 1984. "Implementing Civil Service Reform: Structure and Strategy." In *Legislation Bureaucratic Change: The Civil Service Reform Act of 1978,* ed. Patricia W. Ingraham and Carolyn Ban, 42—62. Albany: SUNY Press.

Campbell, Alan. 1979. "Reflections on Reform." *Civil Service Journal* (April/June):36—39.

Devine, Thomas, and Donald Aplin. 1986. "Abuse of Authority: The Office of Special Counsel and Whistleblower Protection." *Antioch Law Journal* 4:5–71.

Devine, Thomas, and Donald Aplin. 1988. "Whistleblower Protection/The Gap Between the Law and Reality." *Howard Law Journal* 31:401–17.

Huddleston, Mark. 1982. "The Carter Civil Service Reforms: Some Implications for Political Theory and Public Administration." *Political Science Quarterly* 96:607–21.

Ingraham, Patricia. 1984. "Civil Service Reform and Public Policy: Do We Know How to Judge Success or Failure?" In *Legislating Bureaucratic Change: The Civil Service Reform Act of 1978,* ed. Patricia W. Ingraham and Carolyn Ban, 264–78. Albany: SUNY Press.

Kirschten, Richard. 1983. "Administration Using Carter-Era Reform to Manipulate the Levers of Government." *National Journal* 15:732–36.

Luneberg, William. 1988. The Federal Personnel Complaint, Appeal, and Grievance Systems: A Structural Overview and Proposed Revisions (draft).

Murphy, John. 1986. "Striking in the Federal Sector: An Update on the Law." *American University Law Review* 35 (Federal Circuit issue):929–62.

Office of the Special Counsel. 1979. *First Annual Report to Congress on the Activities of the Office of Special Counsel.* Washington, D.C.

———. 1980. *1980 Annual Report of the Office of Special Counsel.* Washington, D.C.

———. 1981. *1981 Annual Report of the Office of Special Counsel.* Washington, D.C.

———. 1987. *Judicial Views/Prosecution of Prohibited Personnel Practices.*

Stahl, O. Glenn, and James McGurrin. 1986. "Professionalizing the Career Service." *Bureaucrat* 15:9–15.

Stanley, David. 1984. "Civil Service Reform, Then and Now: A Sojourner's Outlook." In *Legislating Bureaucratic Change: The Civil Service Reform Act of 1978,* ed. Patricia W. Ingraham and Carolyn Ban, 258–63. Albany: SUNY Press.

Thayer, Frederick. 1984. "Epilogue to 'The President's Management Reforms: Theory X Triumphant.' " In *Legislating Bureaucratic Change: The Civil Service Reform Act of 1978,* ed. Patricia W. Ingraham and Carolyn Ban, 254–57. Albany: SUNY Press.

Udall, Morris. 1982. "Comment" In *Improving the Accountability and Performance of Government,* ed. Bruce L. R. Smith and James D. Carroll, 52–54. Washington, D.C.: Brookings.

U.S. Congress. 1978. Senate. *Senate Report* No. 169. 95th Cong., 2d sess.

U.S. GAO (General Accounting Office). 1982. *Questionnaire Design Problems Limits Usefulness of Results* B-205566. Washington, D.C.

———. 1985. *Whistleblower Complaints Rarely Qualify for Office of Special Counsel Protection.* GGD-85-53. Washington, D.C.

———. 1987. *Merit Systems Protection Board: Case Processing Timeliness and Participants' Views on Board Activities.* B-226858. Washington, D.C.

U.S. MSPB (Merit Systems Protection Board). 1979. First Annual Report.

———. 1980. Second Annual Report.

———. 1981. Third Annual Report.

———. 1982. Fourth Annual Report.

————. 1983. Annual Report for Fiscal Year 1983.

————. 1984. Annual Report for Fiscal Year 1984.

————. 1985. Annual Report for Fiscal Year 1985.

————. 1986. Annual Report for Fiscal Year 1986.

————. 1987. Annual Report for Fiscal Year 1987.

————. 1988. Annual Report for Fiscal Year 1988.

————. 1989. Annual Report for Fiscal Year 1989.

Vaughn, Robert. 1982. "The Opinions of the Merit Systems Protection Board: A Study in Administrative Adjudication." *Administrative Law Review* 34:25–58.

————. 1984. (Supplement, 1986, 1987, 1988, 1989). *Merit Systems Protection Board: Rights and Remedies*. New York: Law Journal Seminars Press.

7. The Federal Labor Relations Authority

David H. Rosenbloom

The Federal Labor Relations Authority (FLRA) was created by Title VII of the Civil Service Reform Act. Title VII is often referred to as the Federal Service Labor-Management Relations Statute.[1] It endorses the principle that "the statutory protection of the right of employees to organize, bargain collectively, and participate through labor organizations of their own choosing in decisions which affect them . . . safeguards the public interest, . . . contributes to the effective conduct of public business, and . . . facilitates and encourages the amicable settlements of disputes between employees and their employers involving conditions of employment." Accordingly, it creates a framework for collective bargaining in much of the federal service.[2]

It also regulates labor unions representing federal employees and the labor relations activities of most federal agencies. The FLRA has responsibility for resolving issues concerning the scope of bargaining, representational arrangements, unfair labor practices (ULPs), and exceptions to arbitrators' awards. Like the National Labor Relations Board, which has a similar role vis-à-vis collective bargaining in the private sector, and like the various state-level Public Employment Relations Boards (PERBs), the FLRA is heavily involved in adjudication, which it prefers to the exercise of its rule-making powers. Consequently, it is appropriate to evaluate the agency in terms of the three criteria offered by Robert Vaughn in chapter 8: efficiency (timeliness), competence (ability to win a high degree of judicial deference), and fairness (evenhandedness with regard to management and labor interests). Additionally, because the Labor-Management Relations Statute looks toward dispute resolution through collective bargaining, the FLRA's impact on the vigor and viability of that process in the federal sector should be considered.

The Federal Service Labor-Management Relations Statute

The Agency

The FLRA is headed by a bipartisan three-member panel appointed by the president with the advice and consent of the Senate. One of the members is designated chairperson by the president. They hold five-year overlapping terms and can be removed by the president "only upon notice and hearing and only for inefficiency, neglect of duty, or malfeasance in office." The panel is referred to as "the authority." Much of the agency's activity is administered by an Office of the General Counsel. The general counsel is also appointed by the president, with senatorial confirmation, for a five-year term. The Office of the General Counsel oversees the FLRA's regional operations. The agency makes extensive use of administrative law judges in processing ULPs, which constitute a large part of its activity. The general flow of work is from the regions to the general counsel and then, if necessary, to the authority on appeal or stipulation. Under the Supreme Court's ruling in FLRA v. Aberdeen Proving Ground (1988. 485 U.S. 409), only the authority can hear and decide some cases involving negotiability. Cases involving negotiability are those concerning the question of whether an agency regulation is supported by a "compelling need."

The Federal Service Impasses Panel (FSIP) is also located within the FLRA. It consists of at least seven presidential appointees, one of whom is designated chairperson. The panel members hold five-year overlapping terms but are removable by the president. The FSIP is empowered to recommend procedures for impasse resolution and to directly resolve impasses itself. It relies on the usual panoply of impasse resolution techniques, including mediation, fact-finding, binding arbitration, and mediation-arbitration. The FSIP predates the Civil Service Reform Act but was strengthened by it.

In fiscal year 1986, the FLRA's budget was approximately $16 million. The distribution of its personnel work years was as follows: the authority, 116; the Office of the General Counsel, 145; and the FSIP, 8 (FLRA 1986:10–11).

The Statutory Regime

The FLRA administers a labor relations system that is defined by four main characteristics.[3] First, the scope of bargaining is extremely limited compared to that prevailing in the private sector and in many public sector jurisdictions as well. The following working conditions are *nonnegotiable:* (a) matters established by law, such as position classifications, Hatch Act enforcement, and pay; (b) governmentwide rules and regulations; (c) rules and regulations of an agency or primary national subdivision, unless the FLRA has determined that there is no compelling need to prohibit negotiations or a union represents a majority of the affected employees (who comprise a single bargaining unit); (d) management rights, including: interpretation of the agency's mission; determination of its budget, organization, number of employees, and internal security; and the right to take personnel actions involving the assignment of work, contracting out, promotions, and emergency actions.

Management may elect to negotiate over the following, which are deemed permissable subjects of bargaining: (a) the numbers, types, and grades of employees or positions assigned to an organizational subdivision, work project, or tour of duty; and (b) the technology, the means, or the methods of performing work. *Mandatory* bargaining subjects include: (a) conditions of employment that do not fall into either of the above categories; (b) procedures for implementing actions within management's preserved rights; (c) appropriate arrangements for employees adversely affected by management's exercise of its reserved rights; and (d) a grievance procedure, which must allow for conclusion by binding arbitration.

The FLRA has confronted the tension between the substantive nonnegotiability of management's rights and the mandatory negotiability of procedures for implementing exercises of these rights by adopting the doctrine that if a union proposal regarding procedures would prevent the agency from "acting at all," then the proposal is nonnegotiable. The theoretical underpinnings of the acting-at-all doctrine have been sharply criticized, and it is uncertain whether it will continue to be sustained in the future (Broida 1987:163–69). However, it allows for more vigorous bargaining, within an already crimped framework, than the management-favored alternative of prohibiting bargaining if the proposal would create an "unreasonable delay" in the exercise of reserved rights (ibid.:164–65).

There is also a tension between the nonnegotiability of management rights and the mandatory negotiability of arrangements for employees adversely affected by the exercise of such rights. Here, by contrast, the FLRA adopted a standard that was found too narrow by the courts. It sought to prohibit the negotiation of proposals that "directly interfered" with management's rights. However, the judiciary over-turned this standard in favor of one requiring bargaining unless the proposal impinged on management's rights to an "excessive degree" (ibid.:171; American Federation of Government Employees Local 2782 v. FLRA 1983. 702 F2d 118-3; Association of Civilian Techni-cians, Montana Air Chapter v. FLRA 1985. 756 F2d 172).

A second major feature of the federal collective bargaining process is the prohibition of concerted union activities, including strikes, work stoppages, and slowdowns. Picketing that interferes with an agency's operations is also prohibited (unless it is constitutionally protected).[4] In 1981, the FLRA decertified the Professional Air Traffic Controllers Organization (PATCO) for engaging in a strike (PATCO v. FLRA 1982. 672 F2d 109; 685 F2d 547).

Third, in the absence of the right to strike, the statutory scheme looks toward third-party intervention as the primary means of resolv-ing impasses. The parties to an impasse may use either the FSIP or, with FSIP approval, an outside arbitrator for this purpose. From FY 1983 through FY 1986, the FSIP received an average of 143 cases per year. In FY 1986, the most prevalent issues of impasse were: hours of work and overtime (38 cases), ground rules of bargaining (18 cases), grievance and arbitration procedures (17 cases), health and safety (17 cases,) official time (15 cases), leave (14 cases), facilities and services (13 cases), and merit promotion (12 cases) (FLRA 1986:132, 135).

Fourth, contract enforcement is to be largely through grievance pro-cedures. Negotiated grievance procedures must be fair and simple, provide for expeditious processing, allow the union or an aggrieved employee to present and process cases, and, as noted earlier, provide for binding arbitration. Grievances cannot pertain to disputes involv-ing prohibited political activities, retirement, health or life insurance, suspensions and removals for national security reasons, examinations, certifications, appointments, and classifications that do not result in an employee's reduction in grade or pay. The grievance procedure may cover or exclude appealable actions, such as breaches of equal employ-ment opportunity regulations, or adverse actions that fall within the jurisdiction of the Equal Employment Opportunity Commission or the Merit Systems Protection Board.

Literally tens of thousands of grievances have gone to binding ar-bitration. These are summarized in the Office of Personnel Manage-ment's Labor Agreement Information Retrieval System (LAIRS).

Awards can include back pay and other make-whole remedies. Exceptions to interest arbitration or grievance awards (not involving adverse actions) may be filed with the FLRA. The agency will overturn awards when it finds them contrary to federal laws, rules, or regulations or if they are considered defective upon some ground that the federal courts have used to reject similar arbitration awards under regulations pertaining to the private sector.

Adjudication by the FLRA

Office of the General Counsel—Unfair Labor Practices

Most of the cases with which the FLRA deals involve ULPs. These are first filed at the regional level and then appealed to the Office of the General Counsel, if a party so desires. From FY 1980 through FY 1987, the agency handled 43,023 ULP cases, or an average of 5,378 per year. Roughly 95 percent of all ULP charges are filed by unions against agencies (ibid.:74). The charges contained most frequently in ULP cases in FY 1986 are displayed in table 2.

Table 2. FLRA Adjudication of ULP Cases, Issues Most Frequently Raised, Fiscal Year 1986

Issue	Number of Cases	Percentage of all ULPs[a]
Agency interference, coercion, restraint	1,875	36.5
Failure to bargain, unilateral agency change	1,519	30.5
Discrimination by agency	736	14.8
Bad faith by agency	625	12.5
TOTAL	4,695	83.6

SOURCE: FLRA: 1986, p. 79.
[a]Cases may raise more than one issue.

The FLRA disposes of ULPs in one of four ways. In FY 1986, 36.7 percent of the cases were withdrawn on the basis that they lacked merit, 27.6 percent were dismissed as lacking in merit, 24.8 percent were settled voluntarily prior to the issuance of a complaint, and formal complaints were issued in 10.9 percent of the cases (ibid.:80). Complaints can result in status quo ante orders by the FLRA under certain circumstances (Bussey 1984:141–42). Alternatively, they may simply require a party to stop engaging in a practice, including refusal to bargain. The parties may also choose to resolve the complaint in a precomplaint or postcomplaint settlement. A summary of FLRA dispositions of ULP charges from FY 1982 through FY 1987 is presented in table 3.

Table 3. Case Disposition of ULP Claims for Fiscal Years 1982–1987

Dispositive Action	1982	1983	1984	1985	1986	1987	Total
Withdrawal (nonmerit)	1,654	1,897	1,711	1,847	1,700	2,014	10,823
Dismissal (nonmerit)	1,625	1,526	1,448	1,522	1,547	1,470	9,138
Party settlement (merit)	1,105	1,235	1,253	1,303	1,172	1,295	7,363
Complaint (merit)	591	726	691	640	549	849	4,046
Informal settlement	143	116	88	95	75	53	570
Yearly total	5,118	5,500	5,191	5,407	5,043	5,681	31,940

SOURCE: FLRA Office of the General Counsel

Agencies or unions may appeal FLRA regional directors' decisions in ULP cases to the Office of the General Counsel. In the mid-1980s, the appeal rate (based on cases not withdrawn or voluntarily settled prior to complaint) was as follows: FY 1983, 37 percent; FY 1984, 35 percent; FY 1985, 30 percent; FY 1986, 31 percent (FLRA 1986:94). Since FY 1984, the regional directors' decisions have been sustained in upward of 90 percent of the appeals. This represents an increase in consistency between the regions and headquarters over the years from FY 1980 through FY 1983, when the directors were sustained in 75 to 86 percent of the cases. In FY 1986, about 3 percent of all ULP cases were transferred from the general counsel's office to the authority for final decision (ibid.:91). The median processing time for ULPs is presented in table 4.

Table 4 indicates that while there has been a reduction in the time taken to resolve ULPs, half the cases still take more than 63 days to process without an appeal and 51 additional days if under appeal. In FY 1986, 649 cases took longer than 90 days to resolve without a hearing and 203 took as much time while under appeal (ibid.:100). Despite the longevity of some cases, the FLRA appears to be timely when compared to New York State's Public Employment Relations Board (PERB), in which it takes an average of 218 days to resolve a

Table 4. ULP Processing Time, Fiscal Years 1980–1986

Fiscal Year	Median Number of Days	
	Prior to Appeal	Under Appeal
1980	81	104
1981	66	125
1982	78	92
1983	74	91
1984	66	62
1985	63	34
1986	63	51

SOURCE: FLRA 1986, p. 101.

ULP at the hearing officer level and another 134 days when appealed to the board (Riccucci and Ban 1989:65).

Office of the General Counsel—Representational Issues

The FLRA also works through the general council with regard to representational issues. Unions or agencies file representation petitions with the FLRA's regional offices. There are seven types of petitions, seeking (1) amendment of recognition or certification, (2) clarification of the existing bargaining unit, (3) determination of eligibility for dues allotments, (4) decertification of a representative, (5) agency requests for clarification of representational matters, (6) exclusive recognition, and (7) unit consolidation. In FY 1986, the FLRA received 319 representational cases. Most of these involved unit clarification (115, or 36 percent) and exclusive recognition (114; 36 percent). Eight cases involved petitions for decertification (FLRA 1986:102–03). Notices of hearings are issued in about one-third of the petitions, but in most of these cases the issues are resolved by the parties without the hearings actually taking place. Table 5 presents the number of representational cases received by the FLRA and the number of hearings held in 1982–1986. Most hearings appear to result in FLRA decisions and orders, as was the case in FY 1986 (31 cases) and FY 1985 (42 cases).

Elections may be held in cases of petitions for exclusive recognition, agency-initiated clarifications of representation, decertification, and unit consolidation. In both FY 1985 and 1986, 87 elections were held. In each year, two elections resulted in decertification. In 1986, 69 elections resulted in exclusive recognition. Turnouts reported by the FLRA ranged from 30 percent to 75 percent of the eligible employees (FLRA 1986:107–08). The median time for processing representation cases

Table 5. Representational Caseload, Fiscal Years 1982–1986

Fiscal Year	Cases	Hearings	Percentage of Cases
1986	319	36	11.3
1985	347	48	13.8
1984	404	49	12.1
1983	364	52	14.3
1982	388	41	10.6
Total	1,822	226	12.4

SOURCE: FLRA 1986, p. 105.

has been declining from 66 days in FY 1980 to 44 days in FY 1986. In the latter year, 12 of 313 cases disposed of took more than three months (FLRA 1986:109).

Adjudication at the Authority Level

Unfair labor practice and representational decisions of the general counsel may be appealed to the authority. The authority also hears agency and union exceptions to arbitration awards regarding grievances and interests. From 1979 to June 30, 1985, the authority reviewed 790 such awards, of which 74 were set aside, 59 were modified, and 9 were remanded (Schuessler-Laux, 1985:122, table 4). Further, it hears cases involving questions of negotiability. Over the years, the authority has earned a reputation for proceeding slowly, though it now tries to handle all cases within six months. At the end of FY 1986, the authority had 389 cases in its inventory. They were distributed as follows: negotiability, 197 (51 percent); ULPs, 115 (30 percent); arbitration exceptions, 71 (18 percent); representation, 5 (1 percent); and one miscellaneous case was reported (FLRA 1986:14).

The FLRA in Court

FLRA decisions are subject to review in all the U.S. Courts of Appeals (circuit courts), other than the Court of Appeals for the Federal Circuit. More than half the cases are handled by the Court of Appeals for the District of Columbia Circuit. Judicial review extends to decisions of negotiability and ULPs. Exceptions to arbitration awards may be reviewed if the dispute involves a ULP. Representational decisions are not subject to review, unless they can be construed as "final orders" for some peculiar reason (Department of Justice v. FLRA 1984.

727 F2d 481). An employer contesting an FLRA decision to certify an agent as an exclusive agent may seek review indirectly by refusing to bargain, thereby committing a ULP (Broida 1987:603).

Between 1979 and May 1987, the FLRA was a party to 108 reported cases in the circuit courts.[5] Analysis of these decisions indicates that, at least in the eyes of the federal courts, the FLRA's rulings do not command great judicial deference. In fact, the outcome of judicial review of FLRA decisions shows almost no relationship to the outcome of the agency's rulings.

Table 6 presents a schema for assessing the FLRA's overall performance in the circuit courts from 1979 through 1987. Cases in which the courts declined jurisdiction are omitted from the table, as are cases remanded to the FLRA on a basis that did not reject the agency's legal reasoning. Remands explicitly faulting the quality of the FLRA's decisions are treated as rejections by the judiciary. Three cases involved two completely separable issues regarding the scope of bargaining, which were ruled on separately by the court (for example, the FLRA was reversed in part). These were tabulated as separate actions. Consequently, the information in the table deviates slightly from the actual number of reported cases receiving judicial review during the period under consideration.

Table 6. The FLRA in Circuit Court, 1979–1987

FLRA Decision	Circuit Court Decisions		
	Affirming FLRA	Rejecting FLRA	Total
For union (agency appeals)	14	25	39
Against union (union appeals)	35	30	65
Total	49	55	104

NOTE: X^2 = 7.15, 1 degree of freedom
      Lambda = .10
        Phi = .25

The table indicates that the circuit courts approved the FLRA's holdings in forty-nine instances (47 percent) and rejected the agency's position in fifty-five (fifty-three percent) of the instances in which decisions regarding the FLRA's actions were reached. When compared to Vaughn's findings regarding the Merit Systems Protection Board, the extent to which the FLRA's decisions have been rejected is startling. The statistical correlations between the FLRA's decisions and the outcome of instances of judicial review, reported in table 6, are so weak as to suggest that there is no substantial association between the outcome of the agency's rulings and those of the circuit courts on review. Nor has the FLRA's level of success on review improved significantly over time. A plausible conclusion, though one contested by FLRA officials, is that in practice the courts seldom defer to the FLRA's interpretation of the governing regulations. Such an interpretation is bolstered by the text of several judicial decisions.

In some cases, the circuit courts have directly questioned the FLRA's competence. For instance, in American Federation of Government Employees, Local 32 v. FLRA (1985. 774 F2d 498), the court noted the burden that the FLRA's inconsistencies place on affected parties. "In light of the apparent conflict between the FLRA's decision in these cases and its decision in [an earlier case] . . . we must set aside the Authority's orders. . . . We remand the cases to the FLRA. . . . On Remand, we expect that the FLRA will address and resolve the conflict candidly and in a manner that persons affected by the Authority's decisions can comprehend" (506). In National Association of Government Employees v. FLRA (1985. 770 F2d 1223), the court attacked the FLRA's logic: "We deem it inappropriate . . . to conclude at this stage that the agency was wrong in finding no violation of the Act; but hold only that it was assuredly not right for the reasons stated. Accordingly, we remand . . . to the Authority. . . . Because of the inordinate delay in the Authority's handling of this proceeding in the past we will provide the appellant further relief if a final decision by the Authority is not forthcoming within ninety days" (1226–27).

In Professional Airways Systems Specialists, MEBA, AFL-CIO v. FLRA (1987. 809 F2d 855), the court strongly criticized the agency's inconsistent holdings: "In the two cases at hand, the effects of the FLRA's failure adequately to set forth its governing rule are clear. With respect to the identical violation, one ALJ awarded back pay; the other did not. . . . The confusion and inconsistency within the Authority is abundantly evident. The FLRA is therefore obliged, on remand, to provide a reasoned explanation for any rule which it chooses to fashion, including an explanation of departures from its own body of law" (860). Another, and in some ways more problematic, critique of the FLRA was voiced in American Federation of Government Employees v. FLRA (1984. 750 F2d 143): "In short, the FLRA's miserly reading of the term 'collective bargaining agreement' finds no support in the plain language or structure of the statute. What is more, the FLRA's strained interpretation creates tension with the purposes of the [statute] itself and with the broad policies of the FLRA'' (148).

FLRA officials take strong exception to the conclusion that the agency's comparatively low success rate is an indicator of incompetence. They maintain that the FLRA faces unique burdens in adjudication. First, unlike other agencies, including the Merit Systems Protection Board, the Equal Employment Opportunity Commission, and the National Labor Relations Board, the FLRA's decisions are very frequently contested in court by federal agencies. In such instances, judicial deference may be mixed, because a court is faced with two federal agencies espousing conflicting views of the public interest. Moreover, the Labor-Management Relations Statute is administered by affected federal agencies as well as by the FLRA. Thus, the FLRA is not in an especially strong position to command deference. Indeed, the information in table 6 indicates that the FLRA was overturned in 64 percent of the cases brought by agencies, whereas it prevailed in 54 percent of those brought by unions. While there are other possible explanations for this disparity, such as the quality of agency and union legal resources, these factors no doubt account for some of the FLRA's inability to win more judicial deference.

Second, the FLRA is frequently involved in hard cases; that is, cases of first legal impression that are law-bound, rather than dependent upon a specific factual situation. This is especially true in terms of negotiability, though it is an apt description of some ULPs as well. On the other hand, some issues have been repeated and all of them involve some aspect of federal personnel administration.

Third, the FLRA is most frequently reviewed by the Court of Appeals for the District of Columbia Circuit, which has a hard-look policy with regard to the actions of federal agencies. The FLRA has been upheld in 43 percent of the cases in which it was a party before this court and rejected in 40 percent, with mixed holdings and remands constituting the balance. The FLRA has been considerably more successful in some circuits, including the third, fourth, and eleventh, and much less successful in others, such as the sixth and seventh. However, these circuits hear far fewer cases involving it.[6]

Based on these considerations, FLRA officials argue that it is inappropriate to compare their agency to the MSPB. The latter, they maintain, deals primarily with fact-bound issues before the Court of Appeals for the Federal Circuit, which is an easier forum in which to obtain judicial deference. In reaching an overall evaluation of the

FLRA's competence, based on its success on judicial review, the following conclusions are reasonable. The ability of an agency to gain judicial deference is an important aspect of its legal competence. The FLRA has faced some unusual—perhaps even unique—and formidable hurdles in this regard. There is no doubt that these partially account for the frequency with which the FLRA has been overturned in court. However, the content of some judicial opinions indicate that the FLRA has shortcomings that are unrelated to its peculiarly difficult adjudicatory burdens. For instance, as late as 1987, a court found the FLRA's legal decision making to be in "disarray" (Professional Airways Systems Specialists, MEBA, AFL-CIO v. FLRA 1987. 809 F2d 855:860). At the very least, when coupled with the FLRA's inability to gain substantially greater judicial deference over the years, such judicial statements strongly suggest that the FLRA is not simply an agency doing the best possible job with a very difficult mission. Rather, they suggest that it is one with a difficult mission whose performance leaves room for improvement.

Evaluation of the FLRA should also consider whether its decisions tend to enhance or inhibit collective bargaining. An examination of its rulings in cases involving negotiability is facilitated by table 7. It indicates that the agency supported the union position in twenty-two (39 percent) of the fifty-six reported instances in which the circuit courts reviewed its holdings on the scope of bargaining from 1979 to 1987. The FLRA rejected the union position in thirty-four (61 percent) of the holdings subject to judicial review. The union position in these cases invariably favors a wider scope of bargaining than that favored by management. In ten cases, the FLRA opted for a more limited scope of bargaining than did the reviewing court. However, in fourteen others its support for the union's view of negotiability was rejected by the courts. Consequently, it cannot be concluded that the FLRA is substantially more or less inclined than the judiciary to support the negotiability of the issues that have been litigated in the cases analyzed here. Again, outcomes of adjudication by the FLRA are only weakly associated with outcomes upon judicial review. The fact that the courts rejected the FLRA's position in about 43 percent of the decisions indicates substantial disagreement between the agency and the judiciary on questions pertaining to the scope of bargaining.

Finally, in assessing the FLRA's success or failure upon judicial review, an analysis of ULP cases is desirable. Table 8 indicates that the circuit courts have rejected the FLRA's holdings in twenty-six (67 per-

Table 7. The FLRA in Circuit Court, 1979–1987, Scope of Bargaining Cases

	Circuit Court Decisions		
FLRA Decision	Affirming FLRA	Rejecting FLRA	Total
For union (agency appeals)	8	14	22
Against union (union appeals)	24	10	34
Total	32	24	56

NOTE: X^2 = 6.58, 1 degree of freedom.
     Lambda = .25.
       Phi = .34.

cent) of the reported thirty-nine ULP cases they reviewed between 1979 and 1987. The table also indicates that the FLRA's interpretations of ULPs tend to be somewhat harsher on unions than those of the circuit courts but that, overall, there is no statistical relationship between the FLRA's holding and that of the courts in the reported ULP cases that have been subject to judicial review.

Table 8. The FLRA in Circuit Court, 1979–1987, Unfair Labor Practice Cases

	Circuit Court Decisions		
FLRA Decision	Affirming FLRA	Rejecting FLRA	Total
For union (agency appeals)	5	10	15
Against union (union appeals)	8	16	24
Total	13	26	39

NOTE: X^2 = 0
    Lambda = 0
      Phi = 0

Conclusion

Title VII of the Civil Service Reform Act placed federal labor relations regarding most general schedule employees on a statutory basis for the first time. The statute established the FLRA and charged it with broad administrative responsibility for overseeing, defining, and refining the federal collective bargaining process. Throughout the postreform period, roughly 60 percent of the work force covered by Title VII has been organized in bargaining units represented by an exclusive agent. In 1980, there were more than 2,600 bargaining relationships (Devine 1981:393), and although changes have taken place through consolidations and the creation of new units, there have been relatively few decertifications. In a sense, collective bargaining has been alive, well, and even flourishing in the federal service during a decade in which unions have faced serious setbacks in the private sector. Yet it would be difficult to conclude that the FLRA has been wholly success-ful in promoting its mission.

As an adjudicatory body, the FLRA has faced difficult hurdles in gaining judicial deference. It has been overruled by the courts more than it has been upheld. Even in a period of searching judicial review (Bazelon 1976), its failure to achieve greater judicial deference to its administrative expertise is unusual. The FLRA deals with difficult le-gal issues and often faces other federal agencies—factors that could be expected to reduce its success upon judicial review. However, in sev-eral opinions, the courts have harshly criticized the FLRA for its in-consistencies and the illogic of its decisions. Such inconsistencies and unclarities in FLRA legal decisions and interpretations make it diffi-cult for the parties to collective bargaining to know what the ground rules are. The FLRA's limited success in court encourages unions and agencies to seek judicial review of its decisions. In a collective bargain-ing system that already depends on third parties for closure, the in-ability of the FLRA to win greater judicial deference prompts additional third-party intervention through appeals. Overall, the FLRA has not yet molded Title VII into a coherent body of law for the creation and regulation of a vigorous bilateral collective bargain-ing system.

The agency has done better in terms of efficiency and fairness. Its timeliness in adjudication has improved substantially since its earlier years. Although some cases continue to encounter long delay, by and large the agency appears to be reasonably efficient when compared to other civil service agencies with heavy caseloads (Riccucci and Ban 1989; Vaughn 1985). Moreover, whatever inconsistencies prevail in other contexts, there is now a high level of agreement between the re-gional directors and the general counsel in ULP decisions. Additionally, based on a review of the FLRA's adjudication and record in the federal courts, there is no reason to conclude that it is strongly biased against either unions or management. In FY 1986, for instance, it issued com-plaints against agencies in 11 percent and against unions in 13 percent of the ULP charges that were brought before it (FLRA 1986:96). In the circuit court cases reviewed here, the judiciary was somewhat more fa-vorable to unions' positions than was the FLRA, but the difference was not great enough to conclude that the FLRA is not more or less even-handed. Thus, whereas the courts supported union positions in forty-four instances and opposed them in sixty, the FLRA was pro-union in thirty-nine decisions and anti-union in sixty-five.

It remains to be seen whether the system of collective bargaining authorized by Title VII can be successful. The narrow scope of bargaining reduces its relevance to federal personnel administration. Its prohibition on concerted action forces unions to rely on political action, arbitration, appeals, and litigation in their quest for influence over working conditions. However, it is the clear conclusion of this analysis that, even within the framework of Title VII, labor relations in the federal service would benefit substantially if the FLRA could command greater deference from the federal judiciary.

NOTES

Robert Kravchuk and Miguel Sapp provided valuable research assistance, for which I am most grateful. I am also indebted to Andrew A. Feinstein, former chief counsel, Committee on Civil Service, U.S. House of Representatives, for his insights and assistance with this analysis.

1. 92 Stat. 1191 (13 October, 1978).

2. Exemptions include the Postal Service, General Accounting Office, Federal Bureau of Investigation, Central Intelligence Agency, National Security Agency, Tennessee Valley Authority, FLRA, and Federal Service Impasses Panel. It covers the Library of Congress and the Government Printing Office, which are in the legislative branch.

3. For discussions of public sector collective bargaining, see Shafritz, Hyde, and Rosenbloom (1986:chaps. 9–10); and Kearney (1984).

4. The extent to which informational picketing is constitutionally protected is unclear. See Edwards, Clark, and Craver (1979:520–21).

5. The cases were generated from *West's Federal Practice Digest*, 3d ed., vols. 114–17; and *Cumulative Annual Pocket* (1987). The latest case included is *American Federation of Government Employees, Local 1923* v. *FLRA*, 819 F2d 306 (19 May, 1987).

6. The FLRA was also reversed by the Supreme Court in *FLRA* v. *Aberdeen Proving Ground* (1988) and *Bureau of Alcohol, Tobacco and Firearms* v. *FLRA* (1983. 464 U.S. 89). *Equal Employment Opportunity Commission* v. *FLRA* (1986. 476 U.S. 19) resulted in a dismissal that was favorable to the FLRA. The cases analyzed are limited to those in which decisions (including remands) were reached and reported. The FLRA's total caseload from its inception to 27 September, 1988 included 484 cases, of which about 30 percent were eventually withdrawn. A few cases were settled or transferred prior to decisions or review. Unpublished decisions could not be analyzed in this study.

SOURCES

Bazelon, David. 1976. The Impact of the Courts on Public Administration. *Indiana Law Journal* 52:101–10.

Broida, Peter. 1987. *A Guide to Federal Labor Relations Authority Law and Practice.* Washington, D.C.: Dewey Publications.

Bussey, Ellen, ed. 1984. *Federal Civil Service Law and Procedures.* Washington, D.C.: Bureau of National Affairs.

Devine, Donald. 1981. The Challenge to Federal Employees Today. *Labor Law Journal* 32:387–94.

Edwards, Harry, R. T. Clark, and Charles Craver. 1979. *Labor Relations Law in the Public Sector,* 2d ed. Indianapolis: Bobbs-Merrill.

FLRA (Federal Labor Relations Authority). 1986. *Eighth Annual Report.* Washington, D.C.

Kearney, Richard C. 1984. *Labor Relations in the Public Sector.* New York: Marcel Dekker.

Riccucci, Norma, and Carolyn Ban. 1989. "The Unfair Labor Practice Process as a Dispute Resolution Technique in the Public Sector: The Case of New York State." *Review of Public Personnel Administration* 9:51–67.

Schuessler-Laux, Renate-Miranda Martha. 1985. "The Impact of the Federal Labor Relations Authority on Labor Arbitration in the Federal Sector." Ph.D. diss., Texas A & M University.

Shafritz, Jay, Albert Hyde, and David H. Rosenbloom. 1986. *Personnel Management in Government,* 3d ed. New York: Marcel Dekker.

Vaughn, Robert. 1975. *The Spoiled System: A Call for Civil Service Reform.* New York: Charterhouse for the Center for Study of Responsive Law.

———. 1989. "The Merit Systems Protection Board." *Policy Studies Journal.*

West's Federal Practice Digest, 3d ed. St. Paul: West Publishing.

Part III THE CIVIL SERVICE
REFORM ACT
Process and Procedure

Introduction

Patricia W. Ingraham

Along with the fanfare of creating new institutions and the lofty promise of greater presidential power and control is a more fundamental reality of civil service reform: the processes and procedures that govern and constrain daily bureaucratic activities, that shape bureaucratic capabilities, and that motivate and reward members of the career civil service. These rules and procedures are the nitty-gritty of reform. They are the part of the reform that caused Jimmy Carter's eyes to glaze over when he was briefed on them. They are also, however, a foundation of effective organizational change.

The Civil Service Reform Act of 1978 contained provisions intended to change many important rules and procedures. The provisions for delegation of examining could have allowed agencies better control over testing procedures for persons seeking employment in the federal government. The new whistleblower provisions in the act were intended to offer greater protection for employees who flagged wasteful or illegal activity inside the organization. Some of the most important procedural provisions of the act were those related to performance appraisal and pay for performance. The move from the stable, predictable, and insular pay practices of the civil service to a system based on performance was a dramatic effort. The creation of the Senior Executive Service, a reform that had been consistently recommended since the second Hoover commission, was also a bold step away from the practices of the past. The elimination of many civil service protections for those who signed the SES contract, the link between performance evaluation and substantial financial bonuses, mobility provisions, and career development opportunities, were intended to create a significantly different senior management cadre. The formal provisions for

159

research and development and for the support of management innovation in the federal service offered the potential for better informed future reforms. Despite their promise and their boldness, however, all of these reforms were implemented in the context of the existing merit system—a system more noted for its 6,000 pages of rules and regulations than for its emphasis on change.

The federal merit system was created by the Pendleton Act in 1883. The purpose of the merit system was to limit political patronage and eliminate political abuse of federal job opportunities. It did so by limiting entrance to the federal service to those who were able to pass competitive examinations for the available positions. (From the beginning, however, there were exceptions to this rule. Veterans are a prominent example.) Initially, the new system covered only 10 percent of the federal work force. The growth of merit was delegated to the president, who was given the authority to extend the system by executive order. Because each president who extended merit denied more patronage jobs to his party, the system grew by fits and starts. But it did grow, however disjointedly. By the late 1930s, about 60 percent of the federal work force was covered by civil service law.[1] In 1940, the haphazard development was corrected somewhat by the Ramspeck Act, which eliminated many exemptions and attempted to bring some order to the underlying philosophy of merit.

The passage of the Classification Act in 1923, which classified federal jobs according to duties and responsibilities and assigned standard compensation levels to those positions across government, added another important component to the merit system. These strongly centralized programs and policies created a system in which many traditional management perogatives—even those as basic as hiring and firing—were removed from federal managers, or were controlled to a significant degree by central personnel authorities. Standardization and central authority, rather than individual flexibility and discretion, were the watchwords of the merit and compensation systems. At the time of the 1978 reform, personnel actions and activities were governed by thousands of pages of rules and regulations, the accretion of nearly one hundred years. These rules and regulations are important to the Civil Service Reform Act because, while they created many of the problems the reform addressed, they also created the environment in which the reform would be implemented. The new delegation authorities created by CSRA, for example, did not simplify or eliminate existing rules and procedures. They merely delegated them from the central authority to the agency level. As one federal manager noted after working with the reform for ten years, "Delegating bad procedures to us does not solve problems!"[2]

The CSRA's process reforms are best understood from the perspective of this procedural maze. Pay for performance, widely believed to be very effective in the private sector, was essentially layered onto existing classification, compensation, and personnel systems. Although rigorous analysis of the transferability of this technique did not occur—Alan Campbell noted a decade after the reform that he had seen no need for experimentation or evaluation because "it was my perception that it worked fine in the private sector"[3]—later analysis demonstrated the lack of fit. The National Academy of Science noted in 1991:

Most of the conditions [for success of pay for performance in the private sector] pose a problem for public sector organizations because of a division of leadership between the political and the career employees; the lack of managerial control over personnel and resource systems; the ambiguity of goals and performance criteria; and multiple authority centers for employee accountability.[4]

The Senior Executive Service, particularly its provisions for performance evaluation and financial bonuses, also suffered from the procedural constraints of the existing system. Because many career SES managers had been at the top of their statutory pay levels for many years, the SES bonus system offered their only real opportunity for increased income. The procedural difficulties of implementing the new performance evaluation system were exacerbated by the fact that many of these evaluations of career managers were conducted by political executives, their organizational superiors. Problems were compounded by congressional and OPM decisions to reduce the total numbers of SES members who were eligible for a bonus annually. In such an environment, it was difficult to develop trust in the new system.

Despite these problems, SES managers were pivotal to the success of the pay-for-performance provisions for the midlevel managers included in merit pay. Because the merit pay program was initially created to be revenue neutral, senior managers had very limited amounts of money with which to reward excellent performers. They would have to have great confidence in performance appraisal techniques and procedures to make the hard decisions required. Absent that confidence, willingness to make decisions based on performance appraisal was unlikely. Since all other aspects of the managers' relationships with their staffs continued to be governed by traditional civil service constraints and protections (such as the well-developed federal appeals procedures), senior management's commitment to the new system was understandably modest.

It is worth noting that the major innovations sponsored by the research and demonstration provisions of the Civil Service Reform Act attempted to remove or bypass many traditional civil service regulations and constraints. Managerial flexibility and discretion was emphasized in all of the demonstrations. New approaches to compensation, which emphasize individual competence and performance, rather than standardization, are common. Pay banding, for example, is frequently a part of the new demonstrations.

Finally, it is important to the history of CSRA that it was overtaken not only by politics and the election of Ronald Reagan in 1980, but by new procedural problems. The abolition of the Professional and Administrative Career Examination left the federal government without a major entry-level hiring mechanism. Hiring efforts for much of the 1980s were chaotic and controversial and contributed to what the Volcker Commission and others called the quiet crisis in the federal government.

Pay was another element of that crisis. At the time CSRA was designed, there were pay problems in the federal government, but comparability with private sector pay was generally adequate.[5] Throughout the eighties, that comparability eroded dramatically. The ability of the federal government to recruit employees in critical occupations and to retain excellent employees was severely damaged. A new centralized entrance examination was put in place in 1990; pay reform legislation was passed in 1991. The long-term impact of both is unclear at this time.

NOTES

1. This was down from about 80 percent prior to Franklin Roosevelt's first term. Roosevelt had many of the New Deal agencies placed outside the civil service system so that he could fill the new positions with persons who were policy experts (and who agreed with his policies) rather than the "neutral competents" the civil service examinations admitted. See Patricia W. Ingraham and David H. Rosenbloom, "The State of Merit in the Federal Government," in *An Agenda for Excellence: The American Public Service*, ed. Patricia W. Ingraham and Donald F. Kettl (Chatham, N.J.: Chatham House, 1992).

2. Ibid., p. 37.

3. Alan Campbell, before the U.S. Subcommittee on Government Operations. See U.S. Senate, *Report of the Joint U.S. Government Accounting Office-Senate Subcommittee on Government Operations Hearing on the Design of the Civil Service Reform Act of 1978* (Washington, D.C., 1988), p. 8.

4. George T. Milkovich and Alexandra Wigdor, *Pay for Performance: Evaluating Performance Appraisal and Merit Pay* (Washington, D.C.: National Academy Press, 1991) p. 161.

5. The primary problem at the time of the reform was the topping out problem, encountered when senior career managers advanced to the statutory limit of their pay level fairly early in their careers and were essentially trapped there. The formal link between pay for members of Congress and pay for senior executives in the federal service severely limited the ability to change the pay scale.

8. To the Threshold of Reform

The Senior Executive Service and America's Search
for a Higher Civil Service

Mark W. Huddleston

The senior executive service (SES) has generated considerable controversy since its inception—though perhaps less than it ought to have
generated given the critical importance of higher administration in
modern government. Commentators have argued about its structure,
its efficacy, the extent to which it has been politicized, and a host of
other issues.[1] One point on which almost everyone agrees, however, is
that the SES today bears little resemblance to what anyone had in
mind for it when it was designed. "It didn't do what I'd hoped it
would do, and what it has done I don't much like" summarizes a
good deal of what has been written and said about the SES. Indeed,
the only people who seemed happy with the SES in 1988 are the ones
who, in 1978, never wanted, or expected, it to do very much.

A major reason for this extensive disappointment is that there was
little consensus in the first place about what the SES was supposed to
accomplish. The framers of the SES brought to the table fundamentally
conflicting ideas about what an American higher civil service ought to
look like—ideas that had, at turns, shaped a series of unsuccessful reform efforts for the preceding thirty years. For some, the SES was to be
the reincarnation of the aborted Senior Civil Service, an elite,
European-style corps of generalist civilian executives. For others, it
was a second chance at a Federal Executive Service, a system that
would help elected officials and their appointees get a firmer political
grip on the vast federal bureaucracy. Still others saw the SES primarily
as a vehicle for bringing the supposed rigor of private sector management techniques to the federal government or as a backdoor way to
increase the pay and perquisites of civil servants.

Rather than try to meet these contradictions head on—and risk
alienating potential supporters—the designers of the SES chose, in

effect, to overlook them. The SES was built and sold like an administrative version of the old F-111, Robert McNamara's something-for-everyone fighter bomber. And like the F-111, the SES has spent more time in maintenance hangers than in the air. It would be facile to suggest that the SES would have been more successful had greater care been taken at the outset to give it intellectual coherence; the landscape of American politics is littered with the carcasses of coherent would-be programs that failed to attract sufficient support. But because strong structures are anchored in clear ideas, it would at the same time be naive to assume that the SES will ever become anything other than an irrelevant designation in personnel files until greater coherence is imparted.

The first step out of this dilemma is full appreciation of the contending visions upon which the SES rests and recognition of the powerful traditions against which it contends. Toward that end, this chapter examines earlier efforts to reshape (or establish, depending on one's perspective) the higher reaches of the American civil service. From a close reading of these efforts, I distill four contending images of the American higher civil service that provided the intellectual raw material from which the SES was constructed. At one level, the chapter may be read simply as an administrative history, a straightforward, chronologically arranged narrative of how we got to the threshold of the SES. At a second, more analytical level, it is intended as a partial field guide to further reform, an admittedly sketchy map of a wilderness area well marked with trails to be avoided. This may be of more than small use, for although history never repeats itself exactly, it has, in this area at least, shown extraordinary—and often distressing—continuity.

Before SES: An Administrative History

The First Hoover Commission and the "Supergrades"

Before the end of the Second World War, there was no American higher civil service, at least not in the sense that our political language contained a discrete construct for such a institution. There was, to be sure, a whole range of civil servants, some of whom held jobs that were higher than others. But scarcely anyone thought or talked as if the men and women who held top positions in the career service constituted a category unto themselves. The rounds of reform that began in the 1870s, culminating in the Pendleton Act, the Classification Act of 1923, and the Ramspeck Act of 1940, were aimed at the civil service as a whole and were intended to advance the idea (or *an* idea) of merit rather than spoils or patronage.

This is not to say that these pieces of legislation, and related executive orders and Civil Service Commission rules, were without consequence for higher administration. The early decision to eschew a British-style, closed career system in favor of open recruitment to jobs at all levels, institutionalized in the Pendleton Act, had profound consequences, all but ruling out, for instance, the development of a self-conscious administrative elite in the federal government. The point is that for a long while higher administration, per se, was not viewed as a problem. Indeed, it was not viewed as anything at all.

The first tentative steps toward recognizing the distinct problems of the higher civil service came just after the end of the Second World War.[2] In 1947, Congress passed Public Law 80-313, which authorized the secretary of war to establish thirty new scientific and technical positions (now commonly known as PL-313 positions) in the War Department that would be compensated at a rate up to 50 percent higher ($15,000 as opposed to $10,000 per annum) than allowed by the existing pay structure for career executives. This action was taken because of the difficulty the defense establishment encountered in recruiting and retaining qualified professionals and can be construed, as a Civil Service Commission report put it, "as recognition of the need to establish a level of career positions above the already existing structure" (U.S. CSC 1971a:5).

Second, and of far greater consequence in terms of framing the nascent debate about the shape of the U.S. higher civil service, were two reports issued in 1949 under the auspices of the first Hoover Commission, which had been established by Congress in 1947 to undertake a thorough review of the structure and managerial practices of the entire executive branch. One report was that of the full commission; the second was the task force report of the commission's Personnel Policy Committee (Commission on Organization of the Executive Branch of the Government 1949: app. A; Personnel Policy Committee 1949). Taken together, these two reports drew attention to a multitude of flaws in the federal government's personnel system that had particularly vexing consequences for upper-level administrators, including uncompetitively low salary ceilings; an absence of planned and predictable promotion opportunities; too few top management positions regularly open to career officials; a negative attitude toward training and development; and a lack of provision for recognition of outstanding performance by top executives (ibid.).

To remedy these defects, the reports urged sharply increased salaries for senior administrators, a greater emphasis by agencies on recruitment, training, and career planning for federal executives, and establishment of a career business manager position in each major agency. This last proposal was especially interesting in light of later developments. As the task force report envisaged the position, the career manager would be the chief operating officer of his or her agency, subject "only to the discretion of the political head of the agency." Moreover,

incumbents of these top career positions should constitute a "common pool" of the most able executives in Government, from which the President, if he chooses, can draw candidates for appointment as agency heads; and from which the heads of departments and agencies can choose key policy and management assistants. If an incumbent is replaced by an incoming agency head, he should be returned to a position of like pay and status to that which he originally vacated—if necessary, retained on the pay roll in the "pool" until he is properly placed again. (ibid.:39)

Although few of these recommendations were implemented, at least to the extent their proponents hoped, they constituted a distinctive, significant, and reasonably coherent vision of what American higher administration might look like.[3]

The third of the postwar steps was the passage of the Classification Act of 1949, which was the legislative vehicle for certain key Hoover Commission recommendations. This law added three new executive pay grades—GS-16, 17, and 18—to the top of a consolidated general schedule structure.[4] These new positions, quickly dubbed the supergrades, were intended to enhance the federal government's ability to attract and keep key senior personnel by raising the effective ceiling on executive compensation.[5]

Finally, in March 1953 President Eisenhower signed an executive order creating Schedule C positions—those of a "policy determining" or "policy recommending" nature, or those involving a close personal relationship between a top political appointee and a staff assistant, such as a speech writer or chauffeur (U.S. CSC 1971a:6). Initially, this new classification had little practical effect, as most positions put into Schedule C were simply transferred from Schedule A, the earlier designation for exempt, policy-making positions.[6] Schedule Cs grew quickly in number, however, both through creation of new positions and through redesignations from the competitive service.

These four activities—the establishment of the PL-313s, the Hoover Commission recommendations, the creation of the supergrades, and the designation of Schedule Cs—clearly did not spring from a common set of assumptions about what an American higher civil service ought to look like. Where the Hoover Commission was edging toward the creation of a strong and reasonably coherent career executive corps, the PL-313s and supergrades were simply an extension to a higher level of the traditional agency-based, specialist-oriented, rank-in-job civil service. The establishment of Schedule C fit with the same general tradition, in that it anticipated a particular kind of career-political system—that is, one in which careerists were kept clearly subordinate and had relatively little access to top jobs.

The Second Hoover Commission and the Senior Civil Service

These images of the American higher civil service that began to appear in the immediate postwar years were like faint pencil sketches, soft and tentative, compared to the vivid canvas presented by the Second Hoover Commission in 1955. This commission, operating like its predecessor through a series of specialized task forces, offered a fundamental critique of the senior executive personnel system and recommended the creation of an entirely new Senior Civil Service (SCS). Because the Hoover proposals—and later incarnations framed by the Civil Service Commission—constituted an especially coherent, fully articulated vision of a higher civil service, and because they met with an equally coherent and equally fully articulated set of opposing views, they and their fate are worth examining in some detail.

The fundamental problem with the civil service, the Second Hoover Commission maintained, was that it emphasized positions, not people: "Jobs are classified, ranked, rated, and paid on the bland assumption that they can always be filled like so many jugs, merely by turning on the tap" (Commission on Organization of the Executive Branch of the Government 1955:49). Although the quality of individual civil servants was judged to be high, the effectiveness of the federal establishment was undermined by a combination of low pay, inequitable and outdated procedures, and a failure to provide for attractive careers for senior executives:

Originating as a reaction against the spoils system, and adapted to the large-scale employment problem of 20th century government, the present civil service has not been well designed to provide professional administrators at the higher levels. The extension to higher posts of concepts and procedures which were designed for large numbers of standardized positions at lower levels has been awkward for both political executives and career administrators, because they disregard so completely both the personalities and the careers of individual men. (ibid.:50)

To address these problems, the commission called for scrapping the extant melange of position and appointment authorities. In its place would be a single Senior Civil Service, composed of some 1,500 to 3,000 highly qualified, politically neutral career administrators who could be shifted from job to job as government needs required. Rank was to inhere in the person, rather than the position, creating enhanced opportunities for mobility and career development. Along with these provisions for the career service, the commission recommended more systematic procedures for the recruitment and use of subcabinet political executives. Proposals for the senior civil service included the following:[7]

• *Personal rank*   Members of the service would have rank, salary, and status vested in them as individuals.

• *Mobility*   Senior civil servants could and would move from one job or assignment to another job or assignment, within or between agencies, without losing pay or status.

• *Responsiveness*   Members of the SCS would be expected to serve each new administration as needed and to fill appropriate positions in Washington, the field, or abroad as needed.

• *Compensation*   Senior civil servants would receive higher pay and would be entitled to salary increments if assigned to positions normally compensated at higher levels.

• *Generalist orientation*   The men and women commissioned as senior civil servants would embody general executive qualities such as "leadership, judgment, adaptability, skill in working with people, and capacity for continued growth, and would be "more than narrow specialists" (Commission on Organization of the Executive Branch of the Government 1955:55, 52).

• *Governance*   Authority and responsibility for setting up and operating the senior civil service would be vested in a full-time bipartisan Senior Civil Service Board within the Civil Service Commission. This board would approve nominations to the service, regularly appraise each member, approve promotions and demotions, and encourage career development.

The Civil Service Commission, which was charged by the Eisenhower administration to study the SCS proposal, reacted to the Hoover recommendations positively but guardedly. Although the commission staff saw considerable merit in the idea of a single career executive corps, they anticipated (quite accurately, as it happened) strong opposition from line departments.[8] In a round of interagency meetings that took place in the early spring of 1955, agency representatives expressed concern that the SCS would thoroughly recentralize the executive personnel function. As a personnel officer from the Federal Trade Commission put it, "If government were one employer, the Senior Civil Service might be workable; the government is not one employer, however" (Chung 1985:144).

Given this skepticism in the agencies (and given the fact that the only two dissenters to the SCS proposal on the Hoover commission were members of Congress), the Civil Service Commission decided that it would be best not to seek broad statutory changes in the structure of the civil service. Instead, they recommended fine-tuning the existing machinery and creating a pilot program to be instituted on a voluntary basis in selected agencies (ibid.:152–83).

Even this conservative strategy came to naught, however, as there proved to be little support among agencies for any program that bore the imprint of the SCS, no matter how limited in scope. At the end of 1956, after nearly a year of negotiations between Civil Service Commission staff and line agencies, a summit meeting in Bethesda, Maryland, attended by top personnel officials of major federal agencies, officially buried the SCS pilot program and suggested the development instead, under the general guidance of the Civil Service Commission, of a career executive program (CEP) (ibid.:193–201). Although the CEP theoretically embodied the goals of the senior civil service, it was in fact stripped of its most important mechanisms, including rank classification, and was to be administered not directly by the Civil Service Commission, but by the quasi-independent Career Executive Board.

Despite continued opposition within some quarters of the executive branch even to the pared-down CEP, the White House decided to grab at what appeared to be a minimal consensus. On 4 March 1958, President Eisenhower issued Executive Order 10758, formally establishing the CEP. At its core was a Career Executive Service (CES) consisting of all federal employees in pay grades GS-16 and above (ibid.:203–30).

Although membership in the CES implied little more than having one's name inscribed on a roster of executive talent that would be made available to agencies, reaction to the executive order by Congress and employee unions was swift and strong. The CES was described as elitist, undemocratic, and even fascistic, smacking "of favoritism and special privilege." It would, critics charged, entrench and further strengthen the bureaucracy, diminish the authority of agency managers, threaten the career chances of specialists, foster the rebirth of political patronage, and generally make life unpleasant for senior executives. Moreover, by issuing an executive order rather than seeking new legislation, President Eisenhower was seen as attempting to circumvent legitimate congressional interests (U.S. Congress 1958:119).

Following several days of hearings, the Subcommittee on Manpower Utilization of the House Post Office and Civil Service Committee passed a resolution in late July 1958 asking President Eisenhower to suspend the career executive program. The White House ignored the resolution and, in fact, shortly thereafter issued another executive order increasing the size of the Career Executive Board. This prompted the chairman of the subcommittee, Congressman James Davis (Democrat of Georgia), to ask the House to attach a rider to an appropriation bill specifying that no money go to support the Career Executive Board. Two such riders were approved the following April.[9] Faced with the cessation of funding for the program, the president admitted defeat, and in Executive Order 10859, dated 5 February 1960, formally terminated the activities of the Career Executive Program.

Kennedy-Johnson Initiatives

Congressional, agency, and union hostility to the SCS-CEP initiatives of the Eisenhower administration did not remove the need to address the problems of the higher civil service. The grand failures of the 1950s did, however, chasten advocates of reform. For the next decade, their proposals were generally modest, their strategies cautious. At least within the government, ambitious schemes to erect vaulting new edifices gave way to limited plans to rehabilitate existing structures.

The Kennedy round of civil service reform began with a report on the federal regulatory agencies prepared for the president-elect by James Landis, who sharply criticized the deterioration in quality of appointees to high administrative office. Too often, Landis argued, careful scrutiny of qualifications was forgone in favor of a consideration of political obligations; rather than advance competent career officials to choice positions, "outsiders not infrequently less qualified were appointed" (U.S. Congress 1960:11).

Kennedy's response was to name John Macy, a former career executive and former executive director of the Civil Service Commission, to the dual role of chair of the Civil Service Commission and personnel advisor to the president.[10] Thus charged with the responsibility of finding the most qualified career and noncareer executives to fill high federal posts, Macy introduced the idea of the Executive Roster. This was a compilation of pertinent information on over 1,000 career executives at GS levels 16, 17, and 18 that could, in theory, be used by agency heads both to fill key positions and to help develop career ladders for senior executives. In fact, though, the Executive Roster was little used either by agency heads or careerists, who found it both cumbersome and soon out of date. During the three years of its existence, only twenty-nine federal agencies used the Roster to fill 134 supergrade positions (U.S. CSC 1964).

Understandably dissatisfied with the impact of the Executive Roster, Chairman Macy assembled a Civil Service Commission task force during the first months of the Johnson administration and charged it with rethinking senior executive personnel management in the federal government. Why, he wanted to know, were the best people not being brought to the top of the government—and what could be done about it? (Boyer and Meckelprang 1973: chap. 2, p. 12). Like Louis, the French police commissioner in the movie *Casablanca*, the task force quickly rounded up the usual suspects—inflexibility, restricted mobility, narrow agency perspectives, underutilization of talent in the career ranks, and so on. The task force discussed a wide range of options, including establishing a new appointment authority that would allow agency managers to appoint career executives to policy-making posts for limited, five-year terms, a proposal that would reemerge, in slightly altered form, at the core of the Nixon administration's Federal Executive Service, as we shall see below. The task force's more imaginative proposals were soon brought to heel, however, by a basic Civil Service Commission decision:

In order to avoid the pitfalls and problems the executive branch had encountered since 1957 whenever it attempted to inaugurate a program that encompassed basic changes in the merit system or process, the Commission would not suggest any basic legal changes. Further, it would not propose doing by

Executive order anything that would raise the issues that in the past had been detrimental to getting such a program implemented. (U.S. CSC 1971:24)

Ironically, at the same time the Civil Service Commission was reining in its task force, an independent group of businessmen and educators was circulating an unusually bold proposal. In a report released in July 1964, the Committee for Economic Development urged that responsibility for senior-level personnel management—career and noncareer—be shifted from the Civil Service Commission to a new Office of Executive Personnel located in the Executive Office of the President. This office would not only maintain an inventory of current and prospective executive talent, but would be centrally responsible for all policies related to senior management, including recruitment, selection, and performance evaluation. The CED report also urged the creation of two new "super-supergrades"—GS-19 and 20—eligibility for which would be "severely limited to career employees with superlative achievement records. These grades would provide both suitable salary recognition and 'rank-in-the-man' status comparable to that of military officers, so that any trouble-shooting or other federal assignment may be taken without loss of pay or status regardless of the job's technical classification." (Committee for Economic Development 1964:47). As one would expect from such a group, the report had a strong corporate flavor, with the job of the president repeatedly likened to that of a corporate CEO who must oversee his management team. Although the CED recommendations had little impact at the time, some of the substance and a great deal of the spirit of the report would soon be reflected first in the proposed federal executive service and later in the senior executive service.

The Civil Service Commission ultimately adopted a more limited plan of its own that called for the creation of an Executive Assignment System (EAS), the heart of which would be an executive inventory comprised of the names and qualifications of over 35,000 federal executives in GS-15 through GS-18 positions. Unlike the Kennedy executive roster, however, the executive inventory and the overall EAS were to serve as more than a passive executive placement agency. Not only would the inventory be computerized and regularly updated, but the EAS would be supervised by a newly created Bureau of Executive Manpower in the Civil Service Commission, which would actively encourage interagency mobility and promote the use of qualified career executives in political positions. On 17 November 1966, more than two years after the commission released its draft report on the EAS, President Johnson established the system by executive order.

According to EAS procedures, whenever a new supergrade position was allocated or an existing supergrade position became vacant, the agency concerned was required to search executive inventory files to identify executives with appropriate qualifications. The three and a half years that this requirement was in effect, from November 1967 to March 1971, produced an impressive number of searches: over 1,300 separate lists of potential candidates for supergrade positions, involving more than 7,000 individual names, were pulled from the inventory and forwarded to agencies. (Boyer and Mackelprang 1973: chap. 2, p. 19).

The problem was that the agencies, not obligated to choose a candidate from the inventory, paid little attention. The inventory search was viewed as just one new piece of commission red tape that had to be tolerated. Indeed, with only approximately 15 percent of all supergrade vacancies during these years filled through EAS procedures, little of the interagency mobility or career development sought by the Bureau of Executive Manpower materialized. When the Civil Service Commission announced on 5 March 1971 that inventory searches would no longer be mandatory, little of value was lost.

The Federal Executive Service

The demise of the executive assignment system did not mark the end of efforts to reshape the higher civil service. In fact, even while the executive inventory was churning out unread lists of candidates, the Civil Service Commission staff was preparing a new initiative, this time at the behest of the Nixon administration.

Soon after he entered the White House, President Nixon asked the commission to undertake an exhaustive survey of the federal government's executive manpower programs. The bulk of the analysis was conducted by the Bureau of Executive Manpower, which, with an eye toward the political difficulties encountered by the earlier senior civil service proposal, assembled an advisory task force of agency personnel directors. After more than a year of study, the commission issued a report that recited the usual litany of problems: Federal executives are governed by an unnecessarily confusing and complex array of personnel systems; no governmentwide system of leadership and responsibility for the management of executive resources exists, with a consequent lack of manpower planning; arbitrary distinctions between career and noncareer executives both limit opportunities for careerists and prevent managers from deploying resources where they are most needed; and political friction between career and noncareer executives inhibits program effectiveness and encourages bureaucratic nonresponsiveness. None of these problems, the commission decided this time, could be remedied within existing law. Instead, legislative action to establish an entirely new personnel system for upper-level officials of the executive branch was deemed necessary. The president accepted the commission's recommendations and, in a special message to Congress on 2 February 1971, outlined his proposal for the creation of the Federal Executive Service (FES).

The FES proposal called for the establishment of a single, integrated personnel system for the approximately 7,000 civilian executives in grades GS-16, 17, and 18. Like the Senior Civil Service proposal of the Second Hoover Commission, the FES broke away from a rigid system of job classification, attaching rank to the person rather than to the position. Similarly, agency heads would have the flexibility to assign and reassign executives as needed. Unlike the SCS, however, the FES was to include a significant number of noncareer executives—up to 25 percent of the service. Moreover, the tenure of FES members would be limited: employment of career executives would be based on renewable three-year contracts, and an FES member whose contract was not renewed by his or her agency would be severed from the service and placed in a GS-15 position.

Initial congressional reactions to the Nixon proposal were favorable, at least compared to the Eisenhower administration's experience on the Hill with the SCS-CES, although employee organizations, incensed by the three-year contract provisions of the FES and disturbed by what they saw as an effort to politicize the civil service, lobbied heavily against the plan. As it happened, however, the FES initiative became overwhelmed by other events. Distracted by Nixon's economic shocks of that year (the wage-price freeze and the abrupt float of the dollar, in particular) the Senate held only one day of hearings on the FES in 1971; the House held none. Although the House did schedule three days of testimony in the spring of 1972, over a year after the FES had been introduced, any momentum that FES proponents might have had was lost. When General Accounting Office officials weighed in at the House hearings with testimony sharply critical of the three-year contract provisions, administration officials began to make plans to reintroduce the legislation following the expected Nixon reelection land-slide in November. Features of the proposed Federal Executive Service included the following (U.S. CSC 1971b):

• *Coverage* The FES was to include approximately 7,000 civilian executives in grades GS-16, 17, and 18 and their equivalents, including both career and noncareer officials.

• *Career and noncareer categories* Noncareer FES members were to be appointed to and removed from the service solely at the discretion of the agency head. Career appointments were to require prior approval of a qualification board.

• *Career-noncareer ratios* No more than 25 percent of the FES governmentwide was to consist of noncareer appointees. Career-noncareer mixes would vary for particular agencies, with authorizations set by the Civil Service Commission and OMB.

• *Compensation levels* Compensation for individual FES members was to be set by agency heads within the range corresponding to GS-16 to GS-18 pay levels, although average FES pay within an agency could not exceed a governmentwide average established by the Civil Service Commission. Salaries could be raised but not lowered for FES members.

• *Assignments* Agency heads would have authority to assign FES members to any job within the scope of the service. Rank would inhere in the person, not in the job. Moreover, no distinction would be made between career and political positions.

• *Employment agreements* Employment of career FES members would be governed by renewable three-year contracts. A career executive not offered contract renewal would have the right to retreat to a GS-15 position, with no reduction in salary for two years.

These administration plans were never realized, however. By the time the Civil Service Commission staff had prepared a revised FES initiative (stripped of the three-year contract provisions) in the fall of 1973, clouds were beginning to gather around the Nixon presidency. After waiting for a more favorable political climate—which never came, at least not during the Nixon era—the commission put the Federal Executive Service proposal quietly on the shelf.

Although the FES resembled earlier reform proposals in certain important respects, it differed significantly in tone. Almost wholly displacing the rhetoric extolling the virtues of a strong and independent career service were attacks—some explicit, some subtly framed—on unresponsive and ineffective bureaucrats. An internal White House memorandum from James McLane, a Domestic Council staffer, to Special Assistant for Personnel Frederick Malek, written on the eve of the release of the president's FES proposal, exemplifies this shift.

The memo begins by arguing that one of the chief causes of "the gap between promise and performance" in American government (a phrase taken from the president's 1971 State of the Union address) is "the inability of a President to exercise control over the Federal government to ensure responsiveness to Administration direction. . . . Inertia or resistance by the bureaucracy has often surmounted brilliant efforts of design." Consequently, McLane insists, the civil service itself needs to be modified, particularly at the higher levels, where one finds the people who have "traditionally developed strong specialized interests in a particular program with its inherent strong ties to particular interest groups and Congressional committees." A main reason that career executives are poorly motivated and have eluded control by the president and his political appointees is the "system's breeding of *certainties*"—for example, beliefs in the transience of political appointees, beliefs in assured advancement over time, and so on—into career employees. The FES would reduce this certainty and ensure that "the executives in the Federal Government are responsive to public policy as enunciated by the President and the Congress and responsive to the top political management, at all times."[11]

Images of a Higher Civil Service

Apart from their purely historical interest, the various reform proposals that antedate the SES are important for what they reveal about how several generations of American policy makers have conceived of the higher federal service. They embody the jumbled set of archetypes, images, or Platonic forms of upper administration on which the framers of the SES were able to draw. An understanding of these archetypes and their assumptions and implications goes a long way toward explaining how the SES was born and why it never matured.

If we construe them as ideal types—that is, as purely analytical constructs that have no one-to-one correspondence with any one reform proposal or any one group's view—it is fair to say that four dominant images of the higher civil service emerged in the postwar period.

Image 1: Higher Civil Service as Congeries of Agency Specialists

The first, and ultimately the most potent, image was what I term the *traditional agency perspective*. This view assumes that the higher civil service is and ought to be simply the name we give to those people who happen to occupy the top job slots in various federal agencies. They have nothing in common other than a pay grade. These upper-level employees are assumed to be professionals and specialists—engineers, scientists, lawyers, physicians, economists—who may (or may not) exercise general managerial authority. Beyond their profession, their primary loyalty is to their bureau or agency. In theory, careers unfold within bureaus or agencies, although in some cases lateral movement within the profession—between the agency and a university, research institute, or industry—is considered appropriate; interdepartmental mobility is not viewed as desirable, as specialized skills are not readily transferable among agencies.

Management, according to this view, is considered both an undefinable, unteachable art and a necessary evil. Good managers—a term to be used advisedly—are always competent specialists first, steeped in the traditions and rituals of the agency and profession; managers seek to retain their identity as professionals and are among the harshest critics of bureaucracy, paper pushing, and red tape. If one has the misfortune to be considered good at management, sooner or later one will be forced away from the laboratory bench or equivalent specialist venue and dragooned into a position of supervisory responsibility.

The more decentralized the personnel system, the better, according to the traditional agency perspective. First the Civil Service Commission, and later the Office of Personnel Management, have been bottlenecks. Far from performing any useful services for agencies, these central staff agencies have simply made it more difficult to get on with the real work of government, especially by making it difficult, through onerous procedures, to recruit and bring on board candidates for top jobs—candidates known and judged by people already in the agency.

The chief problem with the American higher civil service, aside from CSC and OPM interference, is pay. Pay levels are too low to attract and retain the best people. Reform proposals from this perspective, then, are centered on making salary and benefits more competitive with those available to comparable professionals outside the federal government.

Image 2: Higher Civil Service as a European-Style Elite Corps

The second image of the American higher civil service that emerged during this period was sharply at odds with the first. It was what we may call the *elite corps* perspective. According to this view, the federal government is more than a collection of disparate agencies performing discrete, technical, caretaking services for the public. Instead, there is an appreciation of government as a whole and a concomitant understanding that government exists, or ought to exist, to play an active, positive role in society.

This fundamental assumption leads in turn to the belief that administrators, especially higher administrators, need first and foremost to view themselves as guardians of the broad public interest. They need to identify not with the narrow perspectives of an agency or profession but with the central idea of public service. To that end, they need to be set apart from the rest of the civil service and put into a distinctive, governmentwide corps that can provide the necessary socialization and career development. Administrative generalists, not technical specialists, are the mainstay of the higher civil service. This is necessary because only generalists are likely to have both the catholic perspectives and broad skills necessary to translate elusive public purposes into government action. Experts, the aphorism has it, should be on tap, not on top.

This is not to say that the higher civil service is coterminous with some generic idea of management. The elite corps perspective decisively rejects the notion that the private sector is home to some magic managerial potions that can be transferred wholesale to the arena of government, either in the persons of private sector managers or through the import of techniques themselves. Indeed, the core assumption of this perspective is, as Paul Appleby put it, that "government is different." Government management requires far more political acumen, bargaining ability, and sensitivity to diverse constituencies than private management. Most important, it requires a particular commitment to public service and an attitude that one's work is more than meeting some objectified goal or milestone.

The only way these managerial skills can be instilled is through the development of a from-the-bottom-up career system. Great attention must be paid to recruitment, training, and career development. Likely candidates for high administrative office need to be identified very early on, preferably at the time they enter the system as college graduates or holders of newly minted graduate degrees. Much on the model of the military or foreign service, heavy investments in training, both in-house and university based, need to be made throughout the career cycle. And, on the same model, regular rotation from agency to agency, and from field to headquarters, should be the norm. Systematic performance reviews by senior career administrators should be used to reinforce proper public service values, guide career development, and pare down cohorts so that there is ultimately a proper match between the number of higher administrators and the number of available positions.

Given the extraordinary fragmentation of American government, considerable centralization in the personnel system is required to perform these functions. Only a governmentwide staff agency can nurture a governmentwide perspective in senior civil servants. The real problem with the Civil Service Commission and OPM has been not that these offices have retained central authority; rather, it is that they have exercised it poorly, squandering their efforts on developing and overseeing an antiquated system of position classification. A strong and activist executive personnel bureau needs to be responsible for recruiting, selecting, training, placing, and appraising higher administrators.

Finally, this image anticipates a major reduction in the number of political appointees in executive positions. The increased use of political appointees in subcabinet-level jobs has been problematic for two reasons. First, it has diminished the effectiveness of American government by turning over ever greater administrative authority to men and women with little public service experience and, worse, with little commitment to public service. Second, by effectively denying career executives access to some of the most interesting and challenging jobs in government, it has made it more difficult to recruit and retain the most talented public servants. This image rejects simple distinctions drawn between politics and administration and recognizes the extent to which top bureaucrats are inevitably involved in shaping as well as executing public policy. It assumes, however, that central to the role definition of career executives is a belief that, within the law, any elected administration should be served loyally and responsibly.

Image 3: Higher Civil Service as Political Machine

The third image of the American higher civil service that developed during the postwar period shares with the second the idea that the traditional civil service has deteriorated into a congeries of agency fiefdoms, narrow, calcified, and unintegrated. Consequently, it shares, too, the assumption that greater breadth of perspective, flexibility, and coherence should be brought to the system. Where this image parts company is in its insistence that *political responsiveness* ought to be the primary aim of any reform.

Central to this perspective is the belief that bureaucracy is naturally resistant to the authority of elected political leaders. Career executives identify with the programs for which they are responsible. They measure success by their ability to protect and expand their administrative domains and develop close strategic alliances with interest groups and members of Congress who have similar programmatic interests. Consequently, presidents who desire change are frequently stymied. Much of the impetus for the steady increases in the size of the presidential staff in the past fifty years can be attributed to efforts to circumvent the career bureaucracy, as can the tendency to fill greater numbers of jobs within line agencies with short-term political appointees.

The model higher civil service from this perspective is one that would reduce the need for these palliatives. Senior career administrators should be highly responsive to the government of the day— should, in effect, be direct appendages of the president in the agencies. This view is grounded in one powerful (if unsophisticated) strand of democratic theory: in a democracy, free elections are the only legitimate vehicle for the articulation of the public interest. Career administrators have no right independently to make judgments about policy. Because it is impossible rigidly to separate political and administrative roles, it is essential that bureaucrats derive their values from elected officials. It is essential, that is to say, that they be absolutely responsive.

How can such responsiveness be ensured? First and foremost, administrators must be made accountable for their performance. The grip of tenure must be relaxed so that political leaders have the ability to remove nonresponsive or poorly performing executives from office, though not necessarily from the civil service, at will. Second, upper administration should be permeable. While the preponderance of top officials will likely always be drawn from the career ranks, owing to the need for technical expertise, presidents should have wide discretion to make political appointments to administrative offices. Closing the higher civil service to outsiders or reserving key positions for career executives only exacerbates the accountability problem.

Image 4: Higher Civil Service as Corporate Managers

The final image of the higher civil service that emerged during this period bears the stamp of the private sector. According to this *corporate perspective*, American government ought to emulate American business in its managerial practices. Although government is not a money-making activity, it, like business, is primarily about accomplishing goals. The president of the United States is equivalent to the chief executive officer of a large conglomerate, and members of his cabinet are akin to the heads of major operating divisions.

Like any top executives, the president and his appointees cannot be expected to accomplish their goals without full control over the necessary resources, one of the most important of which is personnel. The civil service system bequeathed by the Pendleton Act has been far too insulated and buffered to be an effective management tool. No one would expect the presidents of IBM or General Motors to try to run their respective companies with employees who answer only to an independent commission (and then only minimally), so why should we expect the president of the United States to do so? Personnel administration needs to be recognized as a central management function in the public sector, just as it is in the private sector. The central personnel agency should be headed by a single person, directly responsible to the president, not an independent commission.

A related and even more troublesome problem is the fact that employees have no real incentives to perform at high levels of productivity, as they know that their pay and promotion chances have little to do with their output. Although this is a problem throughout the system, it is especially vexing at the highest levels, where leadership and initiative are critical. Pay for performance should be the guiding principle of the higher civil service, with performance measured by reference to clearly articulated, pre-established goals. To provide even greater incentives, cash bonuses should be available for executives whose performance is clearly exemplary.

Reflecting changes in private sector experience, this perspective has shifted positions over the years on the generalist-specialist question, although the current mainstream view generally de-emphasizes the idea of a manager for all seasons. At the same time, unlike Image 1, there is a strong belief in the value of management and in the relevance of the techniques generated by various theories of management. Hence, this view encourages exchanges, if not permanent lateral movements by executives, between public and private sectors, marking a major disagreement with the closed-career perspective of Image 2.

Political questions that are central to images 2 and 3 are given scant attention by Image 4. What is important is whether an executive is getting the job done, not whether he or she has a political or career background. Because of its emphasis on managerial flexibility, however, this perspective leads by default to a higher civil service that is structurally similar to that proposed by Image 3, the political responsiveness model; that is, tenure is relaxed and at-will employment the rule. The chief difference is that there is an implicit distaste for politics in the corporate model—politics generally being perceived as an extraneous, efficiency-impeding element in management. Thus, Image 4 places greater stress on presumably unbiased, analytically detached measures of job performance, applied to political appointees as well as career executives, which may indirectly come to limit at least certain kinds of responsiveness.

As I noted at the beginning of this section, these four images are ideal types. Although strong traces of the images can be found in the pre-SES reform proposals, I have deliberately not linked them so as to avoid any suggestion of a one-to-one correspondence. The postwar period did not serve up, seriatim, convenient little reform packages just waiting to be analyzed. The Senior Civil Service embodied a considerable chunk of Image 2, to be sure; but Image 2 is also reflected in other proposals, just as the senior civil service incorporated other images.

The advantage of using ideal types is that they exhibit strong coherence, at least if constructed properly. You know that if you accept one set of assumptions, then others naturally follow. For instance, the assumptions of Image 2 about closed careers compel further assumptions about centralized personnel management, mobility, generalism, and so forth—and vice versa. There is, in other words, a strain toward consistency. One can thus predict that assumptions drawn from two or more different images will, in general, create conflict and instability.[12]

Shaping the SES: A Kaleidoscope of Images

Which of these images underlies the SES? The answer is, all of them. More than any other higher civil service reform effort of the postwar era, the SES rests on a kaleidoscope of images, a veritable Mulligan's stew of ideas: a little pay for performance here, a little political responsiveness there, with a splash of opportunity for career executives, and a dollop of decentralization. After a brief recapitulation of the events that led to the inauguration of the SES in 1979, this section of the chapter examines the use of the images in greater detail.

Like other elements of the Civil Service Reform Act of 1978 (CSRA), the immediate roots of the SES are to be found in the work of the Federal Personnel Management Project (FPMP), which was established by President Carter in May 1977 in fulfillment of his campaign pledge to clean up the "horrible bureaucratic mess" in Washington (McGrath 1976:CRS–4). Under the overall guidance of Alan Campbell, then-chairman of the CSC, and Wayne Granquist, OMB's associate director for management, the FPMP was specifically charged with undertaking a "full-scale review of federal personnel management laws, principles, and organization" (U.S. Congress 1978a:21). The day-to-day work of the FPMP, overseen by Executive Director Dwight Ink, was conducted by nine specialized task forces, one of which, Task Force 2, was devoted to studying the "executive service."[13] The task forces completed their work in November 1977, with a final report of their deliberations and recommendations published in December 1977 (FPMP 1977).

An outline of this report was presented to Congress in a presidential message on 2 March 1978, followed the next day by the formal introduction of the CSRA in both houses (H.R. 11280 and S. 2640). As it happened, the senior executive service provisions of the bill slipped through Congress with relatively little controversy, though not without discussion, as congressional attention was focused mainly on labor-management, veterans' preference, and Hatch Act liberalization issues.[14] After almost two weeks of hearings in each house, extending through three months, and following final committee, floor, and conference action, President Carter signed the CSRA into law (P.L. 95-454) on 13 October 1978.[15] As provided by the statute, the SES formally came into being nine months later, on 13 July 1979.

Although it is impossible to reconstruct precisely the collective assumptions and perceptions of the framers of the SES, the documentary record from this period—FPMP issue papers and recommendations, congressional hearings, the SES provisions (Title IV) of the CSRA itself—is quite complete and affords considerable insight into the sorts of images that guided their work. And it is clear that at the very beginning of the discussions about SES a deliberate decision was made to trade intellectual coherence for intellectual balance. Consider, for instance, the following passage from the *Final Report* of the FPMP task force on the SES (FPMP 1977: app. II, p. 9):

The study group gave serious consideration to three complete system designs, each of which has a different focus and each of which received some support among the many groups and individuals with whom we consulted:

1. A system designed to maximize the agency head's autonomy in managing his executive resources—similar to systems prevailing in some large *private sector organizations.*

2. A system establishing *a cadre of professional career managers* along the lines of an officer corps.

3. A system which *balances* the need of agency heads for flexibility in the use of executive resources and the need of employees for career opportunities and protection, with special attention to the rights of the public for effective, efficient and impartial administration of Federal programs (emphasis added).

Although the task force found "some evident advantages" in the first two systems, they decided that the "balance" of the system three, which they labeled "the Executive Service," was of paramount importance. Indeed, members of the task force complained that in discussing various options with over 400 different groups and 200 current executives,

a very common difficulty was the fact that most respondents were unacquainted with the totality of the executive personnel management picture and, consequently, did not recognize the existence of the full range of problems the study group was trying to address. The result in many instances was that such respondents would advance fragmentary systems which would solve the particular problems of which they were aware but would leave others unaddressed or even aggravated. *The study group thus found it impossible to adopt in its totality any of the systems suggested to us. We were, however, able to appropriate many innovative features from the many helpful comments were received.* (ibid.: app. II, app. D, p.1; emphasis added)

So it was that the FPMP panel recommended a system that seemingly had something for everyone, rhetorically and substantively. Image 1 visions were tapped by removing certain noxious central controls over agency autonomy—such as CSC classification of executive positions, CSC approval of the qualifications of agency nominees in cases of movement within the system, CSC case-by-case authorization of spaces, and so on—and by drawing the boundaries of the service broadly enough to include virtually all functional specialties.[16]

Image 2 received its due in passages extolling the virtues of "a highly professional cadre of career managers" and in recommendations for a rank-in-person system, opportunities for career executives to take "noncareer" jobs without jeopardizing their career status, the establishment of "career-reserved" positions, and various protections against political abuses of merit principles.[17] Although the post-Watergate climate of 1977 discouraged some of the more direct and strident rhetorical flourishes of Image 3, the goals of greater political responsiveness did not go unrepresented in the FPMP proposals: agency managers were given greater "flexibility" to fill positions with noncareer appointees and to reassign executives when, in the agency manager's view, such actions become necessary to ensure responsiveness and "to relieve the frustration that the political leadership often feels when confronted with the bureaucracy" (ibid.: vol. 2, app. II, app. C(1), p. 4).

Finally, the FPMP papers are filled with Image 4 allusions: words like "efficiency," "effectiveness," "accountability," and "performance" occur in almost every sentence. Moreover, replacing "longevity pay," which is a "practice that runs counter to that of the private sector," with pay for performance "will make it possible both to reward the outstanding performer and to motivate the marginal and mediocre employee" (ibid.: vol. 1, p. 198).

As one would expect, congressional testimony about the SES was less consistently inconsistent, at least when taken in discrete chunks. As in the story of the blind men and the elephant, scores of individuals and groups drew on these images in supporting the proposal (and more rarely, in opposing it) in ways that revealed wholly different understandings of what the SES was to be about. In fact, if one didn't know better and didn't see the same three letters—SES—used by all who commented, one would come away from reading through the 3,000-plus pages of hearings and supporting documents with the idea that these people must be talking about different reform initiatives.[18]

The remarks of Roy Ash and William Eberle, representing the Committee for Economic Development, for instance, were a virtually pure projection of Image 4, with their constant references to private sector practices and consistent emphasis on "managerial authority" and performance appraisals and financial incentives (U.S. Congress 1978: 92–116). Similar comments were forthcoming from representatives of the American Society for Personnel Administration (ibid.:196–99). For these people and many others, the SES was appealing because it would, in their view, allow the federal government to function more like a large private corporation.

On the other hand, a statement prepared by the National Treasury Employees Union used Image 1 logic to *oppose* most features of the SES, which they deemed highly vulnerable to political abuse: "Though the opportunity existed to return a great deal of personnel authority to individual agencies, where it rightfully belongs, the President has chosen instead to concentrate all power over this 'elite corps' in his own political appointees" (ibid.:173). Almost identical comments were made by representatives of the National Federation of Professional Organizations, who described the proposed SES as "a blatant political patronage grab . . . just as odious as the 1972 [FES] proposal" (ibid.:218), and by spokesmen for the National Association of Supervisors, who viewed the SES as simply adding "8,000 more political jobs" (ibid.:237).

At the same time, Image 1 values were occasionally invoked to *support* (with some reservations) the idea of the SES. Albert Grant of the American Society of Civil Engineers endorsed the system, asking only that the importance of "engineering, scientific and technical expertise" be recognized (ibid.:354), as did George Auman of the Federal Professional Association, who urged that "specialists . . . be afforded the same opportunities for rewards and varying assignments as those in the Senior Executive Service" (ibid.:597). A few others drew on Image 1 to praise the financial inducements in the SES or to note the loosened controls over agency autonomy.

In general, however, it is fair to say that the greatest skepticism voiced about the SES came from those who held Image 1 views of the American higher civil service. In one sense, this is not surprising, as Image 1 represented the traditional way of doing things, while the SES, whatever else it was, was something new, and thus potentially threatening to the status quo. The irony, of course, is that it is this image of the higher civil service that the SES has come most closely to approximate.

One of the strongest Image 3 conceptions of the SES expressed during the hearings, paradoxically enough, came from a member of Congress, Democrat Leo Ryan. In a remarkable extended exchange, worth quoting at length, with James Peirce, president of the National Federation of Federal Employees, and Nathan Wolkomir, former president of that organization, Ryan insisted on the paramount importance of career executive responsiveness to political appointees and elected officials (U.S. Congress 1978:282–83):

Mr. Ryan: Isn't the career employee required to take orders from a person who has been appointed by the President?

Mr. Peirce: Very definitely, but the thing that we pointed out here is that with the approach that is revealed in this SES system, we would most surely have employees . . . afraid to give an opinion based on their expertise and background.

Mr. Ryan: Especially if they disagreed with the person who appointed them, and put them in there to carry out the policies of the President; right?

Mr. Peirce: I think that's true. I think also it restricts . . .

Mr. Ryan: Is that wrong?

Mr. Peirce: The initiative and initiation on their part to bring forth ideas. And this would tend to kill those ideas coming to the surface.

Mr. Ryan: I can think of a particular regional director of a particular Federal agency in San Francisco right now who is diametrically opposed to what the President wants, and so far, he has gotten away with it. Is he right?

Mr. Peirce: He could be.

Mr. Ryan: What is right? What the people want as expressed through their elected officials, or the career employee who doesn't necessarily feel compelled to respond to the sense of the people?

.   .   .   .

Mr. Wolkomir: You are saying because the President is elected, he is infallible.

Mr. Ryan: You are saying, if I understand you, you are saying the career employees should be protected by the politician when he says—

Mr. Wolkomir: We are saying he should have the right for redress. Under the proposal, he has none, and a man in a democracy has got a right to say what he thinks. He has got a right to come to you, hasn't he? Are you saying because he is a Federal employee he should keep quiet and just follow orders, because the President was elected?

Mr. Ryan: He must follow orders of the President and his surrogates in the various departments at the top; you are darn right.

Ralph Nader expressed similar, if more tempered, thoughts about the need for political responsiveness: "Obviously, any form of SES will result in a certain amount of politicization of high level career officials, but we do not believe that all politicization is necessarily bad. When a majority of those citizens who rejected Gerald Ford and elected Jimmy Carter, they announced in a gross fashion that they did not endorse the way the Republicans were running the government" (ibid.:343). As was the case with SES supporters who came at the system using other images, Nader expressed reservations, calling for better protection for whistleblowers in particular. But the point is that he (along with others) supported the SES because he believed it embodied a particular image of a higher civil service he approved of—an image strikingly different from those seen by other SES advocates.

Less conspicuous during the hearings were well-articulated Image 2 analyses of the SES. Although scores of witnesses expressed concerns about undue politicization of the civil service under the provisions of Title IV, almost without exception they did so in a manner that emphasized their commitment to a traditional, Image 1 vision of top executives. The reason for this near lacuna, I suspect, is that language embracing the values of a European-style cadre of elite administrators has little political appeal in general and certainly had little appeal in the antigovernment atmosphere of the late 1970s. Even those who apparently saw the SES in Image 2 terms—especially those academics who supported what the FPMP outlined as a "system two" approach to building a higher civil service (see above)—chose to couch their support mainly in other terms.[19]

Again, what is remarkable about this testimony is not that different people had different reasons for supporting the SES; it is hardly unusual for a piece of legislation to tap multiple motives in various constituencies. What is peculiar is the extent to which the reasons were fundamentally at odds with one another, drawn as they were from contradictory understandings of what a higher civil service should look like.

Table 9 summarizes this paradox by listing the major features of the SES, indicating the images from which each is drawn and the images each contradicts.

Table 9. Key SES Features and Higher Civil Service Images

SES Feature	Supporting Image	Contradictory Image
Governmentwide personnel system	2, 3	1
Rank-in-person	2	1
Decentralization of recruitment and training	1, 4	2
Relaxed tenure, managerial flexibility	3, 4	1, 2
Responsiveness through political appointments to career jobs	3	1, 2, 4
Careerist opportunities through career appointments to political jobs	2	3
Pay for performance	3, 4	2
Emphasis on general management	2	1
Mobility	2	1
Accountability through measurable performance goals and appraisals	3, 4	2

Image 1—Traditional agency perspective.
Image 2—Elite corps perspective.
Image 3—Political responsiveness perspective.
Image 4—Corporate perspective.

Note: Not all images are located on each dimension because, at least as I interpret them, certain dimensions are either irrelevant or not logically required for certain images. For instance, Image 3 doesn't really address the issue of rank-in-person versus rank-in-position, just as Image 1 is neutral on the type of pay schemes.

Table 9 looks too much like a Chinese restaurant menu to resist the hackneyed parallel: it appears as if the SES's designers and supporters had sat around a table in 1977 and 1978, and, in an effort to satisfy everyone's appetite, picked a few dishes from column A, a few from column B, and so on. And of course we were hungry again in no time.

Conclusions

What are the implications of this analysis for the SES? Again, I would not argue that had the SES been more conceptually coherent it would necessarily have been more successful. Most of the evidence, in fact, including the cases reviewed in this chapter, points in the opposite direction. Coherence is probably a necessary condition of success, but it is certainly not sufficient.

Nor would I argue that parts of the SES at least would have been markedly more successful, even given the basic design, if certain things had just broken in the right way. For instance, one popular explanation for the SES's problems hinges on Congress's failure fully to fund the bonus provisions and on the consequent souring of senior executives toward the whole idea. Another has it that if President Carter had won reelection in 1980 and kept Alan Campbell and company on at OPM, things would have worked out. Although I think we would have been better off had both things happened, I doubt either was critical in terms of the SES.

Meaningful administrative change requires basic political change. It requires, for instance, the sort of political realignments that accompanied the rise of the spoils system in the early nineteenth century and the establishment of the civil service more than a half century later, an injection of new groups into politics or a shift in the balance of power between institutions.[20] Reforms short of sea changes are possible in politics, of course—the classification acts of 1923 and 1949 are two examples—but these tend to confirm, rather than challenge, existing distributions of power.

The establishment of an American higher civil service, at least as envisaged in three of the four images discussed above, would clearly be a "meaningful administrative change," a challenge to rather than a confirmation of existing alignments; only the first image, the traditional agency perspective, escapes this dilemma. To pursue the vision of the traditional agency, with its peculiarly restrained conception of elite administration, is to gain victory in name alone. There is reason for optimism, however, and it is to be found in the fact that the system simply doesn't work. Although this has been pointed out by every group from the Hoover commission to the Volcker commission, the breakdowns have become so serious and so regular that sooner or later even the most obdurate opponents of reform will have to pay attention.

My own guess is that it will be sooner. And the character of the breakdowns leads me to believe that Image 2 conceptions of reform will, fortunately, gain support. Why? Because virtually all of the major governmental scandals and policy disasters of the past few years— from the Challenger explosion through the Iran-contra scam to the latest selling of the Pentagon—have derived, in one way or another, from a system of political administration that suppresses the wisdom and values of career professionals and gives free rein to the half-baked ideas and short-term interests of political appointees.[21] This system, which we could never really afford, is getting more costly by the day. And this is why the search for a genuine American higher civil service must—and will—continue.

NOTES

1. For a sample of these commentaries, see U.S. GAO (1985); Clinton and Newburg (1984); Rosen (1981); NAPA (1981); U.S. Congress (1981); U.S. Congress (1983–84); Huddleston (1987).

2. Although the report of the President's Committee on Administrative Management (the Brownlow Committee) complained in 1937 about the operation of the civil service and urged the adoption of sweeping changes in the system (including an OPM-like proposal for the reorganization of the Civil Service Commission into an agency headed by a single administrator responsible to the president), it made no recommendations that bore specifically on the recruitment, organization, or use of top career officials—although Frederick Mosher argues that "the plain implication of its proposals was to lay stress upon generalist administrative qualifications for those holding intermediate and higher positions in the executive hierarchy." See Mosher (1982:85).

3. Paul Van Riper, in his authoritative *History of the United States Civil Service* (1985), is in general quite critical of both the full commission and the personnel policy committee for their failure, in his view, to explore fully some key assumptions about the organization and operation of the civil service. He argues, for instance, that neither report showed evidence of much thought about relations between political appointees and career executives; he also complains that both uncritically assume that promotion from within is to be preferred to greater executive interchange between industry and government. While he is correct that both reports leave much unsaid, both say much more—at least on the subject of the higher civil service—that one would have expected. Hence their significance.

4. Most of the Hoover Commission's civil service recommendations were not aimed at the higher civil service alone, it should be stressed. Central to their proposals were calls for further standardization of pay grades and unification of authority in the Civil Service Commission, with greater decentralization of responsibility for position classification to agencies.

5. Congress initially limited the supergrades, under Section 505 of the Classification Act, to 400 positions governmentwide (300 in GS-16, 75 in GS-17, and 25 in GS-18) and restricted the ability of agencies to classify jobs at these grade levels; only the Civil Service Commission was to have the authority to designate GS-16 and GS-17 positions, and only the president would have the right to determine GS-18 positions. These restrictions, which remained in force with little modification for years, led to the use of the term *505 quota* (or *governmentwide quota*) to refer to job slots authorized by this legislation and later amendments. For a fuller description of these provisions, see U.S. CSC (1954).

6. The new Schedule A became used for other (nonpolitical) positions not subject to examination, chiefly those filled by lawyers.

7. Except as otherwise noted, this list is adapted from U.S. CSC (1971a:7).

8. For the most thorough extant review of the politics of the senior civil service proposal, see Chung (1985).

9. The first rider was to an appropriations bill for the departments of Labor and Health, Education, and Welfare. See U.S. Congress (1959a). A second rider was then attached to an appropriations action for the Civil Service Commission itself the following month. See U.S. Congress (1959b).

10. An earlier two-hat system of this sort had been used in the Eisenhower administration when Philip Young was made the president's advisor on personnel management as well as chairman of the Civil Service Commission in 1953.

11. Memorandum for Frederic V. Malek from James W. McLane on "Civil Service Reform: Broader Development of Executive Level (GS15-18) Civil Servant," 1 February 1971.

12. This is not to suggest that any one ideal type, however coherent, may not contain potentially conflicting elements, a point Max Weber developed to great advantage in his discussion of bureaucracy.

13. Task Force 2 was chaired by Sally Greenberg of the Civil Service Commission; the other members were Jeffrey Caplan (Commerce), Faye Harler (CSC), and Cecil Uyehara (AID). The other task forces were as follows: Task Force 1—composition and dynamics; Task Force 3—staffing process; Task Force 4—EEO and AA; Task Force 5—job evaluation; Task Force 6—labor.

14. For a discussion of the legislative politics of the CSRA, see Nigro (1979). For SES supporters, the only tense moment in the legislative process came when the House Committee on Post Office and Civil Service approved an amendment that sought to limit the system to a two-year experiment in three agencies; this amendment was deleted in the House-Senate conference committee.

15. For a thorough legislative history of P.L. 95–454, see Mosher and McGrath (1978).

16. The task force did urge that the focus of the executive service be kept on managers and that those supergrade members who had no supervisory responsibilities be excluded. It also appears that the task force expected far more discriminating self-selection at the time of conversion than actually occurred. By their estimate, "the number of incumbent managers who would elect to enter the service immediately are on the order of 50–70 percent" (FPMP 1977: vol. 2, app. II, app. A, p. 15). Had OPM not induced a conversion rate close to 99 percent, the expectations of the task force for a more managerially oriented executive service may have been met. It should be noted, however, that the task force's definition of management was fairly loose: "The first or second in command of a significant organizational segment or of a major project" (ibid.: vol. 2, app. II, app. A, p. 3). Moreover, even granting their 50–70 percent projection, absent a more carefully delineated grandfather clause there was no good reason to believe that it would be supergrade managers rather than supergrade nonmangers who would choose to convert.

17. On this last point, see Recommendation 87 in FPMP (1977: vol. 1, p. 196–97).

18. The chief exceptions to this generalization are to be found in the testimony of administration officials. Virtually all of Carter's cabinet officers were sent up to the Hill at one point or another to speak in favor of the CSRA in general and the SES in particular. To a person, they pursued the FPMP strategy of projecting the SES as a system for all seasons, drawing willy-nilly on all possible higher civil service images.

19. Partial exceptions were the representatives of the National Academy of Public Administration, who urged some modest changes in the SES proposal in the direction of increasing

20. Similar examples might be drawn from abroad, such as the Trevalyan-Northecote reforms in Britain in 1854 or the Stein-Hardenberg reforms of the Prussian bureaucracy in the early nineteenth century.

21. This proposition is provocative—although true nonetheless, I am convinced. The great task for students of public personnel administration today, especially those interested in the higher civil service, is to prove its underlying assumption, namely, that public personnel administration makes some sort of difference. One of the reasons that no one outside a fairly restricted circle of professionals gets very exercised about the SES and its fate is that those of us who write about personnel have never taken the time to demonstrate why they should. I was heartened to note that Daniel Schorr, now a senior news analyst for National Public Radio, made a similar point in an op-ed piece recently in the *New York Times* (30 June 1988:A23).

SOURCES

Boyer, William W., and A. J. Mackelprang. 1973. "Federal Career Executives: Manpower Management Policy Development." Unpublished.

Chung, Sung-Ho. 1985. "Politics of Civil Service Reform: The First Attempt to Establish a Higher Civil Service in the Eisenhower Administration." Ph.D. diss., University of Delaware.

Clinton, John B., and Arthur S. Newburg. 1984. *The Senior Executive Service: A Five-Year Retrospective Review of its Operating and Conceptual Problems.* Washington, D.C.: Senior Executives Association.

Commission on Organization of the Executive Branch of the Government. 1949. *The Hoover Commission Report on Organization of the Executive Branch of the Government.* New York: McGraw-Hill.

———. 1955. *Task Force Report on Personnel and Civil Service.* Washington, D.C.: GPO.

Committee for Economic Development 1964. *Improving Executive Manpower in the Federal Government.*

FPMP (Federal Personnel Management Project). 1977. Vol. 1: *Final Staff Report;* vol. 2: *Appendices to the Final Staff Report;* vol. 3: *Supplementary Materials.*

Huddleston, Mark W. 1987. *The Government's Managers: Report of the Twentieth Century Fund Task Force on the Senior Executive Service.* New York: Priority Press.

McGrath, James. 1978. *Federal Civil Service Reform: A Report.* Washington, D.C.: Congressional Research Service.

Mosher, Alice, and James McGrath. 1978. *Civil Service Reform Act of 1978 (P.L. 95-454)*, Issue Brief IB78066. Washington, D.C.: *Congressional Research Service*.

Mosher, Frederick. 1982. *Democracy and the Public Service*, 2d ed. New York: Oxford University Press.

NAPA (National Academy of Public Administration). 1981. *The Senior Executive Service: An Interim Report of the Panel of the National Academy of Public Administration on the Public Service*. Washington, D.C.

Nigro, Felix A. 1979. "The Politics of Civil Service Reform." Paper presented at the 1979 Annual Meeting of the American Political Science Association, August 31–September 3.

Personnel Policy Committee. 1949. *Task Force Report on Federal Personnel [Appendix A]*. City: Commission on Organization of the Executive Branch of the Government.

Rosen, Bernard. 1981. "Uncertainty in the Senior Executive Service." *Public Administration Review* 41 (March/April). pp. 203–211.

U.S. Congress. 1958. House Committee on Post Office and Civil Service. Subcommittee on Manpower Utilization. Hearings, *Manpower Utilization in the Federal Government (Career Executive Program)*. 85th Cong., 2d sess.

———. 1959a. House. Committee on Appropriations. H.R. 302. 86th Cong., 1st sess.

———. 1959b. House. Committee on Appropriations. H.R. 350. 86th Cong., 1st sess.

———. 1960. Senate. Report on Regulation Agencies to the President-Elect. Committee on the Judiciary, Subcommittee on Administrative Practice and Procedure. 89th Cong., 2nd sess. (James M. Landis, author.)

———. 1978a. House. Committee on Post Office and Civil Service. Hearings, *Civil Service Reform*. 95th Cong., 2nd sess. Testimony of Alan K. Campbell. Serial 95-65.

———. 1978b. Senate. Committee on Governmental Affairs. Hearings, *Civil Service Reform and Reorganization Plan No. 2 of 1978, S. 2640, S. 2707, and S. 2830*. 95th Cong., 2d sess.

———. 1981. House. Committee on Post Office and Civil Service. Subcommittee on Civil Service. Hearings, *Senior Executive Service*. Serial 97-7. 97th Cong., 1st sess.

———. 1983–84. House. Committee on Post Office and Civil Service. *Senior Executive Service*. Serial 98-12. 98th Cong., 1st and 2nd sess.

U.S. CSC (Civil Service Commission). *Background of the Supergrade Story, 1923–53*, 4th rev. Prepared by Ismar Baruch. Washington, D.C.

———. 1964a. Federal Career Executives, Three Year's Experience with the Career Executive Roster. Mimeographed report prepared by Mel Bolster. Washington, D.C.

———. 1964a. *Senior Civil Service: Chronological Summary of Internal Activities, Memoranda, Conferences, Notes and Personal Data, March 1955–November 1957*. 3 vols. Washington, D.C.: OMB Archives.

———. *Senior Civil Service: Official Documents and Background Papers, 1957–1958*. Washington, D.C.: OMB Archives.

————. 1971a. *Administrative History of Federal Executive Manpower Management*. Bureau of Executive Manpower. Washington, D.C.

————. 1971b. "The Federal Executive Service: A Proposal for Improving Manpower Management." *Public Administration Review* 31(February):237–52.

U.S. GAO (U.S. General Accounting Office). 1985. *Evaluation of Proposals to Alter the Structure of the Senior Executive Service*. GAO/GGD-86-14. Washington, D.C.

Van Riper, Paul. 1958. *History of the United States Civil Service*. Evanston, Ill.: Row, Peterson.

9. The Merit Pay Reforms

James L. Perry

The merit pay provisions of the Civil Service Reform Act of 1978 (CSRA) were among the most radical innovations in the history of American government personnel practices. They represented a break from the long tradition of virtually automatic salary increases based on length of service. Borrowing from private sector employment practices, Title V of CSRA sought to motivate better performance and to deter poor performance by increasing grade-level 13–15 managers' salaries by amounts designated by their rated performance—much as midlevel managers in the private sector are awarded pay increases based on their companies' profits in the preceding year.[1]

This chapter looks broadly at the operation and consequences of federal merit pay. It begins with brief descriptions of the two merit pay systems that evolved from the 1978 reforms. They are evaluated within the overall context of reform and its intended objectives. Several merit pay demonstrations are also discussed. The chapter concludes by summarizing what we have learned since merit pay's introduction and by identifying unresolved issues.

The Reform Record

The case for merit pay was initially articulated by the President's Reorganization Project (1977). The project's personnel management report concluded that it was difficult to appropriately recognize performance extremes, both high and low. It found that periodic step increases had become virtually automatic, quality step increases and cash awards were used sparingly, and supervisory action to withhold increases often met resistance from affected employees and higher management. The report concluded that this situation fostered mediocre performance.

The Merit Pay System (MPS)

In the period preceding passage of CSRA, federal middle managers received a combination of annual comparability increases and within-grade increases. Although within-grade increases, in theory, could be used to reward performance, they seldom were granted or denied on the basis of differential performance. Two other mechanisms that were designed to reward high performance, cash awards and quality step increases, were used sparingly. The merit pay system (MPS), which became mandatory for grade 13–15 managers in federal agencies on 1 October 1981, altered how incremental adjustments to salary were distributed. Under MPS, employees automatically received only half of the comparability adjustment. The nonautomatic portion of comparability and the within-grade and quality step increase monies that would have been used to adjust pay under the general schedule were pooled and distributed according to performance (U.S. OPM 1981a).

How successful was the MPS in accomplishing the objectives established for it? The results of twelve studies of MPS are summarized in table 10. The table includes both summative and specialized evaluations of MPS. Research that focused on performance appraisal alone (e.g., McNish 1986) or that preceded initial payouts (e.g., Nigro 1982) was excluded from the review. The columns of the table identify the four primary intended outcomes from MPS as specified in OPM's evaluation plan (U.S. OPM 1981b): (1) to relate pay to performance; (2) to provide flexibility in recognizing good performance with cash awards; (3) to motivate merit pay employees; and (4) to improve productivity, timeliness, and quality of work.

The MPS's clearest shortcoming was its failure to establish a demonstrable relationship between pay and performance. This failure is attributable to a variety of causes. One of the chief causes was lack of adequate funding for merit pay. Agencies were required by law to spend no more on MPS than they had under the previous general schedule system. This problem was exacerbated by implementation difficulties. For example, an OPM-GAO dispute about the statutorily permissible size of payouts led, in September 1981, one month before payouts, to a determination by the Comptroller General of the United States (1981) that the OPM formula for calculating merit pay was not in conformance with the statute. The ruling resulted in payouts that provided only small differentials between managers, again undercutting pay-for-performance principles.

The MPS also failed to relate pay to performance because it did not satisfy basic standards of fairness. Managers who performed satisfactorily often found themselves receiving lesser rewards than their nonmanagerial counterparts at grades 13–15 whose pay was set under the general schedule. Nonperformance factors (e.g., the composition of the pay pool) on payouts and arbitrary modification of ratings also diminished the basic fairness of the system. Employees in most agencies perceived no greater likelihood that their performance would be recognized with a cash award after MPS than it had previously. The use of cash award authorities was highly variable across agencies (U.S. GAO 1984). The MPS appeared not to have significantly altered agency behavior with respect to cash awards.

The reported successes of MPS in motivating employees emanated primarily from the performance appraisal requirements of CSRA. Gaertner and Gaertner (1984, 1985) reported that developmental appraisals, those that focused on planning for the coming year and clarifying expectations, were more effective than appraisals that focused only on past performance. However, developmental appraisal strategies were seldom used, and the pay administration role for appraisals tended to undermine this function. In fact, one study (Pearce and Porter 1986) reported a significant drop in the organizational commitment of employees who received satisfactory, but not outstanding, ratings.

The ultimate purpose of merit pay was to improve the performance of government agencies. The most rigorous study of merit pay's effect on agency performance (Pearce, Stevenson, and Perry 1985) failed to find any association between the introduction of merit pay and office performance in the Social Security Administration. No published research to date has indicated that MPS had any positive effects on agency effectiveness.

The Performance Management and Recognition System (PMRS)

Although MPS did not take effect for most federal managers until 1981, it very quickly became apparent that it performed poorly when judged by the objectives established for it. Relief from MPS grew out of legislation introduced in 1984 that proposed a performance management and recognition system (PMRS) (U.S. Congress 1984). PMRS

Table 10. Summary of Empirical Studies on the Federal Merit Pay Systems (MPS)

Study	Intended Outcomes			
	To relate pay to performance	To provide flexibility in recognizing good performance with cash awards	To motivate merit pay employees	To improve productivity, timeliness, and quality of work
Daley 1987. "Merit Pay Enters With a Whimper: The Initial Federal Civil Service Reform Experience"			Merit pay did not heighten survey measures of motivation	Merit pay recipients perceived their agency to be no more responsive or effective than nonrecipients
Gaertner and Gaertner 1984. "Performance Evaluation and Merit Pay: Results in the Environmental Protection Agency and the Mine Safety and Health Administration"	Merit pay not perceived as equitable; raises too small		Improvement in accuracy of performance standards and overall appraisal	No positive impact on perceived agency effectiveness or employee work behavior
Gaertner and Gaertner 1985. "Performance Contingent Pay for Federal Managers"	Not perceived to be rewarding people fairly with significant raises		Performance standards and appraisal improve work planning and accomplishment	No positive impact on perceived agency effectiveness or employee work behavior
O'Toole and Churchill 1982. "Implementing Pay-for-Performance: Initial Experiences"	Subjectivity and lack of resources undermine pay-for-performance relationship		Enhances communication on goals and job expectations	Inconclusive
Pagano 1985. "An Exploratory Evaluation of the Civil Service Reform Act's Merit Pay System for the GS 13–15s"	Sample of pool managers complained monetary reward not worth amount of paperwork and energy expended			

Source				
Pearce and Perry 1983. "Federal Merit Pay: A Longitudinal Analysis"	No improvement in pay-for-performance contingency after merit pay			
Pearce and Porter 1986. "Employee Responses to Formal Performance Appraisal Feedback"			Performance criteria were clearer but may not reflect agency effectiveness · Relatively low (satisfactory) ratings caused a significant drop in organizational commitment	
Pearce, Stevenson, and Perry 1985. "Managerial Compensation Based on Organizational Performance: A Time-Series Analysis of the Impact of Merit Pay"				No significant effect on organizational performance
Perry, Hanzlik, and Pearce 1982. "Effectiveness of Merit-Pay-Pool Management"	Modification of appraisal ratings to achieve agency merit pay goals reduced credibility of system			
U.S. General Accounting Office 1984. A 2-Year Appraisal of Merit Pay in Three Agencies	Provision of cash awards highly variable across agencies	Nonperformance factors influenced size of merit increases more than necessary	Standards perceived to be fair, job-related, and consistent with organizational goals	
U.S. General Accounting Office 1981. Serious Problems Need to Be Corrected Before Federal Merit Pay Goes Into Effect			Performance appraisals have limitations, including overly quanitative standards and lack of pretesting	OPM method for computing merit pay would exceed former costs by $58 to $74 million
U.S. Merit Systems Protection Board 1981. Status Report on Performance Appraisal and Merit Pay Among Mid-Level Employees	Half of all employees perceived a moderate to strong effect on performance		Employees perceived ratings as fair and accurate but not very helpful	

was enacted on 8 November 1984, but the first payout was made retroactive to the fiscal year 1984 performance cycle. Retroactive application created a number of short-term implementation problems (U.S. GAO 1987a).

The drafters of the PMRS legislation sought to retain pay-for-performance principles but to eliminate the dysfunctions of the original system. Under PMRS, employees must be rated at one of five levels, with two levels above and two levels below fully successful. PMRS consists primarily of three monetary components. Employees who are rated fully successful or better are assured of receiving the full general pay or comparability increase. They are also eligible for merit increases that are equivalent to within-grade increases. The size of the merit increase depends on an employee's position in the pay range and performance rating. In addition to these monies, employees rated fully successful or above also qualify for performance awards or bonuses. Beginning in fiscal 1986, performance awards of no less than 2 percent and no more than 10 percent became mandatory for employees rated two levels above fully successful. An upper limit of 1.5 percent of payroll for all performance awards was placed on agency payouts under the system.

The PMRS also created performance standards review boards to review performance standards within an agency, to assure their validity, and to perform other oversight functions. At least half of each board is required to be made up of merit pay employees. The number and functioning of these boards was left to agency discretion, but they are required to report annually to the agency head.

A summary of evaluations of PMRS is presented in table 11. The PMRS appears to have reduced tensions created by the MPS and to have improved the prospects for achieving the outcomes intended for merit pay. There are some indications that PMRS has altered perceptions about the relationship between pay and performance. The U.S. MSPB (1987) reported that just under half of sampled PMRS employees perceived that better performance would lead to more pay. The likelihood that good performance will be recognized with performance awards has also increased. In its second report on PMRS, the U.S. OPM (1988) indicated that most covered employees received performance awards. These findings must be tempered by the findings of other assessments. The General Accounting Office (U.S. GAO 1987a) found that 50 percent of employees surveyed in PMRS's first year found the size of performance awards inadequate. Perry, Petrakis, and

Miller (1989) found significant relationships between lagged measures of monetary rewards and 1986 performance ratings, but the same relationships were insignificant for 1987 performance awards, suggesting a decline in the effectiveness of PMRS over time.

In MSPB's 1986 survey, employees indicated that performance standards were perceived to be fair and accurate. At the same time, GAO and OPM reported shortcomings in the motivational value of the performance appraisal systems because of late issuance and low standards. Although the amount of evidence is too limited to be conclusive, the evaluations of PMRS suggest no improvements, and possibly a decline, in the motivational value of performance appraisals. However, OPM (U.S. OPM 1988) indicates that the performance standards review boards have made a significant contribution to improving the quality of performance standards and the fairness of the process.

The evaluations of PMRS have been silent with respect to the influence of PMRS on agency effectiveness. The MSPB (U.S. MSPB 1988) has identified a tenatative relationship between turnover and performance ratings that suggests that poor performers are more likely than good performers to leave federal service. However, no relationship was found between turnover and performance ratings in an earlier study of the General Services Administration (Perry and Petrakis 1987).

Title VI Demonstrations

In addition to MPS and PMRS, CSRA has spawned several pay experiments (U.S. GAO 1987) under the authority of Title VI. The first of these occurred in the Department of the Navy at two of its laboratories, the Naval Weapons Center in China Lake, California, and the Naval Ocean Systems Center in San Diego, California. These experiments introduced broad pay bands, simpler position classification, and close linkages between pay and performance. The GAO (U.S. GAO 1988b) concluded in its assessment of the experiments that they were implemented to the general satisfaction of managers and employees but that data were not sufficient to verify that the experiments improved laboratory effectiveness, increased managerial flexibility to assign work, or improved employee recruitment and retention. Schay (1988) concluded that the experimental pay-for-performance system was successful in keeping turnover down, increasing employee satisfaction with extrinsic factors, and increasing turnover among low performers. However, Schay noted, as did the GAO study, that mean salaries were

Table 11. Assessments of the Performance Management and Recognition System (PMRS)

Study	Intended Outcomes			
	To relate pay to performance	To provide flexibility, in recognizing good performance with cash awards	To motivate merit pay employees	To improve productivity, timeliness, and quality of work
Perry and Petrakis 1987. "Can Merit Pay Improve Performance in Government?"	Employees achieving high monetary rewards likely to perform at high levels in next rating period	About two-thirds of sample received performance awards		Rewards poor discriminators between stayers and leavers
Perry, Petrakis, and Miller 1989. "Federal Merit Pay, Round II: An Analysis of the Performance Management and Recognition System"	Lagged monetary rewards positively and significantly related to performance ratings	About two-thirds of sample received performance awards		
U.S. General Accounting Office 1987. *Pay for Performance Implementation of the Performance Management and Recognition System*	Nonperformance factors that caused inequities under merit pay continue in PMRS	Fifty percent of respondents found amounts of performance awards inadequate	Performance standards for many employees were issued more than 30 days into the appraisal period	

Source			
U.S. Merit Systems Protection Board 1987. *Performance Management and Recognition System: Linking Pay to Performance*	Slightly less than half of employees perceived better performance leading to more pay	Performance standards perceived to be fair and accurate	Higher turnover rates for employees rated unacceptable and minimally successful
U.S. Merit Systems Protection Board 1988. *Toward Effective Performance Management in the Federal Government*	Same as U.S. NSPB (1987)	Same as U.S. MSPB (1987)	
U.S. Office of Personnel Management 1987. *Performance Management and Recognition System*	Agencies reported reinforcement of linkage between pay and performance	Size and amount of funding for performance awards increased	Quality of performance standards not a problem; not stated in measurable terms and did not differentiate between performance levels
U.S. Office of Personnel Management 1988. *Performance Management and Recognition System: FY 1986 Performance Cycle*	Performance ratings inflated and average rating levels increased with grade level	Performance awards granted to most covered employees	

5 percent higher than at the control labs, raising doubts about the causes of the favorable outcomes.

A demonstration at the Sacramento Air Logistics Center at McClellan Air Force Base is experimenting with gain sharing, which permits employees to share in productivity gains through enhanced earnings. The McClellan demonstration pays incentive bonuses based on the difference between allocated funds and actual costs. Savings are divided equally between the government and employees involved in the experiment.

The National Institute of Standards and Technology (NIST) (U.S. GAO 1988a) has initiated a total compensation demonstration. The project seeks to improve recruitment and retention in NIST by permitting salaries to be set and adjusted based on comparability with total compensation (basic pay, bonuses, allowances, retirement, health and life insurance, and leave benefits) in the private sector. Adjustments to salary are made based on employee performance.

The Defense Logistic's Agency Depot in Ogden, Utah (U.S. OPM 1989b) is planning to test the effectiveness of multiskilled work teams, in which each team member acquires the skills necessary for fulfilling the team's mission. Employee pay will be based on the acquisition of required skills rather than performance of a specific job. The objectives of the demonstration are to show how a participatory work environment and a skill-based compensation system can enhance effectiveness by increasing employee interaction and knowledge.

What Has Been Learned

Although both MPS and PMRS encountered implementation difficulties, the shortcomings of federal merit pay appear primarily to have involved design and fit issues, rather than implementation. The evolution of federal merit pay programs, from MPS to PMRS to the current demonstrations, indicates that federal personnel managers and policy makers have learned some lessons from the experiences of the past ten years.

Zero-Sum Programs Don't Work

The original merit pay program was zero-sum in character at both the individual and organizational levels. At the individual level, it was necessary for some employees to do less well for others to gain financially. It permitted employees performing at a satisfactory level to lose ground relative to their nonmanagerial counterparts. These features of MPS's design were transparent, and employees responded with hostility and disdain. At the organizational level, the norm of budget neutrality eliminated the prospect that demonstrable improvements in agency performance would be recognized with additional financial rewards.

The PMRS reversed the zero-sum character of federal merit pay. Following adjustments to PMRS in 1989 that corrected a glitch for mid-tercile employees who were rated fully successful, managers are no longer at risk of receiving less than their general schedule counterparts. The performance award provisions of PMRS stimulated the payout of substantial numbers of cash awards. Furthermore, because movement through the pay range is defined in absolute terms rather than dependent on the relative ratings of other pool members, the results of individual effort are more predictable and more likely to be perceived as equitable by employees.

The Reward Structure Must Recognize Group and Unit Performance

The individual, fixed contracts required by individually contingent pay programs have a variety of limitations. They become the focus of substantial amounts of administrative energy (paperwork), are prone to manipulation by opportunistic managers, and divert employees from the interdependent aspects of work in public organizations (Perry 1986). These limitations of individually contingent managerial pay are slowly being addressed by designs being used or considered in demonstration programs. The McClellan demonstration is the clearest example of a pay-for-performance system grounded in unit performance.

Bonuses Are Superior to Salary Increments

Organizations must choose whether increments are awarded to employees as permanent adjustments to base pay or as one-time bonuses (Lawler 1981). The traditional method in most government organizations has been to incorporate pay increments into regular salary. In terms of the goal of linking pay to performance, bonuses place larger shares of an employee's compensation at risk, and the increments awarded for performance are more clearly identifiable. The design of PMRS places a larger emphasis on one-time bonuses than did MPS, but empoyees continue to receive substantial adjustments to salary as well. Although there is no clear evidence that PMRS's emphasis on bonuses is the source of improvements in employee acceptance or perceived strengthening of pay-for-performance linkages, some federal managers believe that it has been a factor (McFee and Brumback 1988). Recent experimental evidence also indicates that pay and performance are more likely to be contingent under bonus systems than under salary increment systems (Schwab and Olson 1988).

The Unfinished Agenda

Despite what we have learned since 1978, many important issues remain unresolved, and significant questions are still unanswered. In a recent review of ten years of performance management under CSRA (McFee and Brumback 1988), two high-level federal managers, although acknowledging the learning that has occurred, called for further improvements in the performance management system. In some respects, federal managers and policy makers have learned how to operate merit pay to minimize the pain, but they have not necessarily achieved their strategic goals: improved productivity and effectiveness. This section discusses the unfinished agenda.

What Is an Appropriate Ratings Distribution?

The MPS was initiated with a strong bias for a normally distributed ratings curve. Recent assessments of PMRS ratings note a significant skew in most agencies' ratings, with 68.7 percent of merit pay employees in 1985 receiving ratings above fully successful (U.S. MSPB 1987). These ratings have been viewed with alarm in many quarters, but there is no obvious standard by which to assess the overall distribution of ratings.

The highly concentrated distribution of performance ratings may, in theory, diminish the potential motivational power of merit pay, but it is important to recognize that performance ratings affect more than just monetary awards. Appraisal ratings affect an employee's understanding of the job by providing feedback about performance, self image, organizational commitment, and trust. Although normally distributed performance ratings may be desirable to meet the objectives of the compensation system, they could undermine other aspects of employees' organizational attachments, producing an overall negative effect on motivation. Evidence from several sources suggests that trade-offs exist between the compensation objectives of performance ratings and employees self-image (Meyer 1975), performance feedback (Meyer, Kay, and French 1965), and organizational commitment (Pearce and Porter 1986).

What Is Good Performance and How Is It Measured?

The 1980s began with considerable discussion about how performance in government should be measured (Perry and Porter 1982). As the 1990s began, federal managers were considerably more adept at applying individual performance measurement, but little conceptual progress has been made on fundamental measurement issues. How individual performance is and should be linked to organizational performance continues to be a concern for most federal agencies. Recent scandals raise questions about how ethical considerations are incorporated into individual performance plans (Brumback 1988). More research and development needs to be invested in improving the state of the art of performance measurement before the promise of merit pay can be realized.

What Motivates Government Employees?

Another area that has received scant attention during the 1980s is public employee motivation. We have learned that a poorly designed pay for performance system does not motivate federal employees. However, little systematic knowledge has been developed about what motivational programs work.

The complexity of motivational problems in most government organizations precludes reliance on a single dominant motivational program. Federal agencies must design reward systems that recognize the range of contextual factors—the types of individuals attracted to the organization, the job itself, the work environment, and changes in the external environment—that influence motivation (Perry and Porter 1982). In addition, managers must be prepared to use a variety of informal rewards—those not mandated by the organization—to influence subordinates' actions (Pearce 1989). One of the liabilities of merit pay during its first ten years is that it diverted federal agencies from giving the attention they should to a range of programs to attract and retain members who will perform both reliably and innovatively.

Is There a Better Way?

One of the most important questions about merit pay involves its opportunity costs. If the federal government were to invest the time and energy currently expended on merit pay in a different way, could it get better results? This question is difficult to answer, because so little information is available about the costs and benefits of merit pay.

One of the ironies of merit pay is that it is money intensive at a time when the federal government is under severe pressure to curb budgetary outlays. The logic of merit pay demands that money be expended commensurate with performance. Other motivational programs are less tied to budget outlays and therefore perhaps more appropriate for today's fiscal situation.

Despite doubts about the utility of merit pay for the federal government, the Federal Employees Pay Comparability Act of 1990 extends pay-for-performance principles to all general schedule employees and requires that legislation be enacted to permit implementation by 1 October 1993. The act calls for new systems, including a replacement for PMRS, to be developed by OPM in conjunction with the pay-for-performance Labor Management Committee. The committee consists of twelve members, including OPM, agency, and employee organization representatives. The committee's role is to review studies on pay for performance and to report to OPM about the design of different systems.

Conclusion

In order to fully understand both the past and future of federal merit pay, it must be viewed from both an instrumental and a symbolic perspective (Eisenhardt 1988). From an instrumental perspective, merit pay is perceived favorably by many managers searching for tools to improve productivity. Conceptually, it offers a concrete reward that is valued by many employees. Furthermore, many employees believe, in the abstract, that performance is an equitable basis for the distribution of rewards. In sum, merit pay is perceived by many organizational participants as a valuable tool for performance management.

From a symbolic perspective, merit pay represents an attempt by politicians, administrators, and the public to assert control over bureaucracy (March and Olsen 1983). It is a message from politicians and the public that the governed are in control and things are as they should be. At the same time, it is a way for administrators to communicate that they are responsive to important external constituencies and that they are doing something about perceptions of lagging performance (Tolbert and Zucker 1983). In sum, merit pay is part of the ritual and myth that helps to retain the legitimacy of the governance system, but it may have little consequence for individual and organizational performance.

The truth about merit pay probably lies between instrumental and symbolic interpretations. Regardless of the reasons for its appeal, merit pay is likely to become a relatively permanent part of federal management. Given its likely permanence, the unresolved issues surrounding merit pay deserve attention from managers and policy makers. If they do not, merit pay will surely represent for future generations of scholars and practitioners an example of Wallace Sayre's old adage —"the triumph of techniques over purpose" (1948).

NOTES

1. My familiarity with merit pay is the outgrowth of a research program that began in 1979. The research has spanned the life of the original merit pay system (MPS) and the current performance management and recognition system (PMRS). The initial research was conducted as part of the Office of Personnel Management's organizational assessments of CSRA, and it has been continued with support from the National Aeronautics and Space Administration and assistance from the General Services Administration.

SOURCES

Brumback, Gary B. 1988. "Some Ideas, Issues and Predictions about Performance Management." *Public Personnel Management* 17:387–402.

Comptroller General of the United States. 1981. *Office of Personnel Management's Implementation of Merit Pay (decision B-203022)*. Washington, D.C.: U.S. General Accounting Office.

Daley, Dennis. 1987. "Merit Pay Enters with a Whimper: The Initial Federal Civil Service Reform Experience." *Review of Public Personnel Administration* 7:72–79.

Eisenhardt, Kathleen M. 1988. "Agency and Institutional-Theory Explanations: The Case of Retail Sales Compensation." *Academy of Management Journal* 31:488–511.

Gartner, Karen H., and Gregory H. Gaertner. 1984. "Performance Evaluation and Merit Pay: Results in the Environmental Protection Agency and Mine Safety and Health Administration." In *Legislating Bureaucratic Change: The Civil Service Reform Act of 1978*, ed. Patricia W. Ingraham and Carolyn Ban, 87–111. Albany: SUNY Press.

————. 1985. "Performance Contingent Pay for Federal Managers." *Administration and Society* 17:7–20.

Lawler, Edward E. III. 1981. *Pay and Organization Development*. Reading, Mass.: Addison-Wesley.

March, James G., and Johan P. Olsen. 1983. "Organizing Political Life: What Administrative Reorganization Tells Us About Government." *American Political Science Review* 77:281–96.

McFee, Thomas S., and Gary B. Brumback. 1988. "Reforming Performance Management: Ten Years and Unfinished." Paper presented at the Tenth Anniversary Review and Assessment of the Civil Service Reform Act of 1978, 18–19 May, Washington, D.C.

McNish, Linda C. 1986. "A Critical Review of Performance Appraisal at the Federal Level: The Experience of the PHS." *Review of Public Personnel Administration* 7:42–56.

Meyer, Herbert H. 1975. "The Pay for Performance Dilemma." *Organizational Dynamics* 3:39–50.

Meyer, H., H. E. Kay, and R. P. French, Jr. 1965. "Split Roles in Perfomance Appraisal." *Harvard Business Review* 43:123–29.

Nigro, Lloyd G. 1982. "CSRA Performance Appraisals and Merit Pay: Growing Uncertainty in the Federal Work Force." *Public Administration Review* 42:371–75.

O'Toole, Daniel E., and John R. Churchill. 1982. "Implementing Pay-for-Performance: Initial Experiences." *Review of Public Personnel Administration* 2 (Summer): 13–28.

Pagano, Michael. 1985. "An Exploratory Evaluation of the Civil Service Reform Act's Merit Pay System for the GS 13–15s: A Case Study of the U.S. Department of Health and Human Services." In *Public Personnel Policy: The Politics of Civil Service*, ed. D. H. Rosenbloom, 161–76. Port Washington, N.Y.: Associated Faculty Press.

Pearce, Jone L. 1989. "Rewarding Performance." In *Handbook of Public Administration*, edited by James L. Perry, 401–11. San Francisco. Jossey-Bass.

Pearce, Jone L., and James L. Perry. 1983. "Federal Merit Pay: A Longitudinal Analysis." *Public Administration Review* 43:315–25.

Pearce, Jone L., and Lyman W. Porter. 1986. "Employee Responses to Formal Performance Appraisal Feedback." *Journal of Applied Psychology* 71:211–18.

Pearce, Jone L., William B. Stevenson, and James L. Perry. 1985. "Managerial Compensation Based on Organizational Performance: A Time Series Analysis of the Impact of Merit Pay." *Academy of Management Journal* 28:261–78.

Perry, James L. 1986. "Merit Pay in the Public Sector: The Case for a Failure of Theory." *Review of Public Personnel Administration* 7:57–69.

Perry, James L., M. C. Hanzlik, and Jone L. Pearce. 1982. "Effectiveness of Merit-Pay-Pool Management." *Review of Public Personnel Administration* 2:5–12.

Perry, James L., and Beth Ann Petrakis. 1987. "Can Merit Pay Improve Performance in Government?" Presented at the Annual Research Conference of the Association for Public Policy Analysis and Management, October 30.

Perry, James L., Beth Ann Petrakis, and Theodore K. Miller. 1989. "Federal Merit Pay, Round II: An Analysis of the Performance Management and Recognition System." *Public Administration Review* 49:29–37.

Perry, James L., and Lyman W. Porter. 1982. "Factors Affecting the Context for Motivation in Public Organizations." *Academy of Management Review* 7:89–98.

President's Reorganization Project. 1977. Personnel Management Project. Vol. 1, *Final Staff Report.* Washington, D.C.: Executive Office of the President.

Sayre, Wallace. 1948. "The Triumph of Techniques over Purpose." *Public Administration Review* 8:134–37.

Schay, Brigitte W. 1988. "Effects of Performance-Contingent Pay on Employee Attitudes." *Public Personnel Management* 17:237–50.

Schwab, Donald P., and Craig A. Olson. 1988. "Pay-Performance Relationships as a Function of Pay for Performance Policies and Practices." In *Best Paper Proceedings,* ed. Frank Hoy, 287–91. Athens, Ga.: Academy of Management.

Tolbert, Pamela S., and Lynne G. Zucker. 1983. "Institutional Sources of Change in the Formal Structure of Organizations: The Diffusion of Civil Service Reform, 1880–1935." *Administrative Science Quarterly* 28:22–39.

U.S. Congress. 1984. House. Committee on Post Office and Civil Service. Subcommittee on Compensation and Employee Benefits. Hearings, *Civil Service Amendments of 1984 and Merit Pay Improvement Act.* 98th Cong. 2d sess.

U.S. GAO (U.S. General Accounting Office). 1981. *Serious Problems Need to Be Corrected Before Federal Merit Pay Goes into Effect* (FPCD–81–73). Washington, D.C.

——— . 1984. *A 2-Year Appraisal of Merit Pay in Three Agencies* (GGD–84–1). Washington, D.C.

——— . 1987a. *Pay for Performance: Implementation of the Performance Management and Recognition System* (GGD–87–28). Washington, D.C.

——— . 1987b. *Status of Personnel Research and Demonstration Programs* (GGD–87–116BR). Washington, D.C.

——— . 1988a. *Information on the National Bureau of Standards Personnel Demonstration Project* (GGD–88–59FS). Washington, D.C.

——— . 1988b. *Observations on the Navy's Personnel Management Demonstration Project* (GGD–88–79). Washington, D.C.

——— . 1989. *Pay for Performance: Interim Report on the Performance Management and Recognition System* (GGD–89–69BR). Washington, D.C.

U.S. MSPB (Merit Systems Protection Board). 1981. *Status Report on Performance Appraisal and Merit Pay Among Mid-Level Employees.* Washington, D.C.

——— . 1987. *Performance Management and Recognition System: Linking Pay to Performance.* Washington, D.C.

——— . 1988. *Toward Effective Performance Management in the Federal Government.* Washington, D.C.

U.S. OPM (Office of Personnel Management). 1981a. *Merit Pay Systems Design.* Washington, D.C.

——— . 1981b. *A Strategy for Evaluating the Civil Service Reform Act of 1978.* Washington, D.C.

——— . 1987. *Performance Management and Recognition System.* Washington, D.C.

——— . 1988. *Performance Management and Recognition System: FY 1986 Performance Cycle.* Washington, D.C.

——— . 1989a. *Performance Management and Recognition System.* Washington, D.C.

——— . 1989b. "Proposed Demonstration Project—A Public Sector Skill-Based Compensation System in a Participatory Work Environment." *Federal Register* 54 (64): 13777–94.

10. Research and Demonstrations Under CSRA
Is Innovation Possible?

Carolyn Ban

The drafters of the Civil Service Reform Act (CSRA) were well aware of the negative image of the federal personnel system; it was perceived as overly rigid and rulebound, as outdated in many respects, and as hampering flexible and creative management. A relatively little-known section of the act, Title VI, was aimed at increasing knowledge of personnel management through systematic research and encouraging agencies to try out new personnel systems on an experimental basis via demonstration projects.

This chapter examines the effects of Title VI. It begins with a discussion of the provisions of the legislation and their history. It describes the actual efforts to date under both the research and demonstration provisions of the act. Finally, it explores the challenges of evaluating demonstration projects and of using the results to affect public policy.

Legislative History

The Civil Service Reform Act grew out of the proposals of the President's Personnel Management Project, a group of nine task forces assembled to study the civil service system. Title VI evolved from the proposals of Task Force 1, which examined the composition and dynamics of the federal work force. Their task force report described the problem and the proposed solution in political terms:

Problem: Real improvement in Federal management will require far reaching changes. Such changes, however, involve high risk and will generate opposition from special interest groups. For both these reasons, the President and Congress will be cautious of many proposals coming from the Personnel Management Project.

Recommendation: Authorize selected agencies with demonstrated management ability to experiment with a variety of incentive and penalty approaches with accompanying relief from ceilings, constraints and other disincentives; establish a mechanism (e.g., joint OMB, CSC, GAO review board) for independent monitorship and evaluation and for subsequent extension of proven techniques governmentwide.

Reasons: Experimentation is more likely to be acceptable. It provides opportunity to time-test new concepts, modify them, and, as their feasibility is demonstrated, extend them incrementally throughout the Federal establishment. Legislation is necessary to exempt test agencies from existing constraints. Incorporation of GAO in the oversight body will provide assurance to Congress in the nominations of test agencies and the continuing oversight of them. (U.S. CSC 1977b:47)

The task force described a proactive process in which agencies would be nominated by the review board to conduct a demonstration based upon such criteria as their management record, quality of labor management relations in the agency, and indication of employee support. The review board would also oversee evaluation (ibid.).

The proposals of the task force were incorporated with little change in the *Final Staff Report* of the PMP, which called for "pilot projects, in selected agencies with demonstrated management ability, to test administrative management, initiative and penalty practices" (U.S. CSC 1977a:124). The final report retained the proposal for a joint "Pilot-Project Oversight Group" for independent monitoring and evaluation. The *Final Staff Report* also included a call to "allocate additional resources to all fields of basic and applied personnel research." In support, it pointed out:

While Federal civilian payroll costs are in the vicinity of $32 billion annually . . . the investment in direct research and development of personnel management systems is less than a million dollars a year. In sharp contrast, the Armed Services spend around $100 million annually on military personnel research.

At a minimum, civilian research and development activities must be expanded if the Federal Government is to comply with extremely rigorous test validation requirements of the new Federal Executive Agency Guidelines on Employee Selection Procedures. Moreover, greater experimental resources and authority are essential to maintaining a positive environment for system reform in the future.

A huge investment and large research staff are unnecessary. The Federal Government can make use of research done in the private sector, state and local governments, the military services, and universities, but presently, resources are inadequate for even that approach. The Office of Personnel Management can map out a comprehensive program based on cooperation among Federal agencies and other organizations, and the executive branch can respond with the resources needed for a successful effort. (ibid.:126)

The act reflects the PMP recommendations, with some significant exceptions. The section on research programs calls on the Office of Personnel Management (OPM) to "establish and maintain (and assist in the establishment and maintenance of) research programs to study improved methods and technologies in federal personnel management." OPM is also charged with evaluating the research conducted and with disseminating information on personnel research.

The section in the act on demonstration programs is more detailed. It empowers OPM to conduct and evaluate demonstration projects on a range of personnel management practices that would not be possible under current civil service law and regulation, inluding recruiting and hiring, classification and compensation, assignment of work, discipline, incentives, work hours, participation in personnel decisions, and staff reductions. Up to ten demonstrations can be in operation at any one time, with a maximum of five thousand employees included in each. Some parts of the law, including leave, insurance, retirement, affirmative action, and the Hatch Act are specifically excluded from waiver for demonstration projects (CSRA, Title VI, Sec. 601). Missing from the law was any mention of a joint oversight board; administration of the demonstrations is by OPM alone.

This section of the law was relatively uncontroversial, although in the hearings on the act the president of the National Treasury Employees Union (NTEU) pointed out the "enormous" potential for abuse in suspending civil service law (U.S. Congress 1978). These provisions of the act were in the mainstream of thought about social policy in the 1970s, an era in which government conducted large-scale social experiments in a number of policy areas (Greenberg and Robins 1985). The idea of experimenting with civil service procedures reflected a straightforward, rational view of the policy process in which the government tries out new approaches to what are essentially technical problems, the evaluation of these approaches yields clear-cut results, making it obvious which new methods work well, and the law or regulations are changed as a result. There is reason to believe that this model was based on naive assumptions, both about the policy process in the personnel field and about the nature of social research.

Implementation of the Research Provisions

The Office of Personnel Management, under Alan Campbell, moved aggressively to implement the section of the act calling for research programs.[1] A separate division, the Research Management Division, was established to oversee the research effort. In addition, OPM had active research units in a number of areas, including recruiting and testing, productivity improvement, and evaluation. Some of the Title VI funding went to specific projects being conducted in-house by these research units. In addition, OPM "commissioned State-of-the-Science papers on selected research topics, developed a public grant program . . . [and] continued pre- and post-doctoral public management research support" (Hansen 1983). For fiscal year 1980, "approximately 20 research projects and/or special studies totaling close to $400,000" were sponsored by the Research Management Division (U.S. OPM 1980c:8–9).

In addition, OPM attempted to carry out the act's charge to disseminate research and to encourage and facilitate the exchange of information among interested parties through several mechanisms. Among them were two conferences on personnel issues, jointly sponsored by OMB, GSA, and GAO (U.S. OPM 1980b, 1981). OPM also published a newsletter to disseminate information about public management research being conducted by various federal agencies. In another major effort to collect and disseminate information about ongoing research, OPM contracted with The National Association of Schools of Public Affairs and Administration (NASPAA) and North Carolina State University to develop inventories of research in public management, which were published and widely disseminated (Garson and Overman 1981, 1982).

Many of these efforts were based on a long-term strategy that assumed stable support for the research effort. But this did not reflect the realities of the political situation. In 1981, Reagan appointed Donald Devine to head OPM. Devine, a staunch conservative, made it clear early in his tenure that he was not interested in continuing the existing research efforts. Devine eliminated funding for research under Title VI and eliminated the Research Management Division, as well as many other research units within the agency. Many researchers were either separated or downgraded as a result of a large reduction in force in 1982. Further, the remnants of the research function were moved so often in the frequent reorganizations that took place under Devine that institutional memory has been lost. Not only were contracted research papers not published or disseminated, copies were apparently not archived, and no one interviewed was able to locate them.

There was some resurgence of interest in research under Devine's successor, Constance Horner. She established the Research and Demonstration Division, which oversees both demonstration and research projects. Its main effort in the area of research has been the development of an agenda to spur research in personnel areas that are seen as high priority. The agenda was developed with extensive consultation and input from other agencies, unions, academics, congressional staffs, and professional associations. The agenda was a one-page document that focused on seven areas: work force demographics, recruitment and retention, compensation, performance management, diversity, training and development, and participation. It was broadly disseminated as a mailer with a tear-sheet soliciting responses (U.S. OPM 1988a).

Under the current director, Constance Newman, interest in encouraging research has continued. In the absence of any resources to support research, OPM is attempting to play a broker role, offering scholars assistance "for liaison with other researchers addressing similar issues, for presentation and publication opportunities and for access to Federal data sources" (ibid.).

OPM is also attempting to foster communication among researchers and between researchers and practitioners, by hosting conferences on personnel research (see, for example, U.S. OPM 1989c) and by publishing a research newsletter, *Personnel Research Highlights.*

Implementation of the Demonstration Provision

While the act authorized up to ten demonstration projects, until quite recently only one major demonstration, being conducted by the United States Navy, had been approved. This section begins with a discussion of the management problems that have plagued the demonstration effort. It then turns to a discussion of the navy demonstration and the recent upsurge of interest in demonstrations.

The administrative process that OPM established differed in significant ways from that originally envisioned by the Personnel Management Project. First, there was no involvement of other central management agencies; approval and administration was solely OPM's responsibility. Second, the process was a passive one. OPM did not select agencies for demonstrations or actively solicit proposals; rather, it waited for agencies to come in with proposals, to which it responded. Often, in the early years, OPM's response was that the proposal did not need a waiver of civil service law to implement and so was inappropriate for a demonstration. There was no attempt to support agencies that wished to try new approaches within existing law—to assist them, help evaluate their efforts, or disseminate results. This passive stance occasioned considerable debate within OPM at the time. Indeed, even the navy demonstration had problems receiving approval from OPM staff; the developers of the proposal eventually went over staff heads directly to OPM's director, Alan Campbell.

As recently as 1987, this passive stance was still a problem. In response to a recent General Accounting Office (GAO) survey of agencies to find out why so few agencies chose to carry out demonstration projects, a "common theme in the suggestions was that OPM needed to be less reactive and more proactive in administering the program. . . . Ten of the respondents (38 percent) indicated that OPM should take a more active role in the projects, particularly in the early or initial stages." More broadly, several respondents believed that when Devine was director, OPM was not very supportive of research and demonstration efforts (U.S. GAO 1987: app. 1, p. 16).

Agencies faced other obstacles in developing demonstration proposals. Budget cuts after 1980 meant that fewer agencies had the resources to conduct such experiments. The most common reason given in the GAO survey for not proposing demonstrations was agency unwillingness to commit the time and resources required. Many also mentioned the "difficulty in getting a proposal through the [internal] agency approval process (chain of command)" (ibid.:15). The process of OPM and congressional approval is also cumbersome and time-consuming.

There has clearly been increased support for demonstrations under Constance Horner and Constance Newman. In 1986, OPM attempted to demystify the process by issuing an *Informational Guide* (U.S. OPM 1986b). OPM staff work closely with agencies developing demonstration proposals. And they have attempted, although not yet successfully, to develop a plan for a demonstration and then "sell" it to an agency.

Another possible issue, which was not mentioned by the GAO report, was the daunting model of the navy demonstration project itself.

The demonstration program may have been hurt by the fact that the very first demonstration was an extremely ambitious and large-scale project that affected many aspects of personnel management. This project may have set unreasonably high expectations and intimidated smaller agencies, deterring them from proposing more modest changes via the demonstration process.

On the other hand, the recent upsurge of interest in demonstrations appears to reflect a change in attitude. For many agencies, federal salaries are so far below the market in critical fields, and agencies are having such severe problems in recruiting and retention, that they may see the demonstration provision as one of the few sources of flexibility in the system. They are apparently seeing the costs and hassles of the process as worth putting up with because of the severity of their personnel problems.

The Navy Demonstration

The first—and for many years, the only—major demonstration project was begun in 1980 at two navy labs: the Naval Ocean Systems Center (NOSC) in San Diego and the Naval Weapons Center (NWC) in China Lake, California.[2] Demonstrations normally run for five years; the navy demonstration has been extended twice and now will run until at least 1995.

The navy demonstration is an ambitious one that changed many aspects of personnel administration in order to give line managers a greater role in personnel decisions and to increase the labs' ability to hire and retain high-quality employees. It introduced a simplified, flexible position classification system that grouped occupations into five broad career paths: professional, technical, administrative, technical specialist, and clerical-assistant. Instead of the traditional eighteen pay grades, broad pay bands were established for each career path, with flexible starting salaries and with salary increases linked to performance appraisal. The "objectives-based" performance appraisal system was designed to link the individual's functions to organizational goals (U.S. OPM 1984; see also U.S. OPM 1980a).

The project has been extensively evaluated. OPM's *Summary Assessment* reported positive results: position classification under the new system was simpler and less time-consuming. Employees saw a greater link between pay and performance. Flexible starting salaries increased the ability of the labs to compete with the private sector in hiring, and turnover at the demonstration labs decreased, while increasing at the two labs used as controls. Supervisors perceived more control over both classification and pay, and the performance appraisal system was seen as fairer, more flexible, and leading to improved communication and goal-setting. The evaluation was unable to assess the effects of the project on overall laboratory effectiveness (U.S. OPM 1986a). The most recent study (U.S. OPM 1991) found that it was easier to recruit, and there were some indications that quality of new hires was higher, particularly at China Lake.

An in-depth analysis of survey results from the experimental and control labs from 1979 to 1987 sheds light on the long-term nature of implementing new personnel systems. It found that initial reactions to the demonstration were quite negative at both sites, with only 29 percent of employees in favor of the demonstration. Attitudes changed quite slowly, only reaching the 50 percent support level in 1985. By 1987, 66 percent at NOSC and 72 percent at NWC agreed that they were in favor of the demonstration project (Schay 1988a). In addition, recent analysis of turnover data showed not only that turnover was lower at the demonstration labs than at the control labs, but that the demonstration was meeting its intended goal of aiding in the retention of high performers; turnover rates of superior performers were consistently lower at the demonstration sites than at the control labs (Miller 1988). Turnover at the labs was found to be linked to pay satisfaction and perceived pay equity (Schay 1988b).

One concern about the navy demonstration was the escalation of personnel costs, but a recent study found that, after rising steadily in the earlier years, costs have leveled off at 5–6 percent above the control labs (Simons and Thompson 1990).

The evaluation of the navy demonstration had both management and technical problems, particularly in the early years. The evaluation was begun by the University of Southern California, then contracted out to Coopers and Lybrand, and finally moved in-house to OPM. Partly as a result, the evaluation suffered from what GAO termed "substantial missing data . . . [that] included absent baseline measures, incomplete project data, and limited responses to annual employee surveys" (U.S. GAO 1988b:app. 1, p. 14). GAO also raised questions about the comparability of the two comparison labs as well as about whether the findings could be generalized to other locations.

Table 12. Status of Demonstration Projects

Agency	Year Approved	Year Implemented
Navy	1980	1980
Federal Aeronautics Administration (airway science)	1982	1983
Air Force	1987	1988
NIST	1987	1988
Federal Bureau of Investigation	1988	1988
Federal Aeronautics Administration (pay)	1988	1989
Agriculture	1989	1990

Current Demonstrations and Proposals

For several years, for reasons discussed above, the navy demonstration was the only major demonstration. From 1983 to 1991, the Federal Aviation Administration (FAA) conducted a smaller-scale demonstration, the airway science project, established to help rebuild their work force after the air traffic controller strike. FAA worked with colleges and universities to develop a specific airway science curriculum, graduates of which would be hired through an alternative selection method. Since individuals graduated only in year four of the demonstration, only five graduates had been hired by the end of five years, so the project was extended to permit a full evaluation of graduates' performance on the job (U.S. OPM 1988a, 1983; Kellam 1988b). By 1991, it was evident to both OPM and FAA that the demonstration was not successful, and it was ended by mutual agreement.

Since 1987, the increased interest in demonstrations has become evident. Table 12 lists the demonstrations to date and gives the year they were approved and the year of implementation. Two of the more recent demonstrations clearly show the influence of the navy demonstration. Each includes simplified classification systems and pay banding.

The National Institute of Standards and Technology (NIST) is implementing a project modeled after the navy demonstration, including simplified classification with broad bands and performance-based pay. But they have added several new wrinkles, including total compensation comparability (with annual pay increases based on comparison of pay and benefits to the private sector), expanded direct hire and delegated examination authority, flexible probationary periods, and recruitment and retention bonuses (U.S. OPM 1987a; U.S. GAO 1988a). The agency is attempting to implement the project as "budget-neutral," a significant departure from navy, which saw personnel costs rise by about 1 percent a year during its demonstration (U.S. OPM 1986a).

This demonstration was originally opposed by OPM because it was so similar to the navy's and because it was not budget-neutral. As a result, the agency went around OPM directly to Congress to get approval, but this still counts as one of the ten demonstrations permitted under CSRA, and OPM was charged by Congress with its evaluation. The evaluation effort has encountered problems both because the project was implemented on such a short timetable that there was no time for baseline data collection and because of problems in communication with the agency caused by opposition at the Department of Commerce (Thompson 1989).

Early reports show that NIST is actively using its expanded direct hire authority and that pay for performance has been significantly strengthened, but that recruitment and retention allowances are used sparingly. The director of NIST has chosen not to implement total compensation comparability but rather has given NIST employees the standard General Schedule pay increases (Schemmer et al. 1990).

The air force implemented a demonstration at McClellan Air Logistics Center in 1988. Known as Pacer Share, this ambitious project resembles navy's in its use of classification simplification and pay banding but goes well beyond navy in its focus on participative management methods and on group rather than individual incentives. Perhaps most controversial, the project eliminates individual performance appraisals in favor of measures of organizational performance, including statistical quality control procedures advocated by productivity expert Dr. W. Edwards Deming (U.S. OPM 1987b). Improved organizational performance is rewarded through productivity gain sharing. It is also significant that this is the first demonstration to directly involve a federal union (Kellam 1988a). The goals of the demonstration are improved product and service quality and cost savings through greater productivity and increased staffing flexibility (Gilbert and Nelson 1989; U.S. OPM 1987b).

Pacer Share has encountered some initial problems; budget cuts at the Defense Department were announced just as the project began. The resulting workload reduction has meant that there were no productivity gain sharing payouts for the first year. Further, introducing a broad change in organizational culture is difficult. Negotiations with the unions have been lengthy, and initial employee support is quite low (Kellam 1988a; Schay 1989). More recently, the consolidation of defense logistics installations has meant that Pacer Share staff were split between air force and the Defense Logistics Agency (DLA), which is making administration of the demonstration difficult.

DLA had planned to implement a demonstration in 1990 at a depot in Ogden, Utah, testing skill-based compensation, with staff divided into teams and pay raises linked to acquiring the range of skills needed to perform the team's functions. The goal was improved organizational flexibility (U.S. OPM 1989b). Unfortunately, this demonstration was canceled after four years of planning because changes in DLA's work load and reorganization plans made the project impracticable (Rafshoon 1990).

Two newer demonstrations focus more narrowly on compensation. Both the FBI and the FAA are experimenting with forms of locality pay in an effort to attract people to move to areas where positions have become hard to fill. The FBI's demonstration rewards people to move to, or stay in, the New York City area. It includes lump-sum payments of $20,000 for those who accept direct reassignment to New York and agree to stay there at least three years, as well as pay supplements of 25 percent for those stationed in New York. Those who leave before the three-year period is over must repay the $20,000 bonus. An additional requirement is that participating individuals must agree to live within a fifty-mile radius of New York, since one problem the demonstration was designed to correct was adequate response time. Those who are already working in the New York office get the 25 percent pay supplement but not the initial bonus (P.L. 100–453, 29 September 1988, Title VI; Miller 1989). The initial assessment describes the effects after one year as "dramatic," with sharp increases in the number of experienced special agents transferring to New York and reductions in resignations, especially resignations in lieu of transfer to New York (U.S. OPM and FBI 1990).

FAA's demonstration covers ten sites that are seen as key to the national network. Individuals in safety-related occupations, including not only air traffic controllers but also safety inspectors and maintenance technicians, will receive a retention allowance of up to 20 percent. The Federal Register notice states: "Although it does not require waiver of laws or regulations, this personnel system change is being conducted as a demonstration project because it involves the creation of a new pay system in which retention allowances serve as an alternative to other pay adjustments" (U.S. OPM 1988b:44268).

In fact, both the FAA and FBI demonstrations have come under fire as being less real experiments with new personnel systems than ways to beat the rigidities of the federal pay system. Since those demonstrations were initiated, the federal pay system has been reformed with passage of the Federal Employee Pay Comparability Act (FEPCA). It is too early to assess the impact of FEPCA on the pay demonstrations.

The newest demonstration, at the Department of Agriculture, was implemented in 1990. It is introducing several major changes in the examination and selection process. These include expanded use of direct hire and introduction of a new examination scoring process that replaces numerical ranking with broad "quality groups." In this process, those who meet the minimum qualifications are placed into two categories, "quality" and "eligible." Managers can then hire anyone from the "quality" group. In addition, the current one-year probationary period and three-year career-conditional status are replaced by a provisional appointment of three years for scientists and engineers and two years for other appointments. Finally, Agriculture will be able to use recruitment incentives, including bonuses and payment of relocation expenses. The demonstration is taking place at one hundred sites in the Forest Service and the Agricultural Research Service (U.S. OPM 1989a; Thompson 1989).

The interest in demonstration projects shows no sign of slackening. The most recent inventory of demonstration projects and proposals (U.S. OPM 1989a) lists six projects currently under consideration. (This includes Agriculture, which has since been approved.) Since there are currently seven approved demonstrations and the law sets a cap of ten projects, OPM may soon have to request a change in the law, or it will have to face extremely hard choices between worthy projects. However, interest in new demonstrations may decline temporarily as agencies assess the impact of the 1990 pay reform.

Other changes in the law may also be advisable. Some would urge that more large-scale demonstrations should be permitted. And there is increasing support for permitting demonstrations on leave policy and on benefits (U.S. GAO 1988c). Given OPM's past experience with the research provisions of the act, one important change is to assure that the Records Act is enforced and that proper records are kept so that institutional memory is not lost.

The Policy Impact of the Navy Demonstration

While the other demonstrations are still being conducted and evaluated, the navy demonstration has been in progress for nearly a decade. It has been extensively evaluated and is well known within the personnel community. What effect has it had on policy? An examination of the navy demonstration permits us to address some general questions about the problematic relationship between demonstrations and policy.

OPM sees the navy demonstration as a clear success and has pressed for full implementation on a voluntary basis. This was a high-priority issue for the past OPM director, Constance Horner, and especially for her deputy, James Colvard, a career SES member who came to OPM from navy. OPM introduced bills in 1987 and 1988 calling for an incremental implementation of the navy reforms throughout the federal government. The proposed Civil Service Simplification Act has been faulted for providing few specifics on how this would be done (Marzotto 1988). One key difference was that the administration proposed a budget-neutral implementation, when, as we saw above, the navy reforms increased salary costs significantly.

GAO has opposed such extensions of the navy model on several grounds. First, they feel that flaws in the evaluation mean that the effectiveness of the demonstration has yet to be proven. Second, they point out that a budget-neutral version has never been tested. Finally, they raise general questions about whether demonstration results can be generalized. As they point out, "[T]he fact that a particular program is found to be successful does not mean that its findings can be generalized across different people, settings, and times." They recommend replication of the project to "ascertain its applicability to other settings" (U.S. GAO 1988b:app. 1, 20–21).

There have also been legislative proposals for expanded demonstrations in the pay area, including one bill, the Federal Pay Reform Act (H.R. 3132), introduced by Representative Gary Ackerman, which was particularly controversial because it called for testing use of collective bargaining for setting pay as one of ten experiments.

OPM's current director, Constance Newman, has pushed a different legislative agenda. Broader reform based on the navy demonstration model was placed on the back burner because of the perceived urgency of the pay issue. Newman was successful in getting congressional approval of a pay reform package, the Federal Employees Pay

Comparability Act of 1990, that starts to reduce the disparity between salaries in the private sector and the federal government and that puts into place, governmentwide, one of the key concepts tested in two recent demonstrations: locality pay.

Interestingly, the call for classification reform has moved outside of OPM. The National Academy of Public Administration recently issued a major report entitled *Modernizing Federal Classification: An Opportunity for Excellence*. The broad-banding model they propose clearly owes a great deal to both the navy and NIST demonstrations. It is not clear whether the current OPM leadership will support this proposal.

Demonstrations and Policy: The Uncertain Linkage

The difficulties in implementing the navy demonstration more broadly are far from unique. None of the large-scale social experiments conducted by the government to try out innovative social programs has yet been implemented (Greenberg and Robins 1985:23). Implementation is difficult both because of the nature of the research process and the nature of the evaluation process. The two, in fact, are closely connected.

Evaluation of major demonstration projects will always be difficult, even under ideal circumstances (which almost never exist). First, because of the nature of demonstration projects, a true experimental design with random assignment of subjects is impossible, because the level of analysis is organizational, not individual. But years of experience have shown that "the use of nonrandom comparison groups—the strongest and most widely used of the nonexperimental approaches—often yielded misleading or uninterpretable results" (Orr 1985:578).

Other problems are posed by the complex and changing environment in which the research is conducted. Typically, new projects are continually changed during the implementation, posing problems for researchers. Further, evaluators face serious measurement problems when the goals are such broad concepts as organizational effectiveness or individual productivity, neither of which are amenable to measurement in most governmental settings. Finally, the long time period needed for such studies poses technical problems, such as the attrition of the study population, as well as political problems.

The policy process itself is also an issue. The logic underlying the use of demonstration projects is that, once ideas have been tested and found workable, a consensus to implement them will emerge. This rational model ignores the real-world political environment in which personnel policy is made. In some cases, the technical difficulty in conducting experiments (or demonstrations) increases the conservative effects of conducting experiments:

The availability of scientific evidence shifts attention [from moral issues] to methodological issues that are complex in nature and generally have no clearcut solutions. Controversy then ensues about the merits of the proposed program, creating a cautionary environment that ultimately reduces the probability of eventual enactment of the program. (Greenberg and Robins 1985:25)

In the case of the navy demonstration, controversies about the adequacy of the evaluation and its generalizability to the rest of the federal work force have been major stumbling blocks.

The time lags required for long-term demonstrations also cause problems in the policy arena; by the time a new approach has been tested, the results may be irrelevant because the political environment has changed. This was certainly true for the well-known negative income tax experiments conducted in the 1970s (ibid.:26). In the case of the navy demonstration, the current emphasis on budget neutrality was not anticipated by the demonstration's designers.

Another problem in attempting implementation is that reforms are not seen as simply technical corrections; they are often caught up in a broader political process and are judged according to who is supporting them. Virtually all personnel proposals originating in OPM in Reagan's first term engendered skeptical responses on the Hill and hostile reactions from the unions simply because Devine was so mistrusted and disliked. While Horner did not trigger such strong reactions, personnel issues are now embedded in partisan politics, which affect OPM's ability to get proposals through Congress. Newman's recent success in getting pay reform approved by Congress is an indication both of her willingness to push needed reform and of her ability to forge the political alliances necessary to get legislation passed. It remains to be seen whether OPM will push for further change and whether these coalitions will support future legislative initiatives.

Finally, although there is no sign that this was true of the navy demonstration in particular, we need to recognize that research itself may be a response to a political process. Demonstration projects may be instituted to satisfy an agency constituency (U.S. GAO 1983).[3] Research projects are also begun for symbolic reasons or to delay making a decision (Ban and Ferrara 1988). In such cases, we would obviously expect less than strenuous efforts to push for full implementation.

In spite of all these problems, demonstrations may have significant effects that are more gradual or indirect. Carol Weiss has discussed the "enlightenment model" of evaluation, in which "the concepts and theoretical perspectives that social science research has engendered . . . permeate the policy-making process" (1979:429). This has clearly been the case with the navy demonstration. The personnel community, particularly within the federal government, is very well informed about the navy demonstration model, which has provided a clear alternative to the traditional system and has influenced the terms of the debate.

The NAPA report is clear evidence that this is so. While full implementation has not occurred, two new demonstrations, at the National Institute of Standards and Technology and at McClellan Air Force Base, expand upon and retest aspects of the navy demonstration. And large numbers of agencies have expressed interest in adopting similar systems. As Weiss says, "When the findings and the intellectual structure of evaluation begin to shape the way that decision makers think about an issue—and the elements of it that they think about—evaluation has been 'used' " (1988:17).

NOTES

1. To reveal both my sources and my possible biases, I want to clarify my personal relationship to OPM's research effort. From 1979 through 1982, I served as a staff member and then as acting chief of the division charged with evaluating the Civil Service Reform Act at OPM. This division was housed in the same office as the Research Management Division, and the staffs worked closely together on such projects as the Brookings conferences discussed below. This section of the chapter is based both on personal experience during this period and on interviews with those involved in the research function since 1982.

2. The navy demonstration is commonly referred to as "China Lake," but this is inappropriate because it ignores the participation of NOSC.

3. More than half the HUD demonstrations GAO examined had not been evaluated.

SOURCES

Ban, Carolyn, and Elysa Ferrara. 1988. "Expanding the Concept of Utilization: Case Studies in the Organizational Uses of Evaluation." Unpublished.

Garrison, G. David, and E. Sam Overman. 1981, 1982. *Public Management Research Directory,* Vols. 1 and 2. Washington, D.C.: OPM.

Gilbert, G. Ronald, and Ardel E. Nelson. 1989. "The Pacer Share Demonstration Project: Implications for Organization Management and Performance Evaluation." *Public Personnel Management* 18:209–25.

Greenberg, David, and Philip Robins. 1985. "The Changing Role of Social Experiments in Policy Analysis." In *Evaluation Studies Review Annual,* vol. 10, ed. Linda Aiken and Barbara Kehrer, Beverly Hills: Sage.

Hansen, Michael G. 1983. "Introduction: Linking Public Management Sponsors, Procedures, and Users." *Public Administration Quarterly* 7 (Summer): 132–38.

Kellam, Susan. 1988a. "McClellan AFB Pay Experiment Getting Favorable Reviews." *Federal Times,* 26 September.

———. 1988b. "Varied Pay Projects Awaiting Approval." *Federal Times,* 17 October.

Marzotto, Toni. 1988. "The Fragmentation of the Federal Workforce." Presented at the annual meeting of the American Political Science Association.

Miller, Demaris H. 1988. *Turnover in the Navy Demonstration Laboratories, 1980– 1985.* Washington, D.C.: U.S. Office of Personnel Management.

———. 1989. Interview. Washington, D.C. Research and Demonstration Division, U.S. Office of Personnel Management.

NAPA (National Academy of Public Administration). 1991. *Modernizing Federal Classification: An Opportunity for Excellence.* Washington, D.C.: NAPA.

Orr, Larry L. 1985. "Using Experimental Methods to Evaluate Demonstration Projects." In *Evaluation Studes Review Annual,* vol. 10, ed. Linda Aiken and Barbara Kehrer. Beverly Hills: Sage.

Rafshoon, Ellen. 1990. "Ogden Cancels Pay Test." *Federal Times,* 15 October.

Schay, Brigitte W. 1988a. *Effects of Performance-Based Pay on Employees in the Navy Demonstration Project: An Analysis of Survey Responses 1979 to 1987.* Washington, D.C.: U.S. Office of Personnel Management.

———. 1988b. "Effects of Performance-Contingent Pay on Employee Attitudes." *Public Personnel Management* 17:237–50.

———. 1989. Interview. Washington, D.C.: Research and Demonstration Division, U.S. Office of Personnel Management.

Schemmer, F. Mark, Darrell J. Cira, Kerry Yarkin-Levin, and Arthur Korotkin (University Research Corporation). 1990. *National Institute of Standards and Technology Personnel Management Demonstration Project: the Second Year Evaluation Report: 1989.* PSO-220. Washington, D.C.: U.S. Office of Personnel Management.

Simons, K. Craig, and Paul Thompson. 1990. *Salary Costs Under the Navy Demonstration Project.* Washington, D.C.: U.S. Office of Personnel Management.

Thompson, Paul. 1989. Interview. Washington, D.C., Research Demonstration Division, U.S. Office of Personnel Management.

U.S. CSC (Civil Service Commission). 1977a. "Personnel Management Project." Vol. 1, *Final Staff Report.* Washington, D.C.: USCSC.

———. 1977b. "Personnel Management Project." Vol. 2, *Appendices to the Final Staff Report.* Washington, D.C.: USCSC.

U.S. Congress. 1978. House. Committee on Post Office and Civil Service Hearings on HR 11280. Statement of Vincent Connery.

U.S. GAO (U.S. General Accounting Office). 1983. *Hud Demonstration Programs— Their Use as a Policy Tool.* (GAO/IPE–83–4). Washington, D.C.: U.S. GAO.

———. 1987. *Federal Personnel: Status of Personnel Research and Demonstration Projects* (GAO/GGD–87–116BR). Washington, D.C.: U.S. GAO.

———. 1988a. *Federal Workforce: Information on the National Bureau of Standards Personnel Demonstration Project* (GAO/GGD–88–59FS). Washington, D.C.

———. 1988b. *Federal Personnel: Observations on the Navy's Personnel Management Demonstration Project* (GAO/GGD–88–79). Washington, D.C.

———. 1988c. *Civil Service Reform: Development of Civil Service Reform Proposals by the Carter Administration* (GAO/GGD–89–18). Washington, D.C.

U.S. OPM (U.S. Office of Personnel Management). 1980a. "Proposed Demonstration Project: An Integrated Approach to Pay, Performance Appraisal, and Position Classification for More Effective Operation for Government Organizations." *Federal Register,* 18 April: 26504–43.

———. 1980b. *Setting Public Management Research Agendas: Integrating the Sponsor, Producer and User.* Proceedings of the Public Management Research Conference, 19–20 November, 1979, Brookings Institution. Cosponsored by GAO, GSA, OMB, and OPM. Washington, D.C.

———. 1980c. *Public Management Research 2* (Fall).

———. 1981. *The Changing Character of the Public Work Force.* Proceedings of the 2nd Public Management Research Conference, 17–18 November, 1980, Brookings Institution. Cosponsored by GAO, GSA, OMB, and OPM. Washington, D.C.

———. 1983. "Airway Science Curriculum: Approval of Demonstration Project Final Plan." *Federal Register* 15 July: 32490–99.

———. 1984. *Status of the Evaluation of the Navy Personnel Management Demonstration Project: Management Report I.* Washington, D.C.

———. 1986a. *A Summary Assessment of the Navy Demonstration Project: Management Report IX.* Washington, D.C.

———. 1986b. *Developing Research and Demonstration Projects: An Informational Guide.* Washington, D.C.

———. 1987a. "Personnel Management Demonstration Project: Alternative Personnel Management System at the National Bureau of Standards; Notice of Approval." *Federal Register* 2 October: 370821–96.

———. 1987b. "Proposed Demonstration Project: Pacer Share: A Federal Productivity Enhancement Program: Notice of Final Approval." *Federal Register* 20 November: 44782–810.

———. 1988a. "Research Agenda."

———. 1988b. "Proposed Demonstration Project: Department of Transportation/ Federal Aviation Administration." *Federal Register* 2 November: 44265–71.

——— 1989a. "Inventory of Demonstration Projects and Proposals."

———. 1989b. "Proposed Demonstration Project: A Public Sector Skill-Based Compensation System in a Participatory Work Environment." *Federal Register* 5 April: 12777–94.

———. 1989c. *Personnel Research Conference Proceedings.*

————. 1991. *Recruitment of Scientists and Engineers in Four Navy Laboratories.* Management Report 14. Washington, D.C.

U.S. OPM (U.S. Office of Personnel Management) and Federal Bureau of Investigation. 1990. *First Annual Assessment of the FBI's New York Demonstration Project.* PSO-219. Washington, D.C.

Weiss, Carol H. 1979. "The Many Meanings of Research Utilization." *Public Administration Review* 39:426–31.

————. 1988. "Evaluation for Decisions: Is Anybody There? Does Anybody Care?" *Evaluation Practice* 9, 1 (February):5–20.

Part IV THE LESSONS OF REFORM

Introduction
The Limits of Reform

John A. Rohr

For the originators of civil service reform in the 1970s the limits of reform were surely many, varied, and formidable. Their task of overcoming these limits in order to bring about the reform was far more difficult than my own task of simply looking back over ten years from my academic sanctuary and commenting on but a few of them. Since the chapters included in this collection discuss many of these limits in great detail, I offer a somewhat different perspective by showing how the limits on *any* sort of reform in American government affected the Civil Service Reform Act of 1978. These persistent limits are constitutional, political, and historical.

Constitutional Limits

The most interesting example of a constitutional limitation on reform concerns the sensible effort to treat personnel questions rationally by vesting management powers in one agency, the Office of Personnel Management (OPM), and by creating another agency, the Merit Systems Protection Board (MSPB), to defend the integrity of the merit principle. The management agency, though technically independent of the president, was really under his control and was intended to be so. The protection board was to be independent of the president in both a technical and practical sense.

There was a commendable rationality behind this plan, but it soon encountered problems emanating from the cardinal constitutional principle of separation of powers. No one could seriously expect Congress or even the courts to lose interest in personnel management matters simply because of the creation of a new office tasked with directing personnel affairs. This became quite apparent in an interesting controversy over the president's constitutional powers to remove the director of the Office of Government Ethics (OGE).

OGE was established by the Ethics in Government Act of 1978. The office was headed by a director appointed by the president with the advice and consent of the Senate. OGE was housed in the Office of Personnel Management and, under the logic of the Civil Service Reform Act (CSRA), was therefore firmly under the control of the president. In 1983, OGE underwent the customary five-year review required by the sunset statute. Not surprisingly, congressional critics of OGE questioned the propriety of an ethics office being under the control of the president. Discussion focused in particular on the president's unfettered power to remove the director of OGE.

A Senate bill proposed limiting the president's removal power over the director by imposing a "for cause only" requirement. This brought a sharp rejoinder from the Justice Department, arguing that the director was clearly an executive officer and therefore Congress could not constitutionally condition the president's power to remove him. Defenders of the bill argued that the director of OGE should be independent of the president. This debate mirrored in miniature the CSRA debate of 1978 and showed how difficult it is in principle to define *personnel management.* Is the director of OGE a person who should be managed by the president's personnel office? Are questions of ethics appropriately put under presidential management? If so, then who will guard the guards when the ethics of the president himself or his closest associates are under review? If not, how can one justify removing ethical standards from presidential control without impairing the president's solemn constitutional obligation to "take care that the laws are faithfully executed"?

The upshot of this debate was an unsatisfactory compromise that blurred the issue by conferring a five-year statutory term upon the director, on the one hand, and by permitting the president to remove him at any time within that five-year period, on the other. As a consolation prize, OGE won a budget line independent of OPM's line. Eventually, during its second sunset review in 1988, OGE became a fully independent agency. The vagaries of OGE point to the larger problem of stating with any precision just what is meant by a personnel management issue under a regime driven by separation of powers.

Political Limits

One of the most startling aspects of the debate over CSRA was the candor of its proponents in defending the proposed senior executive service (SES) on the grounds that it would increase the political responsiveness of career civil servants. One might challenge the wisdom of such legislation, but no one can deny that this was a fundamental consideration in the creation of the SES. The career civil service has been partially but significantly politicized *by law*. This was a fundamental change in the civil service tradition of the United States, but, unfortunately, students and practitioners of public administration have been remiss in developing a new normative theory of public administration to fit the new legal realities. This I attribute to the political limitations on reform.

Even ten years after CSRA's legal politicization, we still speak uncomfortably of "administrative statesmanship"; but this is clearly what the new, politicized role of the senior civil service requires. Prudence urges caution in trumpeting the new statesmanship role for civil servants, and this is a consequence of the political limitation on reform. It is not politically expedient to use this sort of language. As a consequence, the reform is in place but we have not yet developed a set of normative standards that will enable it to work. We still talk about the civil service as though nonpartisanship were the appropriate norm, when clearly it is bipartisanship.

Thus far the political accountability of career civil servants bears little resemblance to statesmanship of any kind. To date, we have seen little more than the unedifying spectacle of political bullies punishing and humiliating institutional weaklings. One reason for the institutional weakness of senior civil servants is the absence of a normative theory to ground principled, partisan support for the president and principled resistance as well. The absence of sound theory has created a vacuum that has been filled by raw executive power; political accountability has been perverted into cringing subservience.

Ten years after CSRA might be the time to overcome the limits politics has imposed on reform. The worst excesses of the bureaucrat-bashing era are probably behind us. The Volcker Commission report heralds a happier day. For a start, we might recall Alan Campbell's statement that one of the goals of the SES was to render "appropriate responsiveness to the government's political leadership, while resisting improper political influence." Perhaps we are now ready to put some specific content into Campbell's Delphic utterance. Perhaps we are ready to assemble and analyze cases and principles that will help us to identify "appropriate responsiveness" on the one hand and "improper political influence" on the other. It would seem that the academic wing of the public administration community should take the lead in this matter. Academics are not nearly as vulnerable to political reprisals as their practitioner confreres. There would be a certain justice in this as well, because of the salient role academics played in bringing us CSRA in the first place. With a convincing bipartisan theory of public administration in place, we could look forward to the day when senior executives will gather with impunity during presidential campaigns to prepare position papers on how their agencies could implement the policy positions advocated by the leading candidates.

Historical Limits

If I were to single out the one moment during the Syracuse conference that made the most lasting impression on me, it would surely be the revelation that all the talk about generalists in the senior executive service was just "academic pablum" the proponents of reform "fed the professors" to keep them happy. I was well aware, of course, that the senior executives had not become generalists over the past ten years, but I was quite surprised to learn that support for this idea in 1978 was disingenuous. The "academic pablum" remark occurred during the discussion of one of the conference papers and came from a person exceptionally well qualified to discuss the origins of CSRA. There was no demur to this assessment from any of the conference participants who had firsthand knowledge of the CSRA story.

The reason I was so impressed by this revelation was that I was one of the academic consumers of the reformers' pablum. I took the generalist idea seriously even if they did not. There seemed to be an informal consensus among those present at the Syracuse conference that the generalist idea was not very likely to ever find its way into practice in the United States. The reason was historical. We were told— correctly, I suppose— that American public administration has come down firmly and definitively on the specialist side of the generalist-specialist debate. No one went so far as to say that history is destiny, but it surely qualifies as a limit to reform. We will not have generalists because we have never had generalists.

I still happen to think that generalists in public administration would be desirable, even though I am ready to concede that our history makes it unlikely that this will ever come about in the United States. One reason I would favor it is that it would accommodate nicely the legitimate political role of senior civil servants under the CSRA. A senior civil servant who had made himself obnoxious to the president because of his views on the environment might be able to get a fresh start in defense procurement or social security. If such transfers were made routinely and without any embarrassment, there would be impressive institutional support for civil servants to act like statesmen without running intolerable risks.

History can be a wholesome limit on reform because it counsels prudence, restraint, and common sense. Unfortunately, however, it can also stifle our institutional imagination. To be sure, we are a nation of specialists and so we should not find it remarkable that our administrative practices mirror this national trait; but this is no excuse to adhere mindlessly to our own ways of doing things. Perhaps a judicious use of comparative administrative studies might enable us to consider alternatives without forgetting what our past has made us.

During the debates over CSRA, there were occasional references to the British model to support the generalist idea. These references were quite general. As far as I know, there was no careful study of just how the British model might pertain to generalist administrators in the United States in the absence of a parliamentary form of government. This neglect was unfortunate. Had serious comparative studies been available, the generalist idea might have been taken more seriously. Or it might have been dismissed with candor.

It is not too late to undertake such studies. Indeed, Mark Huddleston's contribution to this volume is an important step in this direction. At the very least, Huddleston makes a convincing case that our senior executive service is not a service at all. French administrative practice might well prove as enlightening as that of the British. Through its corps system, especially the *grands corps,* French public administration is specialized. However, French administrators often leave their corps temporarily to serve in various ministries with activities pertinent to the specializations of the various corps—engineering, law, finance, diplomacy, and so forth. This broadens the administrator's perspective without forcing him to abandon his professional expertise. The French system is not without its problems. Critics complain about the way the *grands corps* "colonize" the ministries. Americans, however, who study such institutions do not intend to adopt the entire French administrative system. The goal is not imitation but a highly selective adaptation and integration into our own institutions of practice that seem useful.

I mention the French practice only to support the broader point that we undertake comparative administrative studies in order to mitigate the limits that history places on reform. Comparative studies have the merit of forcing us to look beyond our own traditions, but, precisely because other nations are involved, such studies caution against slavish imitation. Students of American administrative history are well aware of the Anglophile excesses of the original civil service reformers. We can imitate their cosmopolitan interests without imitating their uncritical acceptance of what they found in other nations.

11. Representative Bureaucracy and the EEOC
Did Civil Service Reform Make a Difference?

J. Edward Kellough and David H. Rosenbloom

The problem of equal employment opportunity (EEO) has been a focus of concern in public administration at least since the 1940s, but as time has passed, government policy toward EEO has evolved through several distinct stages.[1] Early programs relied almost exclusively on procedures for processing complaints of discrimination. More recent efforts, however, also require affirmative action (AA), which directs special attention to the employment of minorities and women. The principle of affirmative action has proved to be one of the most contentious public personnel issues of the past two decades.[2] This chapter examines the impact of the civil service reform of 1978 on discrimination complaint processing and affirmative action in federal employment.

The EEO Reforms

The Civil Service Reform Act (CSRA) of 1978 and accompanying reorganization measures embodied former President Carter's effort to restructure the federal personnel system and increase managerial efficiency in the federal bureaucracy. In the process of reform, the important issue of federal EEO was significantly addressed. The 1978 reform restructured the federal EEO-AA program and added additional components to the effort in an attempt to further increase the representation of minorities and women in middle and upper levels of the federal service.

The importance of the CSRA for the concept of EEO is reflected in the act's introductory language, which endorses the notion of representative bureaucracy by calling for a "work force reflective of the Nation's diversity" (United States 1978b:1112). To help achieve that goal,

Section 310 of the act, known generally as the Garcia Amendment, established a new EEO recruitment effort that was subsequently titled the Federal Equal Opportunity Recruitment Program (FEORP) (ibid.:1152). The Equal Employment Opportunity Commission (EEOC) was directed to formulate guidelines for this program, but it was to be implemented under supervision of the Office of Personnel Management (OPM).

FEORP requires that federal agencies conduct affirmative recruitment activities aimed at correcting the underrepresentation of minorities and women in middle and higher level occupations and grades. Section 310 defines "underrepresentation" as "a situation in which the number of members of a minority group designation . . . within a category of civil service employment constitutes a lower percentage of the total number of employees within the employment category than the percentage that the minority constituted within the labor force of the United States" (ibid). Agencies are required to "conduct a continuing program for the recruitment of members of minorities for positions in the agency to carry out the [EEO-AA] policy . . . in a manner designed to eliminate [such] underrepresentation" (ibid). Although many agencies were already conducting minority and female recruitment efforts as part of their ongoing EEO agendas,[3] this new program grounded in statutory law was intended to add impetus to those efforts.

A second element of the 1978 reform designed to advance federal EEO is Section 405 of the CSRA. In setting forth performance evaluation criteria for members of the senior executive service, this section suggests that success in "meeting affirmative action goals and achievement of equal employment opportunity requirements" should be one of the standards for satisfactory performance (United States 1978b:1168). Inclusion of this factor among the other suggested criteria for performance appraisal was clearly an attempt to underscore further the importance of EEO-AA accomplishments.

Perhaps the most dramatic aspect of the 1978 reforms with implications for EEO, however, was the transfer of authority for supervision of the overall internal federal EEO-AA effort from the government's central personnel agency to the EEOC. The transfer was accomplished through Reorganization Plan No. 1 of 1978, rather than through the CSRA itself (United States 1978a). The major impetus for this shift in responsibilities came from a growing disenchantment with the rather slow rate of progress in minority and female employment in higher bureaucratic positions achieved under the Civil Service Commission's guidance of the program during the 1960s and 1970s. In fact, in his message to Congress regarding the transfer of responsibility to the EEOC, President Carter argued that the Civil Service Commission (CSC) had been "lethargic in enforcing fair employment requirements within the Federal government" (U.S. Congress 1978:4).

The EEOC and Federal EEO-AA

The decision to vest general oversight of the federal service's EEO-AA efforts in the EEOC posed considerable risks. Although it was broadly supported by civil rights and minority group organizations—some of whom had favored transferring the EEO program from the CSC to the EEOC in the early 1970s—the agency's ability to absorb a large, new, and complex function was very much in doubt.[4] The commission was created by the Civil Rights Act of 1964 to enforce equal employment law in the private sector. But throughout its existence, the EEOC seemed to lack the capacity to do its original job effectively.[5] As Eleanor Holmes Norton, who was appointed chair of the EEOC in June 1977, exclaimed: "When I came to the EEOC I found an agency pretty much on its knees, largely because the function was unprecedented in the federal government. Nobody in the federal government takes 80,000 potentially complicated complaints every year and deals with them in a timely manner" (American Enterprise Institute 1979:7–8). Indeed, at various times the commission had a backlog of over 150,000 cases. Expanding the EEOC's responsibility threatened to inundate it with still more cases to process.

An even greater challenge to the EEOC is the fact that it has had to share responsibility for federal EEO-AA with other agencies. As mentioned earlier, the reform act gave the Office of Personnel Management authority for FEORP, which is "designed to eliminate underrepresentation in employment through a process of need assessment and intensive recruitment focused directly at underrepresented groups" (U.S. OPM 1980). To a substantial extent, therefore, the success of federal EEO-AA depends upon OPM's efforts and cooperation with the EEOC. Furthermore, except for a pilot program under Norton that was later terminated by the Reagan administration, individual agencies have retained authority to handle much of the EEO complaint process (Lavelle 1989). They can even reject the recommendations of an EEOC administrative law judge should a case ever reach one.

Nevertheless, designating the EEOC as the lead agency for federal EEO fit the coalition politics of the reform well by attracting the support of women and minority group members. It also wrenched total control of the EEO-AA program from the government's central personnel agency for the first time since 1965, thereby eliminating the organizational conflict of interest that exists when an agency, such as the CSC, is responsible for policing its own policies and procedures. Consequently, it was hoped by supporters of the decision to make the EEOC the lead agency for federal EEO-AA that such an institutional arrangement would facilitate elimination of those barriers to equal opportunity that were embedded in the federal personnel system.

In evaluating the impact of the civil service reform on EEO-AA, attention must be devoted to the two major components of the federal EEO program that have developed since the government first adopted a policy of nondiscrimination based on race, color, creed, or national origin in 1941. These are (1) a system for handling complaints of discrimination and (2) affirmative action to achieve proportional gains in the employment of members of minority groups (and, since the 1960s, of women) in regions, agencies, occupations, and ranks in which their employment interests have suffered due to discrimination.

The Complaint System

The system for adjudicating complaints of prohibited discrimination brought by federal employees has been called "A system of failure" (ibid.).[6] It has failed to resolve cases on a timely basis, and it gives all the appearances of favoring the interests of agencies over those of their employees.

Although discrimination cases are supposed to be closed within 180 days, the governmentwide average is about 1.5 years. In some agencies, including the departments of Justice, State, Health and Human Services, and the Environmental Protection Agency, it takes more than two years, on average, to close cases. Even in NASA, which apparently resolves complaints faster than other agencies, it takes an average of 218 days per case. Some delays are legendary: "Seven General Services employees filed an age discrimination complaint in 1980. It took six years for the agency to decide one issue—timeliness."

A major reason for the failure to resolve cases in a more timely fashion is the complexity of the complaint processing system. For example, figure 4 displays a flow chart of OPM's internal discrimination complaint process. In theory, OPM ought to be a model of good personnel

Figure 4. OPM's Internal Discrimination Complaint Process

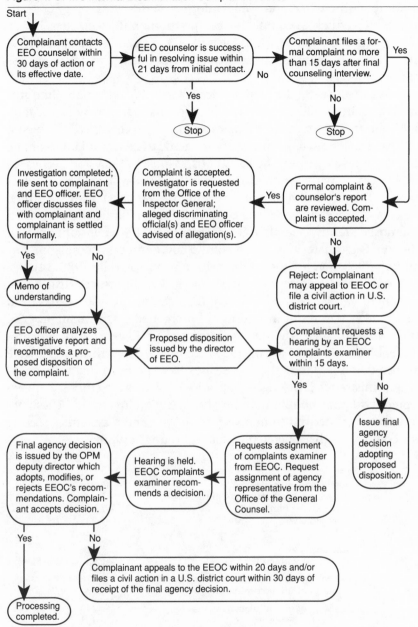

practice for other agencies. Its system relies heavily upon EEO counselors to fashion fair and rapid informal settlements of EEO complaints. Nevertheless, complaints can go through thirteen steps before
OPM reaches its final decision. Even then, the case may be appealed to
the EEOC or brought before a federal district court. The whole process
can be arduous.

Governmentwide, the civil service reform offered no absolute improvement in timeliness over the prereform system, in which it took
only about 200 days to judge cases on their merits (Rosenbloom
1977:131). Nor did it diminish a two-decade trend toward taking more
time to resolve cases: in the late 1960s, it took 144 days on average to
resolve cases (with a formal time limit of 90 days), and in 1974, it
took 200 days (with a formal time limit of 180 days) (ibid.). Further,
the cost of processing a federal complaint is now about $8,000, which
is almost certainly more than it was prior to 1978 (in constant dollars).
The EEOC estimates that it costs only $800 to process complaints un-
der its jurisdiction arising in the private sector (Lavelle 1989:34).

Nor do more lengthy cases seem to yield more justice. Historically,
the chief indicator of the fairness of EEO complaint systems has been
their tendency to result in findings of prohibited discrimination. Prior
to the reform, such findings were reached in 13 percent of all cases
(Rosenbloom 1977:134). In 1987, findings of discrimination were
handed down in 244 of the 1,478 cases (16.5 percent) that were heard
by administrative law judges, but only 91 of these decisions were accepted without modification by the agencies involved.[7] These 91
decisions were derived from a very large base and a system of sorting
out complaints that operated as follows (Lavelle 1989):

Total complaints filed	17,014
Cancelled—claimant doesn't follow up	−1,575
Rejected—filing errors	−2,668
Withdrawn	−3,519
Settled	−4,828
Appealed	4,424
Decided without hearing	−2,946
Hearings held by administrative law judge	1,478
Findings of no discrimination	−1,234
Findings of discrimination	244
Rejected by agency	−131
Modified by agency	−22
Accepted by agency	91

Both Norton and her successor, Clarence Thomas, appointed by President Reagan, were critical of the complaint system. Each sought to simplify the complaint process by consolidating much more of it directly under the EEOC and accordingly reducing the role of individual agencies in processing cases (ibid.:35).[8] Opposition to revamping the system seems to focus on the short-term costs of such a reorganization. Aside from timeliness, fairness, and cost, the complaint system has been criticized for its inability to sort out the trivial from the serious complaints. Nevertheless, the system may also deter individuals from filing legitimate complaints. For instance, they may be dissuaded by EEO counselors or unable to find attorneys who will take their cases on a contingency basis. In fiscal 1987, 0.5 percent of the 2,942,981 federal employees covered by the EEO program filed complaints. Interestingly, the EEOC itself had the highest rate of filings, with 71 (2.3 percent) of its 3,100 employees lodging complaints. This may suggest less that the agency is given to discrimination than that it does not place substantial barriers in the way of employees who want to file formal complaints.

In sum, the evidence indicates that the civil service reform did not improve the handling of complaints of discrimination within the federal service. The current system is not efficient in terms of timeliness. Nor does it inspire confidence that outcomes will be fair. Lacking substantial control over much of the complaint process and unable to mount the political strength necessary to gain it, the EEOC has been unable to make the system operate more efficiently than it operated under the CSC prior to the reform. Norton called the federal complaint process "the most frustrating experience I had at the EEOC" (ibid.:34). Here, as in other areas, much of the reason why the reform did not achieve its aspirations lies in faulty design.

Affirmative Action

Federal affirmative action requires programmatic effort to overcome the effects of past and present discrimination in government employment practices. Prior to the civil service reform, federal agencies developed annual affirmative action plans outlining steps that would be taken to ensure equal employment opportunity. In the mid-1970s, agency affirmative action plans contained both an assessment of EEO problems within the agency and a statement of actions that would be undertaken to correct problems identified.[9] The EEO assessment focused on issues such as the organization of agency EEO activity, employee recruitment and upward mobility programs, and supervisory and managerial commitment to EEO-AA. The CSC provided guidance for evaluating these concerns.

For example, regarding EEO program organization, the CSC specified that the agency director for EEO should have "direct access to top management and lines of communication to agency supervisors." With respect to employee recruitment, the CSC indicated that agencies should have programs in which "EEO officials provide technical assistance to the personnel office and monitor (or participate in) recruitment efforts." Agencies were also instructed to review the composition of their work force "by racial, ethnic and sex groupings at the various grade levels." When such programmatic criteria were not met, "affirmative action" was required to correct the situation. There was no requirement that numerical goals and timetables for minority and female employment be developed, but agencies were permitted to do so when "circumstances clearly indicat[ed] that they would be appropriate and useful."

Upon assuming control of the federal EEO program following the 1978 reform, the EEOC significantly changed the nature and format of agency affirmative action plans, shifting the focus more decidedly to the use of numerical goals and timetables. Explicit instructions were given by which federal agencies would determine minority and female underrepresentation, and numerical goals and timetables were required in instances where agencies found underrepresentation to exist (U.S. EEOC 1979: III.3–III.5). Agency plans were also shifted to a multiyear format that was to include annual goals, timetables, and program strategies for a five-year interval. The first multiyear period ran from fiscal year 1982 through fiscal year 1986.

The Reagan administration initially retained the emphasis on numerical employment targets, although many conservatives were opposed to affirmative action in the form of goals and timetables. In a management directive issued early in 1983, however, the EEOC stressed that the accomplishment of goals was not mandatory, arguing in part that "it may not always be possible to attain all goals according to the agreed-upon timetables, despite vigorous and goodfaith efforts" (U.S. EEOC 1983:3). Early in 1986, the EEOC abandoned requirements for goals and timetables in settlements with private sector employers, and there was concern at that time that goals and timetables would be dropped from the federal sector EEO-AA program as well.[10] When new guidelines for federal EEO were issued by the EEOC in

1987, agencies were in fact no longer required to develop goals and timetables in response to the underrepresentation of minorities and women. They were permitted to do so, however, at their discretion (U.S. EEOC 1987:13–14). The policy regarding numerical goals and timetables was shifted back to what it was in the 1970s under the CSC.

Impact on Employment Trends

Research Design and Methodology

To assess the impact of the 1978 reform on federal employment trends for minorities and women, it is necessary to examine employment patterns for those groups prior to and following the reform. A quasi-experimental, interrupted time-series research design as discussed initially by Campbell and Stanley (1966:37–43) and later by Cook and Campbell (1979) is used. The period under analysis runs from 1972 through 1986. Extending the analysis farther back into time is inappropriate because of the different nature of federal EEO before 1972. The 1972 Equal Employment Opportunity Act shifted internal federal EEO from an executive order to a statutory basis, and a 1971 decision by the Civil Service Commission first permitted the development and use of numerical goals and timetables in annual affirmative action plans for the year 1972.

The analysis examines employment trends for blacks, Hispanics, and women in general schedule and equivalent grades 9–12 and 13–18. Problems of minority and female underrepresentation have been focused primarily in those grades since the early 1960s. Data are obtained from reports on minority and female employment in the federal service compiled by the Civil Service Commission and the Office of Personnel Management.[11] Unfortunately, reports published since 1982 include approximately 150,000 part-time and intermittent workers not covered in earlier reports. These employees comprise about 7 percent of the total work force reported during the 1980s. However, many part-time and intermittent workers are located outside of general schedule (GS) and equivalent pay systems, and for those in GS and equivalent positions, most are below the GS 9 grade level. Very few are at or above GS 13. Consequently, the change in coverage has minimal impact on analysis in this chapter.

Because of the nature of the various employment series analyzed, an ordinary least squares (OLS) regression model provides the most

appropriate method of data analysis for this research.[12] In other interrupted time-series studies, autoregressive integrated moving average (ARIMA) models as developed by scholars such as Box and
Jenkins (1976) are more suitable than OLS regression. ARIMA analysis controls for seasonal trends or autocorrelation in the data and will
provide a better assessment of policy interventions under some circumstances. However, ARIMA is not appropriate in studies where
there are relatively few preintervention observations or where there is
no clear indication of serial correlation of the error terms.[13]

In the interrupted time-series regression model developed here, the
annual percentage of black, Hispanic, or female employment in targeted grades is regressed on time in years, scored 1 for the first year
examined, 2 for the second, 3 for the third, and so on. Additional independent variables are added to the model to assess the short- and
long-term impacts of the 1978 intervention. The model is represented
by the following equation:

$$Y_t = b_0 + b_1 X_{1t} + b_2 X_{2t} + b_3 X_{3t} + e_t.$$

The dependent variable Y_t represents the percentage of positions in
targeted grades held by blacks, Hispanics, or women in a given year.
The variable X_{1t} is the counter for year, coded 1 for 1972, 2 for 1973,
3 for 1974, and on to 15 for 1986. This variable accounts for trends
in black or female employment over the entire series and provides a
baseline against which change may be assessed. The variable X_{2t} is a
dichotomous dummy variable coded 0 for observations before the intervention and 1 for observations after. The variable X_{3t} is a post-
intervention counter for time that is scored 0 for observations prior to
the intervention and 1 for 1979, 2 for 1980, and on to 8 for 1986.

The OLS regression is designed to uncover any of four possible effects of the 1978 civil service reform on black, Hispanic, and female
employment trends: (1) no observable impact (i.e., no change in the
employment pattern following the reform); (2) an immediate change
in the number of black, Hispanic, or female employees followed by a
return to the preintervention rate (i.e., a shift in the level of the series
suggesting an immediate but short-term, effect of the reform); (3) a
change in the average annual rate of gain (or decline) in black, Hispanic, or female employment; or (4) both an immediate shift and a
change in the average annual rate.

If the 1978 reform had no clearly observable impact on progress in
federal EEO; that is, if the reform is not followed by an immediate shift

or a change in the rate of black, Hispanic, or female employment, then postreform employment will be a direct extrapolation of prereform employment. There will be no shift in the postreform intercept, and the postreform slope will show no change from the prereform slope. If the reform has only the effect of an immediate change in employment levels, then an increase or decrease in employment will accompany the introduction of the reform, but thereafter the trend will remain the same as before the reform. If the reform changes only the rate of black, Hispanic, or female employment, then the postreform slope will be different from the prereform slope. If both an immediate change and a change in the rate occur, then an immediate increase or decrease in employment accompanying the reform will be followed by a postreform change in the slope.

In the model specified above, the parameter b_0 estimates the level or intercept of the prereform series. It is the estimated level of black, Hispanic, or female employment for 1971, the first year preceding the years examined. The coefficient b_1 estimates the slope of the series prior to the 1978 intervention. The average annual rate of black, Hispanic, or female employment for the series preceding the 1978 changes in EEO-AA policy, is indicated by b_1. The parameter b_3 adjusts this slope, as necessary, to account for change in the postreform period. Thus, the estimated slope for the postreform years is given by $b_1 + b_3$. Finally, the coefficient b_2 estimates any change in the level or intercept from the pre- to the postreform years and provides an assessment of immediate short-term impact of the intervention.[14]

Time-series analysis inevitably faces the problem that something other than the intervention under study produces observed changes in the dependent variable. However, in this model, the trend variable X_{1t} is a proxy for other social forces that may be influencing black, Hispanic, or female employment patterns across the series. The impacts of variables such as trends in minority and female enrollment in institutions of higher education; the rate at which blacks, Hispanics, and women enter the labor market; the general state of the economy; and broader changes in social attitudes are reflected in X_{1t}.[15]

Results

Table 13 summarizes results of the regression analysis of effects of the 1978 reform on the employment of blacks, Hispanics, and women in grades 9–12 and 13–18. The very high values for R^2 suggest the strength of the linear employment trend over time. The values for the

Table 13. Regression Analysis of Effects of the 1978 Reform on the Federal Employment of Blacks, Hispanics, and Women

Employee Group	Regression Equation
Blacks, GS 9–12	$Y_t = 5.20 + .43X_{1t} + .22X_{2t} - .15X_{3t} + e_t$ (61.90)* (22.62)* (2.12)** (−6.23)* $R^2 = .9969$ D.W. = 1.72
Blacks, GS 13–18	$Y_t = 2.64 + .21X_{1t} + .36X_{2t} - .08X_{3t} + e_t$ (24.89)* (8.87)* (2.75)* (−2.52)* $R^2 = .9850$ D.W. = 1.92
Hispanics, GS 9–12	$Y_t = 1.47 + .14X_{1t} + .36X_{2t} + .03X_{3t} + e_t$ (32.76)* (14.22)* (6.56)* (1.93)** $R^2 = .9970$ D.W. = 2.13
Hispanics, GS 13–18	$Y_t = .80 + .07X_{1t} + .22X_{2t} + .02X_{3t} + e_t$ (21.39)* (8.11)* (4.76)* (2.10)** $R^2 = .9930$ D.W. = 2.12
Women, GS 9–12	$Y_t = 15.09 + 1.26X_{1t} + .60X_{2t} - .003X_{3t} + e_t$ (80.91)* (30.33)* (2.64)* (−.07) $R^2 = .9989$ D.W. = 2.32
Women, GS 13–18	$Y_t = 3.77 + .34X_{1t} + .18X_{2t} + .49X_{3t} + e_t$ (43.22)* (17.57)* (1.64) (19.61)* $R^2 = .9990$ D.W. = 2.67

NOTE: Figures in parentheses are t-values; R^2 is the coefficient of multiple determination, and D.W. is the Durbin-Watson statistic. Significance levels are based on a two-tailed test. For a definition of the variables and interpretation of the results, see the text.
*Significant at .05 level.
**Significant at .10 level.

Durbin-Watson statistic indicate that autocorrelation is not causing difficulty and estimates of statistical significance can be accepted.

Black Employment in GS and Equivalent Grades 9–12. In these grades, black employment increased from 5.5 percent in 1972 to 8.1 percent in 1978 and 10.6 percent in 1986. This trend in the employment of blacks is illustrated in figure 5. In table 13, the slope for the years 1972 through 1978 is estimated at .43, meaning black employment in these grades rose at an average rate of slightly more than 0.4 percent per year before the reforms. The coefficient b_2 suggests that following the reforms there is an immediate positive change in the level of the series. Such change is consistent with an immediate but short-term increase in the number of blacks employed in these grades. The coefficient b_3 suggests, however, that the average rate of increase in black employment dropped slightly for the years following 1978 (see figure 4). The slope for the years following the reforms is reduced to .28 (.43 − .15).

Figure 5. Black Employment, 1972–1986

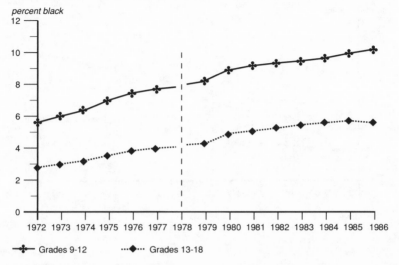

percent black

1972 1973 1974 1975 1976 1977 1978 1979 1980 1981 1982 1983 1984 1985 1986

—✦— Grades 9-12   ···◆··· Grades 13-18

Black Employment in GS and Equivalent Grades 13–18. Black employment patterns in these grades are also illustrated in figure 5. In 1972, blacks held 2.8 percent of the positions in these grades. By 1978, blacks occupied 4.1 percent of these positions, and by 1986, black employment increased to 5.4 percent. Table 13 indicates that the slope for the years prior to the civil service reforms is .21. This suggests that black employment in grades 13–18 increased at an average rate of approximately 0.2 percent per year in the years before the 1978 reforms. The coefficient b_2 suggests that immediately following the reforms there was a significant increase in black employment in these grades. This increase lifted the postreform series to a level higher than the prereform series. The slope for the period following the reforms is, however, reduced to .13 (.21 − .08). This difference in prereform and postreform slopes suggests that following the EEOC's assumption of responsibility for federal EEO-AA and the other changes made in 1978, the average rate of increase in black employment in these grades dropped. While this decline in the employment rate is not very large, it is noticeable in figure 5.

Hispanic Employment in GS and Equivalent Grades 9–12. The employment of Hispanics in grades 9–12 increased from 1.6 percent in 1972 to 2.5 percent in 1978 and 4.1 percent in 1986. These employment patterns are presented in figure 6. Regression analysis (see table

Figure 6. Hispanic Employment, 1972–1986

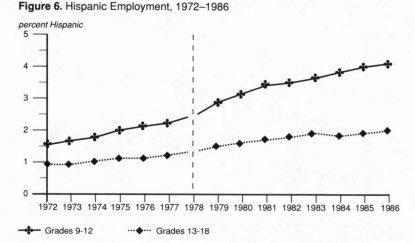

percent Hispanic

—✶— Grades 9-12   ····◆··· Grades 13-18

13) suggests that before the civil service reform, Hispanic employment increased at an estimated rate of 0.14 percent per year. The b_2 coefficient suggests that an immediate increase in Hispanic employment followed the reform, but thereafter the rate of growth in employment returned to essentially what it was before the reform. The postreform slope increased over the prereform slope only 0.03 percent per year, yielding a rate of increase for the period following the civil service reform of only 0.17 percent annually (.14 + .03). Consequently, no substantial long-term impact of the 1978 reform can be found.

Hispanic Employment in GS and Equivalent Grades 13–18. In the higher grades, Hispanic employment stood at only 0.9 percent in 1972, as illustrated in figure 6. Hispanic employment in these grades increased to 1.3 percent in 1978 and finally to 2.2 percent in 1986. Table 13 indicates that the rate of increase in Hispanic employment prior to the civil service reform was 0.07 percent per year. There is, again, an immediate increase in the postreform employment of Hispanics estimated by the coefficient b_2. This rise in Hispanic employment shifts the postreform series to a slightly higher level, but the rate of increase in employment in the years following the 1978 reform is not considerably different from the rate before the reform. The postreform slope increases to only 0.09 percent annually, according to regression estimates.

Figure 7. Employment of Women, 1972–1986

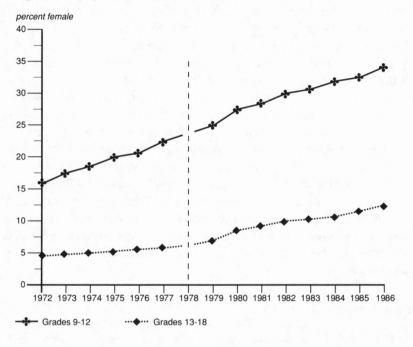

percent female

Grades 9-12   Grades 13-18

Female Employment in GS and Equivalent Grades 9–12. In middle level positions, female employment rose from 16.4 percent in 1972 to 24.4 percent in 1978 and 34.5 percent in 1986 (see figure 7). From table 13, it can be seen that, during the period before the civil service reform, the employment of women in these grades rose an average of 1.26 percent per year. The coefficient b_2 in this regression indicates that, after the EEOC accepted the responsibility for the federal EEO program and the other reforms were initiated, there was an increase in the number of women employed, raising the level of the postreform series, but this shift is difficult to see clearly in figure 7. The average annual rate of female employment in these grades following the reforms is estimated to be essentially the same as before the reforms. There is a very small and statistically insignificant drop in the postreform slope indicated by the coefficient b_3. Given the nature of these results, it seems most appropriate to conclude that the policy reforms may have had a short-term effect but no long-term impact on female employment in these grades.

Female Employment in GS and Equivalent Grades 13–18. In the top grades analyzed, the employment of women rose from 4.2 percent in 1972 to 6.3 percent in 1978 and finally to 13.0 percent in 1986, as illustrated in figure 7. Before the civil service reforms occurred, female employment in these grades is estimated to have increased an average of 0.34 percent per year (see table 13). The coefficient b_2 is positive, suggesting a small immediate increase in the employment of women in these grades following the reforms, but the coefficient does not achieve statistical significance. In the years following the EEO changes, however, the rate of growth in the employment of women increased considerably. The slope for those years is 0.83 (0.34 + 0.49), indicating an average increase in employment of 0.8 percent per year. However, as of 1986 women were still considerably underrepresented in these grades. Should the postreform rate estimated here continue, it will take approximately forty-five years for the representation of women in these grades to equal their representation in the national population.

Conclusion

This study finds that the transfer of responsibility for federal sector EEO to the EEOC, and other aspects of the 1978 civil service reform that were designed to enhance federal EEO, were not followed by increases in the rate of black employment in middle and higher level positions. There appears to have been a short-term gain for blacks in grades 9–12 and 13–18, but thereafter, the rate of increase in black employment actually declines moderately, as illustrated in figure 5.

Regarding the employment of Hispanics, it appears that there were immediate short-term increases but no substantial long-term change in the rate of increase in Hispanic employment. In grades 9–12 and 13–18 there is no substantial change from the prereform slope estimated by the regression analysis.

For women, a short-term increase in employment in grades 9–12 is observed, but the average annual rate of employment in those grades is virtually the same for the prereform and postreform years. In other words, as for Hispanics, the reform did little to change the long-term employment trend for women. The higher grades (13–18) reveal no significant short-term effect, but the average annual rate of growth in employment of women increased considerably in grades 13–18 following the 1978 reform.

The indication that immediate increases in employment were followed by declining or essentially unchanged rates of employment for all but one of the groups studied here may lead to pessimism regarding the EEO impact of the 1978 reform and progress toward equity in the higher levels of the federal service during the Reagan years.[16] It is certainly fair to say that the Reagan administration was not enamored of affirmative action through numerical employment targets. In 1984, the Department of Justice, the Federal Trade Commission, and the National Endowment for the Humanities, for example, all refused to develop numerical goals and timetables for the employment of women and minorities—a violation of the EEOC regulations then in effect.[17] At the Justice Department, William Bradford Reynolds, chief of the Civil Rights Division, became an outspoken critic in the early 1980s of "statistical formulae designed to provide non-victims of discrimination preferential treatment."[18] Whether a reduced commitment to goals and timetables frustrated additional EEO progress during the Reagan administration is an interesting but difficult question.[19]

Other factors, however, may also explain the absence of more impressive progress in EEO following the reform of 1978. We have already seen that the complaint processing system was not improved under EEOC supervision. Furthermore, federal budget reductions and lower personnel ceilings during the early 1980s probably reduced opportunities for targeted groups. Success in increasing the representation of minorities and women in higher positions is more difficult during periods of retrenchment, when fewer job openings are available and restrictions are placed on hiring from outside, than during periods of stability or expansion. Under such circumstances, an adverse impact on the employment of women and minorities is likely because reductions in force are required to be accomplished in reverse order of seniority. Minorities and women are still disproportionately represented among the most recently hired in higher-level positions and are, therefore, most likely to be the first to go under circumstances requiring layoffs.

The fact that women in grades 13–18 apparently fared better than other groups during the cutbacks of the early 1980s is intriguing. The performance of women may be due in part to the possibility that women as a group have suffered somewhat less than blacks or

Hispanics from "economic and cultural deprivations," and thus, have been better able to achieve upper-level positions when attempts to counter sexual discrimination were undertaken (Rosenbloom 1980).

It is also interesting that employment rates did not begin to decline significantly for blacks in grades 9–12 until they began to approach parity in terms of representation. Blacks were no longer significantly underrepresented in grades 9–12 in 1981, when they achieved 9.3 percent of those positions, and it is at that time that a noticeable decline in the rate of increase in black employment began (see figure 5). As indicated earlier, agencies were required to develop goals and timetables for the employment of targeted groups during the early 1980s, but only when such groups were underrepresented. When the underrepresentation of blacks began to be less of a problem, it could be expected that efforts to increase their representation would diminish. Goals and timetables could not be used in the absence of underrepresentation. The smaller decline in the rate of gain in black employment in grades 12–18 may also be at least partially a function of the group drawing close to parity in the 1980s, although, depending on how parity is defined for those positions, blacks may not have actually reached it.

The rate of growth in the employment of women and Hispanics in grades 9–12 also failed to increase considerably during the 1980s, as they too drew closer to parity. This pattern is consistent with the view that as representation increases, pressure for recruitment is reduced. Underrepresentation has been most dramatic for women in grades 13–18, and appropriately, it is in those grades that we witness the only significant increase in the postreform rate of gain in employment.

The lack of dramatic progress in EEO following the 1978 reforms is, therefore, open to differing interpretations. One view is that the reform could not overcome the Reagan administration's aversion to affirmative action coupled with budget reductions and restrictions on hiring in the early 1980s. An alternative perspective, however, is that the declines in the rate of increase in black employment and the absence of a substantially increased rate of employment for most other employees studied here were more a function of the groups drawing closer to parity in representation. This view seems particularly persuasive in the case of blacks in grades 9–12. From this interpretation, it may appear that the reforms were not necessarily unsuccessful. This view raises the question, however, of how to properly define parity for the representation of minorities and women in higher bureaucratic positions.

NOTES

1. For a discussion of the development of federal EEO policy, see Rosenbloom (1977).

2. A recent survey of city managers, for example, found approximately 60 percent opposed to affirmative action through numerical goals and timetables. See Slack (1987).

3. For example, see McVeigh (1968).

4. This section relies on Rosenbloom (1977) for the history of EEO-AA prior to 1978. See also Vaughn (1975).

5. See U.S. Commission on Civil Rights (1975:643–46). See also U.S. Commission on Civil Rights (1977:ch. 4).

6. Unless otherwise noted, the facts and quotations in this and the next paragraph are drawn from this source.

7. Lavelle (1989) concluded, "Of the 17,014 discrimination charges handled through the required bureaucratic procedures in 1987, only 91 of those cases were decided clearly and finally in favor of the individual pressing the complaint" (p. 1). The number of settlements and decisions without hearings in which discrimination was found and complainants were favored is apparently unknown, though it could be substantial.

8. The remainder of the factual information in this paragraph is drawn from this source.

9. See U.S. CSC (1977b). All quotations in the next paragraph are drawn from this source.

10. See "EEOC Abandons Hiring Goals, Timetables," and U.S. Congress (1985).

11. Data used in this study are from the following documents: U.S. CSC (1972–1975a); U.S. CSC (1972–1975b); U.S. CSC (1976–1977a); U.S. OPM (1978–1980); U.S. OPM (1982; 1984; 1986).

Data for 1981, 1983, and 1985 are estimated by averaging employment statistics from adjacent years. This was done because the government did not issue reports for those years, and comparable data are unavailable from the Office of Personnel Management or other sources. Subsequent analysis rests, therefore, on the assumption that calculations for 1981, 1983, and 1985 are reasonable estimates of actual employment levels. The assumption is not unrealistic given the incremental nature of minority and female employment increases over time, but the actual values for the missing years remain unknown. Calculating the regression model without the estimated data points in the analysis produces substantive results that are of the same direction and nearly identical in magnitude to those illustrated in table 13. With respect to statistical significance, very small differences are observed: the coefficient b_2 for blacks in grades 9–12 does not retain statistical significance at the .10 level—significance drops to .15. Also, the coefficients b_2 and b_3 for blacks in grades 13–18 are significant at .07 instead of .05, and the coefficient b_2 for women in grades 9–12 is significant at .08 rather than .05. There is no change for women in grades 13–18 or for Hispanics in either category of grades.

For the years following 1978, the grade 13–18 category includes senior executive positions that had earlier been equated to GS grades 16–18.

12. The model is widely used under conditions similar to those in this study, since it makes the best possible use of the available data. For applications see Legge (1985) or Lewis-Beck (1979). Further explanation of the model is available from Lewis-Beck (1986); Mohr (1988:151–54); and Welch and Comer (1988: 289–94).

13. See Cook and Campbell (1976:274–75) and Legge (1985:52).

14. See Lewis-Beck (1986:215); and Legge (1985:54).

15. For example, college and university enrollment for blacks is correlated with the time trend variable X_{1t} at .885. The correlation between female enrollment and X_{1t} is .987.

16. Because the civil service reform and the Reagan administration are separated by only about two years, it is not possible to control statistically for the impact of the Reagan administration while at the same time assessing the possible effects of the reform.

17. See U.S. EEOC (1983). See also U.S. Congress (1985).

18. Statement by William Bradford Reynolds, quoted in William Raspberry, "Fill in the Numbers Please," *Washington Post*, 15 July, 1983.

19. Gregory B. Lewis finds a decline in the rate of gain in employment for blacks and Hispanics during the Reagan years, but Lewis reports that other groups, specifically white women and Asian Americans, made more rapid progress under President Reagan than they did under Carter. Lewis concludes that overall progress toward EEO "seems to have continued at the same rate" during the Reagan administration as during the Carter presidency (Lewis 1988).

SOURCES

American Enterprise Institute (for Public Policy Research). 1979. *A Conversation with Eleanor Holmes Norton*. Washington, D.C.

Box, George E., and Gwilyn M. Jenkins. 1976. *Time Series Analysis: Forecasting and Control*. San Francisco: Holden-Hay.

Campbell, Donald T., and Julian C. Stanley. 1966. *Experimental and Quasi-Experimental Designs for Research*. Chicago: Rand McNally.

Cook, Thomas D., and Donald T. Campbell. 1976. "The Design and Conduct of Quasi-Experiments and True Experiments in Field Settings." In *Handbook of Industrial and Organizational Psychology*, ed. Marvin D. Dunnette. Chicago: Rand McNally.

———. 1979. *Quasi-Experimentation: Design and Analysis Issues for Field Settings*. Boston: Houghton Mifflin.

"EEOC Abandons Hiring Goals, Timetables." 1986. *Public Administration Times*. 1 March.

Lavelle, Marianne. 1989. "A System of Failure." *National Law Journal* 24 April, pp. 1, 34, 35, 36.

Legge, Jerome S., Jr. 1985. *Abortion Policy: An Evaluation of the Consequences for Maternal and Infant Health*. Albany: SUNY Press.

Lewis, Gregory B. 1988. "Progress Toward Racial and Sexual Equality in the Federal Service?" *Public Administration Review* 43 (May/June): 700–07.

Lewis-Beck, Michael S. 1979. "Some Economic Effects of Revolution: Models, Measurement, and the Cuban Evidence." *American Journal of Sociology* 84 (March): (1227–49).

———. 1986. "Interrupted Times Series." In *New Tools for Social Scientists: Advances and Applications in Research Methods,* ed. William D. Berry and Michael S. Lewis-Beck. Beverly Hills: Sage.

McVeigh, Edward J. 1968. "Equal Job Opportunity Within the Federal Government: Some Experiences of the Department of Labor in Establishing Positive Measures to assure Full Compliance with Civil Rights and Executive Orders." *Employment Security Review* (July–August): 42–47.

Mohr, Lawrence D. 1988. *Impact Analysis for Program Evaluation.* Chicago: Dorsey.

Rosenbloom, David H. 1977. *Federal Equal Employment Opportunity: Politics and Public Personnel Administration.* New York: Praeger.

———. 1980. "The Federal Affirmative Action Policy." In *The Practice of Policy Evaluation,* ed. David Nachmias. New York: St. Martin's.

Slack, James D. 1987. "Affirmative Action and City Managers: Attitudes Toward Recruitment of Women." *Public Administration Review* 47 (March/April): 199–206.

United States. 1978a. *Federal Register.* Vol. 43, No. 90. pp. 19807–09.

———. 1978b. *Statutes at Large.* Vol. 92.

U.S. Commission on Civil Rights. 1975. *The Federal Civil Rights Enforcement Effort, 1974.* Washington, D.C.

———. 1977. *The Federal Civil Rights Enforcement Effort—1977: To Eliminate Employment Discrimination—A Sequel.* Washington, D.C.

U.S. Congress. 1985. House Committee on Education and Labor, Subcommittee on Employment Opportunities. 99th Cong., 1st sess. serial No. 99-24, *The Equal Employment Opportunity Commission Collection of Federal Affirmative Action Goals and Timetables and Enforcement of Federal Sector EEO Complaints.* Washington, D.C.

U.S. Congress. 1978. House Committee on Government Operations, 95th Cong., 2nd sess. House Document No. 95-295, *Reorganization Plan No. 1 of 1978: Message from the President of the United States.* Washington, D.C.

U.S. CSC (Civil Service Commission). 1972. 1973. 1974. 1975a. *Study of Minority Group Employment in the Federal Government.* Washington, D.C.

———. 1972. 1973. 1974. 1975b. *Study of the Employment of Women in the Federal Government.* Washington, D.C.

———. 1976. 1977a. *Equal Employment Opportunity Statistics.* Washington, D.C.

———. 1977b. *FPM Letter 713-40.* Washington, D.C.

U.S. EEOC (Equal Employment Opportunity Commission). 1979. *Management Directive 702.* 11 December.

———. 1983. *Management Directive 707.* January.

———. 1987. *Management Directive 714.* 6 October.

U.S. OPM (Office of Personnel Management). 1978. 1979. 1980. *Equal Employment Opportunity Statistics.* Washington, D.C.

———. 1982. 1984. 1986. *Affirmative Employment Statistics.* Washington, D.C.

———— . 1980, Pamphlet EM-1. Washington, D.C.
Vaughn, Robert. 1975. *The Spoiled System.* New York: Charterhouse.
Welch, Susan, and John Comer. 1988. *Quantitative Methods for Public Administration: Techniques and Applications.* 2d ed. Chicago: Dorsey.

12. The Senior Executive Service After One Decade

Kirke Harper

The concept of a federal corps of executives was first suggested in the 1950s to replace a patchwork of laws and regulations and improve the treatment of the highest level of government employees.

The introduction of a new personnel system that affects more than six thousand people working in hundreds of locations for more than seventy different departments and agencies is very complex and time-consuming. It is complex because each agency has to develop new procedures for recruiting, selecting, evaluating, rewarding, and managing personnel under the new system. Time is required for the employees to understand the system and for its operators to sort out problems and unintended impacts. The new senior executive service system was barely in place in 1981 when the government underwent a transition to a new president who had a mandate to make extensive changes in the operation of government.

The first years of the SES were traumatic, and many people formed opinions of the system during those early years. Despite the problems of the initial years, when the SES is judged against the objectives set forth at the time the system was proposed to Congress, and when viewed from the perspective of years of operation, the argument can be made that the SES is a successful personnel system.

In the initial years of the SES, study after study pointed out failures and weaknesses in the new system (U.S. OPM). The SES has not lived up to all the expectations created when it was established in 1979. Beyond those unfulfilled expectations, the SES became a lightning rod for feelings and frustrations about compensation, respect in the workplace, and the treatment of government employees.

Many of the complaints about actual and implied promises made in 1979, concerning, for example, the availability of performance awards, compensation increases, and increased opportunities for mobility and executive development, are valid. Congress reacted to the first bonus payments by reducing the number of future bonuses that could be paid. Greatly expanded mobility and executive development opportunities did not occur. Compensation increases aimed at keeping pace with inflation and with private sector salaries did not occur because of Congress's unwillingness to increase its own salaries. Many executives understandably feel disappointed about these aspects of the senior executive service. The mixed and negative feelings of SES members are real, and the problems cannot be denied; however, the SES was established to overcome a variety of longstanding problems with the management of executive resources. The years since the inception of the SES have seen substantial progress on nearly all of those problems.

Despite the continued existence of issues that were not resolved by the SES, the emergence of new issues since 1979, and implementation problems in the first years of the system, there has never been a serious call to abolish the SES.

This chapter briefly reviews the origins and objectives of the SES, describes some recent improvements in its management, and presents some descriptive information about the status of the SES in 1990.

The Origins and Objectives of the SES

Mark Huddleston's background paper in the 1987 Report of the Twentieth Century Fund's Task Force on the SES provides an excellent brief history of systems for employing executive-level personnel in the federal government (Huddleston 1987). The Second Hoover Commission was the first group to recommend a new approach to the executive personnel process. In 1955, the commission recommended a system, to be called the senior civil service, as a way to provide attractive careers, improve low pay problems, and shift the emphasis from positions to people (Commission on the Organization of the Executive Branch of the Government 1955). Efforts by the Civil Service Commission and the Eisenhower administration to implement the senior civil service were strongly opposed by the personnel community, people who would have been subject to it, and by Congress. The Eisenhower administration quietly abandoned the concept in 1960 (Huddleston 1987).

Another attempt to reform the executive personnel system came in 1971, when the Nixon administration proposed the establishment of a federal executive service (U.S. CSC 1971). The FES would have employed executives on three-year contracts, allowed for up to 25 percent noncareer appointments, and given authority to agency heads to assign and reassign executives. The FES aroused less opposition than had the SCS, although the renewable contract feature was unpopular with potential members. The proposal died with the Nixon presidency, but the idea of a new approach to executive resource management was becoming part of the accepted thinking in Washington.

The proposal to establish the senior executive service resulted from the recommendations of the Federal Personnel Management Project (FPMP), one of several government reorganization efforts established by President Carter in 1977 (U.S. CSC 1977). The FPMP established an elaborate process of task forces, public hearings, and peer review that involved thousands of people. Among the problems identified by the FPMP was "the jumble of laws, regulations, and special provisions affecting executive positions [that] makes it very difficult for agency heads to utilize their top staff most effectively, to hold managers accountable for program accomplishment, and to reward or remove them on the basis of performance. There is virtually no mobility of senior executives among Federal agencies."[1]

The overall objective of the establishment of the senior executive service was to create "a fully effective governmentwide system . . . for selecting, assigning, developing, advancing, rewarding, and managing the men and women who administer the hundreds of Federal programs that are vital to the Nation" (U.S. Congress 1978:37). Ten specific improvements were listed as the expectations the new system was designed to meet:

1. Provide better management of the number and distribution of executive personnel.

2. Treat in a more realistic fashion the career-noncareer relationships at the executive level.

3. Offer increased advancement opportunities to career executives.

4. Give agency managers greater flexibility in assigning executives where they are most needed.

5. Ensure the management competencies of those entering the service.

6. Make executives more accountable for their performance, and remove those whose performance is not satisfactory.

7. Simplify the multiplicity of laws and authorities governing the executive levels.

8. Establish more efficient procedures for staffing executive positions.

9. Provide equitable compensation linked with performance.

10. Increase opportunities for minorities and women to enter the executive levels.

Implementation of the SES System

The SES was launched with an intense public relations campaign aimed at federal executives. Membership in the SES was voluntary, and, for this reason, OPM sought to convince eligible supergrade employees to join. The staff of OPM's Bureau of Executive Manpower prepared extensive materials that explained the new system and its operation. The advantages of the new system, real and potential, were explained and discussed in meetings in the departments and agencies. Disadvantages were carefully considered. In the end, 98 percent of the eligible employees decided to join the SES. Only 81 of the approximately 6,919 eligible employees declined President Carter's invitation to become charter members of the SES.

The SES was the subject of extensive examination in 1983 and 1984, when the Congress conducted a mandatory five-year "sunset" review of its implementation (U.S. Congress 1983). More than twenty witnesses gave very candid and critical assessments of the system's implementation shortcomings. It is important to remember that no one called for the elimination of the SES or a return to prior methods of executive resource management. The testimony of John Macy, former chairman of the Civil Service Commission, established a perspective for the changes that had been made. Macy said that there was "excessive criticism of the preexisting conditions, and a kind of halcyon expectation from . . . [CSRA'S] . . . enactment. There was not an adequate appreciation . . . of the problems that are involved in implementing any sweeping Federal program change, and particularly one of this magnitude" (ibid:319).

In the sunset review, compensation of senior executives was a major factor that colored attempts to analyze the impact of the SES. It is nearly impossible to separate the compensation issue from other features of the personnel system. The compensation difference between average federal executive pay and the average for comparable private industry occupations was $14,315 in 1979 and grew to $25,392 by 1987 (President's Commission 1988:17).

Another important factor in the early years of the SES was the attitude of many elected officials toward career employees. Hugh Heclo characterized the atmosphere in this way: "The Act of 1978 was born with a split personality. On the one hand, it was the culmination of several generations of efforts by good government types to produce a high level role for senior civil servants. On the other hand, the Act was responding to a more recent surge of anti-Washington Government-is-the-problem sentiment" (U.S. Congress 1978:339).

The implementation of the SES personnel system suffered from the political atmosphere that characterized its early years. While impossible to quantify, much of the anger and frustration revealed in surveys of executive personnel during that time are due in large measure to the atmosphere in those years.[2] The atmosphere had begun to improve by 1986, when Constance Horner replaced Donald Devine as director of the Office of Personnel Management. One of the themes of the new director and her deputy, James Colvard, was changing the rhetoric about government service and government employees.

Horner and Colvard were also concerned about improving the image and morale of the senior executive service. In 1986, OPM and the President's Council on Management Improvement invited selected agencies to send representatives to a meeting to discuss the future of the SES. This conference, held at Hunt Valley, Maryland, from 30 September to 2 October 1986, was the first public indication of the increased attention to SES concerns. While the results of that meeting were never published, a list of corrective measures recommended for improving the SES was circulated among the meeting's participants and became the initial agenda for OPM's efforts to move the SES closer to the initial design. The participants recommended creating a governmentwide executive advisory board and taking a series of steps aimed at building a stronger identity in the SES, attracting and retaining quality executives, improving career-noncareer relationships, and improving career development activities.

Improvements in the SES Since 1987

Shortly after the Hunt Valley meeting, OPM began making changes in its management of the SES. In January 1987, OPM removed its requirement that agencies secure approval before paying annual bonuses. An advisory board, composed of career and noncareer SES members, was established in February, and by July the board had given Constance Horner a list of specific recommendations. In March, agencies were invited to increase nominations for the Presidential Rank Award from 6 percent to 9 percent of their SES members. In June, OPM dropped the 35 percent limit on the number of executives who could receive annual performance bonuses. In December, department and agency heads were encouraged to establish voluntary executive mobility programs. Also in December, restrictions that prevented individuals from receiving both an annual bonus and a Meritorious Rank Award in the same year were dropped.

In 1988, a series of communications devices were developed to improve the quality and availability of information among SES members. The first *Annual Report of the Status of the SES* was published in August 1988. Orientation programs for new career and noncareer appointees were developed. More than seven hundred new SES members have attended orientation sessions. OPM prepared a two-hundred-page *Handbook on SES Operations* for agency personnel officers that incorporates a synthesis of over eight hundred pages of previously issued guidance.

A continuing focus on SES issues was signaled by the new administration in January 1989, when President Bush made his first speech outside the White House to the SES assembled at Constitution Hall. In April, President Bush proposed ethics reform legislation that included pay increases for executive branch employees. The act that finally passed, P.L. 101-194, the Ethics Reform Act of 1989, provided the framework for increasing SES pay by 18 to 25 percent in January 1991.

Status of the SES in 1990

This section contains information on selected indicators for the SES from OPM's governmentwide data base.

Resource Allocation. Prior to the SES, resource allocation was a cumbersome process that frequently required legislation to increase the number of executives. The SES allocation process has now operated for ten years without a need for any additional legislation. The limit of

Figure 8. Noncareer SES Appointments

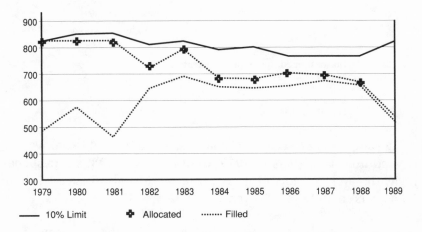

——— 10% Limit   ✚ Allocated   ⋯⋯⋯ Filled

10,777 SES and GS 16–18 positions, established in 1979, was never exceeded.[3] Allocations to many agencies were reduced by nearly 10 percent during the early 1980s (see figure 8). These reductions were an attempt to narrow the wide gap that existed between allocated and filled positions. Allocations were increased again starting in 1987. In September 1989, the total number of positions allocated for SES and GS 16–18 was well below the congressional ceiling of 10,777:

Positions	SES		GS 16–18		Total
Allocated	8,167		655		8,822
Established	8,076		569		8,645
Filled	7,305	(89%)	528	(81%)	7,388
Vacant	771	(9%)	41	(6%)	812

The congressionally imposed ceiling on noncareer appointments of 10 percent of the number of career positions has not been violated, and in September 1989 the number of noncareer appointees stood at 523, 5.9 percent of the 8,822 allocated SES positions (see figure 8).

Education Levels. The education level of SES members in 1989 was slightly higher than SES equivalent executives in 1977, as shown in the table below.

| | Percentage | |
Education	1977	1989
Doctor of philosophy		17
Doctor of medicine or jurisprudence		15
Masters'		33
Total	63.4	65
Bachelors'	29.9	30
Less than Bachelors'	6.6	5

Age and Years of Service. The average age of federal executives increased from 49.8 years in 1979 to 50.1 years in 1989. Correspondingly, the average years of government services also increased, from 20.4 years in 1979 to 21.6 years in 1989.

Women and Minorities. Reflecting changes in other segments of the work force over the past ten years, the number of women in the SES nearly doubled, from 5.1 percent to 10.1 percent. The numbers of women holding positions at GS 13–15 and in the presidential management intern (PMI) program, were also higher, creating an expectation of continued growth in the number of women in the SES. Figure 9 presents the percentage of women in feeder groups.

The number of minority members of the SES increased only 1.3 percent between 1979 and 1989, from 5.7 percent to 7.0 percent. Minority members of grades 13–15 and the PMI program were somewhat higher. Blacks and minorities make up 17.6 percent of the national work force and 21.8 percent of the federal work force. The percentage of minority persons in feeder groups is given in figure 10.

Separations. Each year since 1979, an average of 643 career executives left the SES. (See table 14.) Retirements made up slightly more

Table 14. Separations from the SES, July 1979 to December 1989

Type	Number	Average	Percentage
Retired	3,651	365	57
Resigned	1,711	171	27
Voluntary downgrade	665	66	10
Involuntary removal	123	12	2
Other	282	28	4
Total	6,432	643	100

SOURCE: U.S. Office of Personnel Management, Executive Information System.

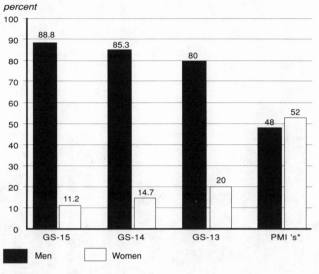

Figure 9. Women in SES Feeder Groups
September 1989

percent

Men · Women

*PMI Data 1978–1988

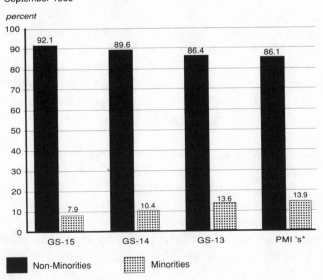

Figure 10. Minorities in SES Feeder Groups
September 1989

percent

Non-Minorities · Minorities

*PMI Data 1978–1988

Figure 11. Career SES Leaving Federal Service
July 1979–December 1989

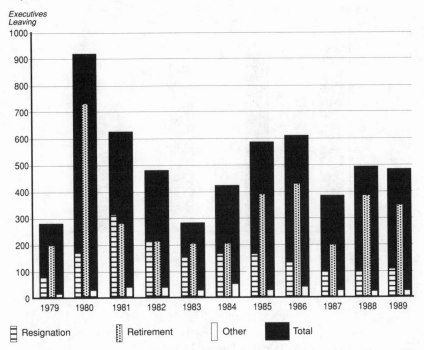

than one-half of those who left. Another 27 percent of those who left resigned to pursue other opportunities outside the federal government, while 10 percent voluntarily left the SES and returned to lower-graded federal positions. The number of career executives who leave each year has remained remarkably stable over the years, with exceptions for election years and the years that fall three years after pay raises when retirement benefits are highest (see figure 11).

Performance Appraisal. One of the major purposes given by Carter administration spokesmen for establishing the SES was the improvement of productivity by increasing accountability. The major mechanism used to increase accountability has been an annual, highly objective appraisal of performance. In exchange for greater accountability and risks of transfer and removal, executives were given the opportunity to compete for annual performance awards and Presidential Rank Awards. While the processes for performance appraisal adopted by the agencies differ widely, and have been criticized

Table 15. SES Performance Appraisal, Fiscal Year 1987

Levels	Career		Noncareer	
	Number	Percentage	Career	Noncareer
1. Unsatisfactory	2	<1	0	0
2. Minimally satisfactory	16	<1	3	1
3. Fully successful	639	11	115	26
4. Above fully successful[a]	2,261	40	100	22
5. Highest[a]	2,682	48	228	51
Total	5,600		446	
Average rating	4.36		4.24	

SOURCE: See table 14.
a. Levels 4 and 5 were not named in the statute. They are given different names by agencies, e.g., "Outstanding."

for being paper-intensive and time-consuming, people appear to have become accustomed to an objective performance appraisal. Agencies by and large are generous graders. Governmentwide ratings in 1988, the latest year for which figures are available averaged 4.43 for the agencies that used a five-point scale. A total of 90 percent of career SES members were rated above the fully successful level. Starting in 1989, agencies were again free to choose three-, four-, or five-point systems. Table 15 shows performance appraisal for fiscal year 1987.

Removals. Since the beginning of the SES in 1979, only 33 executives have been removed for performance reasons; another 28 have been removed for bad conduct or refusal to accept a geographical reassignment. A total of 123 executives have been removed for all possible reasons: reduction in force (RIF), adverse actions, performance during a probationary period, and performance (see table 16).

Bonuses. One of the most criticized aspects of the SES has been the availability of annual performance awards (bonuses). After initially authorizing bonuses for 50 percent of the SES, Congress reduced the limit to 25 percent in 1980 and instructed OPM to limit payments to not more than 20 percent. SES members understandably felt that a promise had been broken. By 1984, the percentage had been raised to 35 percent. Congress, late in 1984, changed the payment limitation to a pool of 3 percent of the salaries paid in each agency, but OPM retained an overall limit of 35 percent of the

Table 16. Removal from the SES of Career Appointees

Type of Removal	Number
Probationary Period (7/79–9/88)	11
Performance (7/79–9/88)	22
Adverse Actions (7/79–9/88)	28
Conduct: 8	
Refusal to accept geographical reassignment: 20	
RIF (8/81–9/88, certified to OPM)	62[a]
Placed at GS 15 or below: 20	
Separated: 42	
Total Removals	123
Average per year	12.3

SOURCE: See table 14.
a. Another 35 were placed in other SES positions.

SES who could receive a bonus. That limit was removed in 1987, and in 1989, 2,535 executives, 40 percent of the SES, received an average bonus of $5,478 (see figure 12). Another 5.4 percent of the SES, 349 executives, received a Presidential Rank Award in 1989 (see figure 13). The Distinguished award, which includes a prize of $20,000, was presented to 63 executives, and 286 received the Meritorious award of $10,000. These numbers were dramatic increases over the number of awards given in the early SES years.

Figure 12. Performance Bonuses
Number Presented

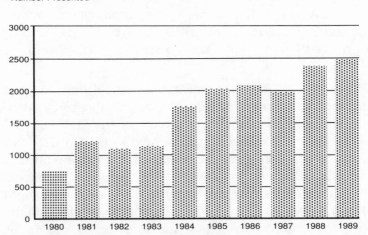

Figure 13. Presidential Rank Awards
Number Presented

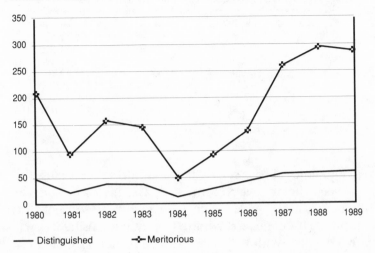

— Distinguished   ✛ Meritorious

The combination of bonuses and Presidential Rank Awards totaled 2,884 awards and $18,005,676 in 1989. This is the largest number of awards and amounts of money ever granted to SES members (see figure 14).

Compensation. Until the increases authorized by the Ethics Act of 1989, compensation remained the area of largest concern to SES members (see table 17). As the president's pay commission pointed out,

Figure 14. Performance Bonuses and Rank Awards
Total Dollars Awarded

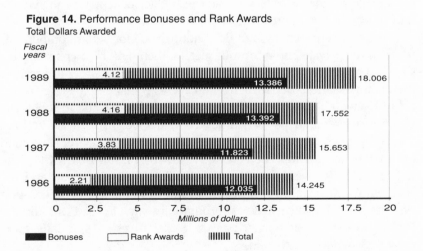

■ Bonuses   ☐ Rank Awards ||||||| Total

Table 17. SES Basic Compensation (in dollars)

SES Level	July 1979	January 1989	January 1991
6	47,500	80,700	108,300
5	47,500	78,600	104,600
4	47,500	76,400	100,500
3	47,500	74,900	95,300
2	47,500	71,800	91,200
1	47,500	68,700	87,000

SOURCE: See table 14.

despite a number of base salary increases during the 1980s, the salary gap between the average SES member and his or her private sector counterpart nearly doubled from 1979 to 1987 (President's Commission 1988:7). If Congress is willing to continue raising its own salary level to keep pace with inflation, SES compensation should not be an overriding concern in the 1990s.

The Future of Executive Personnel Systems

The SES legislation was designed to solve longstanding problems with the Civil Service Commission and the management of executive personnel. It has relieved many of them. The problems of the 1990s are not the same as the problems of the late 1970s. Our expectations of government and, in fact, of all institutions are different today. The emergence of new issues, such as the budget deficit, has altered the nature of many relationships.

If the compensation system does not provide for better comparability with the private and nonprofit sectors, there will be increased pressure to remove groups of employees from the SES in order to increase their compensation. Departments and agencies that employ large numbers of scientific and technical employees will continue to lobby the Congress for separate pay schedules for their specialists. In 1989, three federal agencies left the SES in connection with the savings and loan industry restructuring. The Federal Home Loan Bank Board (now the Office of Thrift Oversight), the Comptroller of the Currency, and the National Credit Union Administration have established compensation systems similar to other federal corporations, such as the FDIC and the Federal Reserve System, that pay their executives substantially more than SES members are paid.

Pay reform legislation passed in 1990 established a senior biomedical research service within the Department of Health and Human Services and authorized the establishment of up to eight hundred critical pay positions that could be paid up to the salary of cabinet secretaries. The legislation also provided authority for recruitment and relocation bonuses and retention allowances of up to 25 percent of basic pay. The impact of these provisions will not be known until they are fully implemented.

The Ethics Reform Act of 1989 also established a triennial process for recertifying the competencies of SES members. This process will be implemented for the first time in 1991, followed again in 1994. Many SES members are concerned about how recertification will be applied across the departments and agencies.

There should not be extensive structural changes in the SES system in the near future. Additional efforts will be made to encourage agencies to expand internal mobility opportunities in order to develop more widely experienced executives. OPM will attempt to improve mobility between agencies. Executive development and training should be more available as executives prepare themselves for recertification.

NOTES

1. Testimony of Alan K. Campbell, in U.S. Congress (1978:22).
2. See, for example, U.S. MSPB (1984).
3. The 10,777 limit was eliminated by the Federal Employees Pay Comparability Act of 1990, P.L. 101-509, November 1990, which replaced grade levels GS 16, 17, and 18 with an ungraded senior level position system and established separate pay systems for administrative law judges and board of contract appeals judges.

SOURCES

Commission on the Organization of the Executive Branch of the Government. 1955. *Task Force Report on Personnel and Civil Service.* Washington, D.C.
Huddleston, Mark. 1987. "Background Paper." In *The Government's Managers.* Twentieth Century Fund. New York: Priority Press.
President's Commission (on the Compensation of Career Executives). 1988. *Report.* Washington, D.C.
U.S. Congress. 1978. House. Committee on Post Office and Civil Service, Hearings: "Civil Service Reform." 95th Cong., 2d sess.

————. 1983. House. Committee on Post Office and Civil Service, Subcommittee on Civil Service, Hearings: "Senior Executive Service." 98th Cong., 2d sess.

U.S. CSC (Civil Service Commission). 1971. *The Federal Executive Service.* Washington, D.C.

————. 1977. *Personnel Management Project.* Washington, D.C.

U.S. MSPB (Merit Systems Protection Board). 1984. *The 1984 Report on the Senior Executive Service.* Washington, D.C.

U.S. OPM (Office of Personnel Management). 1989. *The Status of the Senior Executive Service, 1988.* Washington, D.C.

13. A Comparative Lesson:

The Senior Executive Service in Australia

John Halligan

The 1970s and 1980s were a time of ferment in Australian public administration. The several public services experienced the most intensive period of change since the beginning of the twentieth century, as governments reformed structures and processes within their executive branches. These fundamental changes were both a response to the rapidly expanding demands on executives and a consequence of moves by reformist governments to redistribute power within executive branches. As a consequence, traditional administrative modes of operating were supplanted, as both management and political leadership became increasingly important. These trends were of course international: the ascendancy of managerial and political executives is a familiar process in Western democratic countries.

A distinctive manifestation of these changes in Australia can be seen in personnel management. It has become fashionable for state and federal governments to reconstitute the senior public service and to replace the Public Service Board with central agencies under political direction.[1] Such changes in Australian public services reflect a number of influences and reform movements, of both indigenous and overseas origins; but the influence of the U.S. Civil Service Reform Act of 1978, whether direct or indirect, is unquestionable. The major changes—the establishment of a senior executive service and the reformulation of central organization for personnel management—were implemented throughout Australia during the decade after the passage of this act. There is another sense in which the American experience has been salient for Australia. It provided the most distinctive and best-known alternative to the British model (which historically has been the touchstone in guiding Australian practice). Consequently, departures from tradition have been interpreted as American, and recent changes have been depicted as propelling Australia down the U.S. path of politicization.

Before we proceed, the main points of comparison between U.S. and Australian personnel systems should be noted. The U.S. higher civil service has generally been depicted in the literature as differing from other systems in the strength of the specialist and the role and extent of political appointments, the most striking contrasts being with the British system. The Australian system falls between the two. The Australian senior public service has, following the British tradition, not provided for noncareer (i.e., political) appointees. Like the U.S. system, the Australian personnel service has been based on a career service and on the specialist (although the latter has had to compete with the generalist administrator for senior positions). The semblance of an administrative elite has been cultivated in recent decades, although never comparable to the British administrative class. The Australian system can be seen, therefore, as a distinctive type that corresponds to neither the U.S., British, or European system.[2]

This chapter examines the application of CSRA principles in Australia, focusing on the senior executive service. The federal experience is examined—with reference to the role of contending conceptions of the senior public service—and some lessons are explored.

1883 and 1978: Australian Echoes of Pendleton and CSRA?

There have been two major periods of intensive administrative change in Australia. Both periods were characterized by experimentation, attention to system design, and the emergence of a distinctive paradigm. The first pattern arose from the great period of modernization between the 1880s and the 1920s, which also produced the reconstitution of the colonial systems into six states and a national government within the Australian federation. The second pattern is still emerging from the second great period of change (1970s–1990s), which involved the systemic reform of all seven public sectors. As a consequence, the paradigm that has dominated for most of this century has been largely displaced by a second framework, one that has yet to be fully implemented and tested but that has nevertheless secured wide acceptance (Halligan and Power 1991; Halligan and Wettenhall 1988).

The main product of the earlier period was the provision of centralized personnel control for the public service and decentralized management within the public sector. Both were designed to disengage politicians from administrative processes. The second period has been characterized by the dismemberment of the centralized personnel function and the managerializing of the public service. The political executive has been regenerated as an active participant in the executive branch. At the beginning of each period of change in Australia was a major change of direction in the United States. The years 1883 and 1978 assume significance in both countries: 1883 signaled a shift toward a new approach to personnel management, while 1978 represented the demise of a policy that issued from the first—the fall of the central personnel agency that had dominated the intervening years.

The year of the Pendleton Act in the United States, 1883, was also pivotal in Australian administrative history because it both produced the first significant legislation for central personnel management and saw the public corporation emerge as an organizational form. Neither innovation was immediately successful, but each supplied a model that other governments drew on and refined over the following generation. The significance of these developments lay in the formulation of the relationship between politicians and bureaucrats based on the notion of removing a range of personnel and technical decisions from the direct influence of politics.

The move to institute personnel systems in the Australian colonies arose from the lack of uniform rules governing personnel and, in particular, was a reaction against the prevalence of patronage in recruiting staff. The Victorian Public Service Act of 1883 made explicit for the first time the main principles of public service recruitment and control, but the transition was not accomplished until later legislation was passed in New South Wales (1895) and by the new federal government (1902). This legislation had two important effects. First, it expressed the idea that personnel administration could be divorced from both financial administration and government policy. Second, it established a pattern consisting of a career service, recruitment from school at base grade on an open and competitive basis, and central control by an independent board or commissioner with full control of the public service (Caiden 1964; Spann 1979).

The second U.S. landmark year also had resonances in Australia as well as long-term effects of profound importance. The Civil Service Act of 1978 inaugurated a new period of personnel management in the United States. Its main components—the senior executive service and the Office of Personnel Management—found imitations in

Australia almost immediately.[3] The U.S. approach, and Australia's, "emphasized the values of management flexibility and efficiency and downplayed the traditional public personnel values of equity and procedural uniformity" (Ban and Ingraham 1984:2).

In Australia, the mounting pressure to strengthen the political executive led a state government to initiate the first major break with past practice. In New South Wales, the public service had been subject to the dictates of the most powerful central personnel agency in the country. The Public Service Board, an independent authority, had statutory powers that covered recruitment and promotions, establishments, industrial relations, and the efficiency and economy of public service administration. In 1979, the Labor state government formally moved to curb its power and to assert the paramountcy of the government. Subsequently, public service boards in all states, and eventually at the federal level (in 1987), lost their powers, their independence, and usually their very existence. The most common practice was to differentiate the functions of the former board and assign them to new agencies. A most important outcome was that personnel management came under political direction in all public services (although special provision was generally made for merit protection). This occurred by designating a central agency as responsible to the prime minister or state premier and through the delegation of responsibilities to departments subject to ministerial direction.

The diffusion of the SES concept in Australia also occurred in the 1980s. A senior executive service was introduced in the state of Victoria in 1982 and federally in 1984. Two other states, Western Australia in 1987 and New South Wales in 1989, followed. Each case was accompanied by a more general swing toward political management that was based both on private sector methods and on extending political influence over the public service.

At the federal level, the job of implementing this approach fell to a new government in 1983, which was susceptible to the appeal of the political and managerial conceptions. With the success of state Labor governments in combining political reconstruction with managerialist ideology in the 1980s, the combination became irresistible to the federal Labor government when the need for solutions became pressing. The intensification of fiscal austerity produced a need for tighter resource use, which could not be satisfied by the process-oriented traditional approach. The government chose to accelerate the introduction of managerialism because it complemented its political agenda. Managerialism offered both a new approach for directing the public service and a rationalization for exerting greater ministerial control.

A senior executive service was a central component of the reform program. In studying the development of the SES it is difficult to isolate it from the broader program of change. In the first phase of the SES (1984–87) implementation was permissive, but following extensive departmental reorganization in 1987, a phase of involuntary change commenced. It is necessary, therefore, to establish whether the SES objectives were achieved and to explore to what extent the conceptions of the SES, discussed below, were realized in practice.

Three Conceptions of the Senior Public Service

In the early post–Second World War period an American visitor reported that "both the Australian and United States Services are based on a similar classification concept, give wide scope to the specialist, and are founded on a strong and valuable egalitarian tradition" (Scarrow 1957:139–40). The strength of the Australian tradition was subsequently tested. Three conceptions contended for recognition prior to the emergence of the senior executive service in the federal public service.[4]

The Elite Conception

The British administrative class has long served as a model for Australian reformers. Its basis was a group of generalists specifically recruited from universities and displaying certain qualities. The elitist conception did not take root in the Australian environment, where egalitarianism flourished with the support of the union movement and the Labor party. Traditionally, senior positions were open to both specialist and generalist. At various times, official inquiries recommended developing the senior public service along the lines of the administrative class, but only when the development of a senior service became pressing were there moves in this direction. With the vast expansion in the role and size of the federal government during and following the Second World War, new regulatory mechanisms and policy-making processes were required. The higher public service expanded as greater specialization and a larger second division—those senior officials immediately below department heads—became necessary (Scarrow 1957).

The Committee of Inquiry into Public Service Recruitment (1959) recommended an administrative class modeled on the British system. This was to involve the direct entry of recruits to the training classes of an enlarged second division. While this recommendation was made with the British administrative class in mind, it differed in a number of respects (e.g., a degree was not prescribed, and the British social context did not exist in Australia). Even if the concept differed from the British administrative class in its recruitment policy, in terms of purpose there was a close resemblance. The proposal envisaged senior public servants who would focus on policy, relationships with politicians, and processing the work of program specialists: "The Committee wanted to give recognition to the 'thinking' function of the Service or policy-planning, which had been recognized only on a piecemeal basis rather than comprehensively. The Service should recruit people who would be able to devote themselves to policy-making directly into the Second Division, which up until then had been conceived mainly as managerial" (Caiden 1965:419). The influence of egalitarianism, however, remained too entrenched for an elitist concept to receive support, even from the conservative and Anglophile government of the day. It endorsed the committee's objectives but preferred different means to achieve them.[5]

An administrative elite, nevertheless, emerged as the result of incremental moves toward cultivating the senior public service. The constraints on recruiting graduates were relaxed, and the education of staff was given greater recognition. The numbers of graduate entrants with general rather than specialist degrees increased. Specialist skills were still recognized at this level, but from persons who were primarily policy advisors, managers, or administrators. The graduate generalist acquired a more prominent role than the specialist. The second division was crystalized as "a corps of top administrators and/or managers" by giving it "explicit and systematic recognition." It became official policy to develop the "corporate identity of the Second Division" (Wheeler 1964:293–94; Crisp 1970).

Canberra's variant of an administrative and policy elite became a reality. Under the coalition government (1949–1972), the senior public service reached its zenith. The power of the senior public service increased, and the Canberra mandarin became entrenched. Thus a royal commission argued:

The administration, especially in its higher echelons, has an exaggerated conception of its proper role in the processes of government; that it believes, consciously or unconsciously, that, independently of Parliament or the government, it is the guardian of "the public interest" as opposed to sectional or vested interest, of continuity and stability in government administration, and of assumed social consensus about certain basic "supra-political" values. (RCAGA 1976:18–19)

Political Responsiveness Conception

The pressure to expand the influence of the politicians intensified in the 1970s. The bureaucracy was seen as too elitist, too independent, too unrepresentative, and insufficiently responsive. The reaction was to challenge the public servants' monopoly over advice to ministers and to question their indispensability to the processes of government. Alternative sources of advice and assistance were increasingly relied upon by ministers, mainly in the form of greater numbers of ministerial advisors, who were often public servants.[6] Overt political appointments to top positions in the public service occurred, but there were only a few (if celebrated) examples. Up until the early 1980s, then, there was experimentation with several options for expanding ministerial influence.

There were, however, proponents of greater change. Wilenski, a key adviser to Labor governments and disseminator of North American ideas within Australia, focused on the issues for a "democratic socialist government": the need to reestablish ministerial control and greater responsiveness—an American concept—to government policies and priorities. This was part of a political framework that promised to increase "democracy"—by allowing the minister to have greater influence, and by expanding the accessibility and diversity of the public service and diminishing the roles of the public servant. The essence of the argument was that the top positions were already politicized because the incumbents were "heavily involved in political decision making, and many appointments [were] politically influenced." Accordingly, the role of public servants should be recognized by converting covert to overt political appointments. Wilenski became the primary advocate of "a far more radical step . . . a move towards the United States system"—the appointment of senior public servants by the government (Wilenski 1980:27–28; Wilenski and Yerbury 1983:160–61; Wilenski 1986).

This type of advice was influential in the framing of the Labor party's 1983 election platform (with which it won control of the government). The platform argued for greater opportunity to appoint
"officers with special expertise . . . to create a more open and responsive service." It proposed a political tier within the senior ranks of the
public service. This was to be a special division composed of all departmental heads (who made up the first division) and up to 5 percent
of the second division, with provision for variations according to circumstances. The appointments would be made by the cabinet on the
recommendation of individual ministers. It was expected that most appointments to the special division, at least in the short term, would be
public servants, because there would be insufficient persons elsewhere
with the appropriate skills and experience. There was no requirement
that this be the case in practice.[7] In essence, this scheme represented
the most significant challenge to the tradition of public service neutrality since the formation of the federal government. The formulation
specifically sought to place the control of policy direction in the hands
of political appointees within the public service. It also meant a departure from the evolving convention which was that the minister's
office should be developed.

Managerial Conception

The managerial model was crystalized in the early 1980s as consensus rapidly emerged about the deficiencies of the public service.
This occurred in the context of fiscal austerity when the private sector
had again become a fashionable source of inspiration for the public
sector. But the factor that most influenced attitudes was the failure of
management in specific agencies (the details of which were exposed
through a series of politically embarrassing public inquiries).

A bipartisan view emerged that the management skills of the senior
public service were deficient. According to this argument, management skills had been undervalued relative to policy and administrative
skills. In addition, the emerging orthodoxy among many public administrators was that managerial approaches should be adopted. There
were growing pressures within the public service for managers to have
greater freedom from procedural constraints and for departments to be
able to manage more independently of central agencies. These sentiments were reflected in a parliamentary report and a review of federal
administration that saw the need to refashion the federal public service
to reflect private sector modes of operating and give prominence to

management skills. In particular, they advocated greater emphasis on mobility, external recruitment, flexibility in deployment, staff appraisal, appointment to levels rather than specific positions, and a servicewide approach.[8]

Implementing the Senior Executive Service

The new scheme envisaged the reshaping of the second division into a unified group entitled the senior executive service (SES). The Australian public service scheme was mandatory: all members of the existing second division were automatically included in the SES. Emphasis was to be placed on the active deployment of senior staff across the public service. At this systemic level, the quality of public service management was to be enhanced by greater movement of senior managers within the service and by recruiting lateral entrants. At the departmental level, there was to be greater opportunity for deploying senior staff. Staff development and staff appraisal were to receive greater emphasis.

The scheme was depicted at the time "as an attempt to bring together the best of our systems with the best practices in some overseas services and those that are alleged to prevail in private sector organisations."[9] The title of the new group was acquired from the U.S. SES, and U.S. principles were followed (although a senior executive category had previously been recommended for the Australian public service) (RCAGA 1976:249, 272).[10] The basis of the concept was an executive group that was to operate as a servicewide, corporate entity, rather than simply as the sum of departmental and agency members. The major contrast with the U.S. system was the lack of a bonus package as an incentive to performance.

The Public Service Act now referred to the SES as providing a group of officers who: "may undertake higher level policy advice, managerial and professional responsibilities" and may be deployed by secretaries within departments, and by the Public Service Board (before its closure in 1987) within the Australian public service. The initial implementation of the program occurred within the first three years of its inauguration on 1 October 1984. Its progress can be considered by examining three main objectives: openness and competitiveness, mobility, and performance evaluation.[11]

One central objective of SES arrangements was that positions in the public service should become more open and more competitive.

Greater openness in the service was to be achieved by inviting applicants both inside and outside the Australian public service to apply for vacancies in the SES. A particular goal was to inject persons from the private sector into the public service. To facilitate the entry of outsiders, the opportunity for fixed-term engagements was provided. There was no pronounced increase in external appointments following the introduction of the SES. The proportion of such appointments was 15 percent in 1984–1985, 10 percent the following year, 8 percent in 1987, and 5 percent in 1988. The majority of SES appointments continued to come from intradepartmental promotion. Most disheartening for the advocates of increased external recruitment was the failure to attract more than a few persons from the private sector. The most compelling reason for failure was the poor salaries offered relative to the private sector (or the Victorian senior executive service). The government had recognized the difficulty but could not resolve the conflict between higher salaries for senior executives and its general industrial policy of wage restraint. In addition, a shortage of funds limited the scope and scale of the advertising for the positions, despite the Public Service Board's claim that "extensive public advertising of senior executive positions is essential to achieve an open, competitive SES" (Public Service Board 1986:29).

The second thrust of the new system was to increase staff mobility at senior levels. Moreover, this mobility was to apply between departments, between central agencies and departments, and between policy and managerial work. The arguments were that people favored promotions rather than transfers and that departments were concerned with filling positions but not necessarily with servicewide needs. These problems were to be overcome by loosening the relationship between people and positions (abolishing tenure for positions), placing more emphasis on general skills (management and policy) relative to specialized knowledge, and by inaugurating a staff mobility program. However, for the initial years of the scheme only about one-fifth of movements were interdepartmental.

The problems with the mobility objectives were twofold. First, there were strong pressures within the system to counter its full implementation. Departmental secretaries were reluctant to lose senior staff who had acquired specialized knowledge of an operational sphere. Officers, for reasons previously mentioned, were not stimulated to transfer. Second, the tension between system needs and specialized requirements of components was not properly taken into account in the design of the SES program. A large number of positions required specialists, despite their designation as part of the SES. As governments have learned in the United States, there must be a balance between systemwide and specialized needs (Sherwood 1986: Uhr 1987).

The third component of the original SES concept—performance appraisal—was developed at a leisurely pace. Departments were to be required to establish schemes for staff appraisal while working within Public Service Board guidelines designed to ensure enough uniformity for a servicewide approach. The Public Service Board developed options for staff appraisal schemes and conducted a pilot program to test models. The board viewed staff appraisal as "an essential component of the Government's plans for improving senior management" (Public Service Board 1986:33) but did not accord it priority. There appeared to be neither much commitment to formalized schemes nor much prospect of a move toward performance assessment. The successor to the board, the Public Service Commission, expected that its current approach to performance evaluation (which seeks to link goals and indicators to corporate planning) would eventually provide a model for the service. Nevertheless, five years after the establishment of the SES there was still no servicewide appraisal scheme.[12]

In the first three years, the overall changes to the Australian Public Service (APS) at the senior executive level were limited. It was unclear in what respects the SES could be clearly differentiated from the old second division. A common view among members of the SES was that the changes have had little effect on them personally. The government experienced relatively little success in developing generalist, government-wide perspectives on the part of its senior executives. Executive development was limited, voluntary mobility between agencies did not increase, lateral recruitment remained modest, and performance appraisal was not taken on.

Immediately following the 1987 election, the prime minister instigated a major program of change for the public service. For the senior executive service there were two important developments. The first was a massive reorganization of departments that reduced their number from twenty-eight to eighteen. The creation of the so-called megadepartments produced fewer senior positions. The second was the intensification of cutbacks in staff, which demonstrated that the SES could no longer be immune from reductions. Departments were also reworking their internal structures to reflect new program structures, and the top-down pressures to apply program budgeting, efficiency scrutinies, and resource management were now unavoidable (Halligan 1987; Wettenhall 1989).

Toward Political Management

To what extent have the managerial and political conceptions of the SES been realized in practice? What are the results of these managerial and political pressures to change the senior public service? These questions cannot be answered with precision at this time because of the lack of published studies, although some tendencies are clear.[13]

How Managerial?

The main elements of the managerial model were the infusion of managerial skills and private sector values and techniques. The need for senior executives to conform accelerated after the 1987 reorganization of departments, as the pressures to manage intensified and as managerial objectives developed (the notion of risk management, for example, rapidly became a hallmark of managerialism). The extraordinarily intensive process of change destabilized the senior public service and forced its members to confront the new framework. Senior positions in departments were vacated through reorganization or managerial rationalization and were filled by a process that saw many SES members displaced and a substantial number retrenched (about 10 percent). The result was something of a transformation of the senior executive service. Those who survived this process were generally required to demonstrate a degree of adaptation to a managerial culture. The four main trends are as follows.

First, the SES continues to be based on internal promotion. This means that there is a reliance on converts, particularly in the most senior positions: persons who served during the premanagerialist era and were capable of fitting into the new culture. Many senior public servants have experienced difficulties in reconciling the old values with the new. The relatively modest impact of external recruits is apparent. Second, those who have successfully adapted to the new framework and survived the purge are not primarily managerial specialists (e.g., computers, personnel, financial management). They have had to justify their candidature in terms of SES competencies (consisting of general managerial skills). The most successful have been public servants with training in economics, because they have adjusted more easily to the rigors of an economic rationalist environment and the requirements of resource management.

Third, there is a greater attachment to instrumentalism among many senior executives. This reflects both the instrumental emphasis of managerialism and the pragmatics of survival under a government that emphasizes ministerial influence. This instrumentalism can also be seen as an extension of the "can do" ethos that has been prevalent among central agency executives and diffused with their movement into line departments.[14] But it principally results from the combination of managerialism and top-down political direction, which provides strong incentives for public servants to be responsive.

Fourth, this mix of generalist manager, economic rationalist, and central agency can-doer has been directed at the policy specialist in line departments, with decisive impact in some cases. The top management of departments has been displaced by persons without a background in or commitment to departmental policy concerns. The consciousness of senior public servants about managerial skills has been enormously improved, but whether they have become skilled managers remains to be demonstrated. The central agency breeding ground for many senior public servants is not necessarily conducive to producing persons capable of managing megadepartments with major responsibilities for delivering services. Resource management has received priority, but other managerial skills remain underdeveloped (Baker 1989; Public Service Commission 1989).

How Politically Responsive?

The central element of the politically responsive conception was not implemented. Nevertheless, the practice suggests that the intentions were largely realized. The government gave prominence to political direction, and this was reinforced by tight fiscal controls (and relatively limited scope for new policy for much of the 1980s).

Much of the pressure for formal political appointments within an SES was rechanneled by the creation of a new position, the ministerial consultant. The new Hawke government, mindful of the disruptions produced by its activist Labor predecessor (the Whitlam government, 1972–1975), settled for a compromise by creating this new mechanism for augmenting ministerial resources and influence. Ministerial consultants were to provide ministers with assistance from persons who either shared the party's values and objectives or offered special skills. In providing ministers with further support, the consultant offered a Labor government some relief from its concern about dependence on the permanent public service. The government's case for institutionalizing the practice of appointing ministerial consultants was based on two arguments. It was claimed that there was a legal need for formalizing the practice of such appointments (contract appointments having become commonplace during the last decade) and that there was a need to separate legislative provisions for political appointments from those for the career service. The result was a statutory scheme for engaging ministerial consultants with a process of appointment different from that of the public service (Halligan 1988).

Instead of introducing political appointments into the senior public service on a prescribed basis, the government chose to expand the ministerial office. Part of the compromise was a provision for ministerial consultants to work in departments (rather than the minister's office), but in practice this option was rarely used. Thus the appearance of politicization was avoided. The government also sanctioned the move toward interposing more political appointments between (or within) the bureaucracy and politicians. Ministerial staff (including both consultants and advisors) perform some roles previously undertaken by senior public servants and may be directly and routinely involved in departmental processes.

Appointments to the SES (and of departmental heads) continue to be largely from the public service. Ministerial influence on appointments occurs but is inclined to assume the form of negative acts—the vetoing of incompatible candidates—rather than positive interventions that reflect the minister's preferences. If contract employment becomes more established, the potential for patronage will test the continuing validity of traditional public service values.

Australian Lessons

A broadly similar concept was applied in both Australia and the United States: the schemes were designed to enhance management capacity, to emphasize the generalist manager, and to expand political control under the guise of responsiveness. Both concepts incorporated external recruitment, mobility, performance appraisal, and the corporate identity of the service. The Australian SES lacked two significant features of the U.S. scheme: performance appraisal (finally applied in the 1990s) and merit-based pay. There were also commonalities in the patterns of experience that emerged: six Australian lessons echoed the American experience.

First, the original concept placed emphasis on the need for expanding managerial skills. However, the enthusiasm for importing the notion of mobile generalists suggests misconceptions about the realities of work at senior levels. The focus on general competencies ignored the range of tasks performed in practice. General competencies were seen to be applicable across the public service. The generalist manager was really an illusion. The balance between generalist and specialist has yet to be resolved.

Second, there were inherent conflicts built into the original design. These derived from the mix of agendas: the desire to make the senior service more responsive and managerially competent, while seeking to preserve a career system based on public service values. As U.S. observers have indicated (Ban and Ingraham 1984; Huddleston 1988; Newlands 1988), there are inherent contradictions and conflicts between responsiveness and neutrality or management and other skills.

The third matter centers on implementation. In both countries there was a failure to follow through on the original concept: to implement integral aspects of the scheme. Remuneration that was more comparable to the private sector failed to materialize. In Australia, the Labor government's commitment to wage restraint led it to resist intense pressures to increase salary packages to reflect market realities. But other key aspects have yet to assume significance: performance appraisal remains experimental (and unsupported by performance pay), while contract employment has yet to be widely used.

A fourth lesson is that responsiveness may be exacted without imposing a formal layer or quota of political appointees. The cost is political appointments that are not formally and overtly recognized as such. There is still a *higher* public service that offers prospects for career public servants, even if senior executive roles are more constrained than before.

Fifth, the changes have not been accomplished without significant costs. This experience suggests the difficulty of achieving significant change without destabilizing the public service and impairing morale. The incentives of senior executives have become confused. Traditionally, they have received great satisfaction from proximity to political power, involvement in national policy roles, and public service. Now they are exhorted to focus on performance and to respect private sector values, but without the associated rewards of business executives.

Sixth, the Australian experience suggests the need for careful attention to balancing objectives, competencies, and values in reforming senior executive systems. A number of questions about what is appropriate for the development of the senior executive in the APS remain unresolved. Among the outstanding questions are how to reconcile the needs of a generalist, centrally administered SES system with those of a decentralized, more specialized public service; and how to balance the administrative, managerial, and policy roles of senior executives.

The senior executive service has been significant as a symbol and facilitator of change. It has been represented as a change mechanism for accelerating the shift toward a results-based public service and for developing the management skills of the senior public service. However, there is an argument that an SES was not essential to either, and the extent of its contribution has yet to be established. It has not had the impact of the SES in the state of Victoria, where substantial numbers of senior executives were brought in from outside the public service and performance plans and merit pay were integral (Halligan and O'Grady 1985; Cullen 1986). Compared to other SES schemes, the Australian federal experiment has been unenterprising. In the longer term, some merit may be discerned in this cautious approach, but it is not apparent yet.

Conclusions

There remains the question of the prospects for the Australian senior public service as an SES. It was indicated earlier that Australia had developed a distinctive service that shared characteristics with both U.S. and British models. Can it retain distinction in its new, but still evolving, form?

The Australian federal experience suggests that it is possible to accomplish change within the executive branch without heavy-handed politicization; that it is possible to exact responsiveness from career public servants without the imposition of partisans on the bureaucracy; that reliance of ministers on their offices can provide sufficient leverage over the public service; and that it may still be possible to reconcile responsiveness and relative neutrality in the public service if the extent of covert appointments can be contained. In these respects, the Australian senior public service may continue to remain distinctive.

There is greater uncertainty with the managerial side. The SES is currently in limbo. This is a problem of both conception and practice. The senior public service is suspended uneasily between the traditional service approach and ideas influenced by the private sector. The reconciliation of conflicting objectives, of old and new values, is far from being accomplished. Australia has yet to achieve a balance that effectively combines performance and public service integrity.

NOTES

1. In order to discuss recent public service change in Australia, it is necessary to consider both the states and the federal government. The states number only six (plus two territories) and are much larger relative to the other two spheres of government than their counterparts in the United States. Following the adoption of an income tax during the Second World War and the rapid expansion of its responsibilities, the federal level eclipsed the state level and developed a professional senior public service. During the 1980s, the states initially set the pace in administrative change.

2. One further contrast is that while the Australian public service has been the subject of criticism and intense pressure to reform, it has not suffered the denigration that the U.S. service has. Comparative studies of higher civil services include Fesler (1987) and Smith (1984).

3. There were other examples, such as the Victorian Department of Management and Budget, which was based on the U.S. Office of Management and Budget.

4. Each of the conceptions has been reported as exercising influence in the United States. See Huddleston (1988) and Ingraham and Ban (1988).

5. See Thompson (1989). Thompson also notes that the example of the U.S. Hoover commission was a factor that influenced the establishment of the inquiry (p. 148).

6. Since the ministerial advisor became a general feature, around half have been drawn from the public service, but the proportion of politically active nonpublic servants has been increasing (Walter 1986).

7. See the Labor party paper by Hawke and Evans (1983), discussed in Nethercote (1984).

8. An example is Commonwealth Parliament, Joint Committee of Public Accounts (1982). For an overview of the inquiries, see Nethercote (1984).

9. According to a then member of the Public Service Board, G. Glenn, "Senior Executive Service," speech to Department of Territories (October 1984).

10. The Canadian public service's management category was also closely studied.

11. The government's objectives are specified in Hawke and Evans (1983). See also Halligan (1988).

12. Performance appraisal was eventually introduced in the 1990s by departments operating within guidelines produced by the Public Service Commission. See also Enfield (1989:26).

13. Several academic surveys of the SES have been conducted, but have not yet been properly reported upon. The following observations are informed by interviews with senior executives from central agencies and line departments that have been conducted by myself and Colin Campbell, but which await systematic analysis. An initial report of one study is Pusey (1988). See also Nethercote (1988).

14. A matter that has been the subject of debate in Canberra has been the extent to which the heads of line departments have been appointed from persons who have served in the Department of Prime Minister and Cabinet. See Kelleher (1989).

SOURCES

Baker, John. 1989. "From Management to Leadership: A Comparative Perspective on Leadership in the Australian Public Service." *Australian Journal of Public Administration* 48 (3):249–64.

Ban, Carolyn, and Patricia Ingraham. 1984. "Civil Service Reform: Legislating Bureaucratic Change." In *Legislating Bureaucratic Change: The Civil Service Reform Act of 1978,* ed. Ingraham and Ban, 1–10. Albany: SUNY Press.

Caiden, G. E. 1964. "The Independent Central Personnel Agency: The Experience of the Commonwealth Public Service of Australia." *Public Administration* (London) 42 (Summer):133–61.

————. 1965. *Career Service.* Melbourne: Melbourne University Press.

Committee of Inquiry into Public Service Recruitment (Chairman: R. Boyer). 1959. *Report* Canberra: Commonwealth Government Printer.

Commonwealth of Australia. 1983. *Reforming the Australian Public Service: A Statement of the Government's Intention.* Canberra: Australian Government Publishing Service.

Commonwealth Parliament, Joint Committee of Public Accounts. 1982. *202nd Report: Selection and Development of Senior Managers in the Commonwealth Public Service.* Canberra: Australian Government Publishing Service.

Crisp, L. F. 1970. "Specialists and Generalists: Further Australian Reflections on Fulton." *Public Administration* (Sydney) 29 (3):197–217.

Cullen, R. B. 1986. "The Victorian Senior Executive Service: A Performance Based Approach to the Management of Senior Managers." *Australian Journal of Public Administration* 45 (1):60–71.

Enfield, John. 1989. "The Objectives of Reform in Public Sector Personnel Management." In *Public Sector Personnel Policies for the 1990s,* ed. D. C. Corbett, C. Selby Smith, and R.F.I. Smith, 7–31. Clayton: Public Sector Management Institute, Monash University.

Fesler, James W. 1987. "The Higher Public Service in Western Europe." In *A Centennial History of the American Administrative State,* ed. R. C. Chandler, 509–39. New York: Macmillan.

Halligan, John. 1987. "Reorganising Australian Government Departments 1987." *Canberra Bulletin of Public Administration* 52:40–47.

———. 1988. "The Australian Public Service Reform Program." In *Hawke's Second Government: Australian Commonwealth Administration 1984–1987,* ed. Roger Wettenhall and J. R. Nethercote, 27–84. Canberra: CCAE/RAIPA.

Halligan, John, and Michael O'Grady. 1985. "Public Sector Reform: The Victorian Experience." *Australian Journal of Public Administration* 44 (1):34–45.

Halligan, John, and John Power. 1991 "A Framework for the Analysis of Recent Changes in Australian Executive Branches." In *Handbook of Comparative and Development Public Administration,* ed. Ali Farazmand, 91–99. New York: Marcel Dekker.

Halligan, John, and Roger Wettenhall. 1988. "Major Changes in the Structure of Government Institutions." Keynote address to National Conference of the Royal Australian Institute of Public Administration, 200 Years of Public Administration—Retrospect and Prospect, Melbourne, 26–28 October.

Hawke, Bob, and Gareth Evans, 1983. *Labor and Quality of Government Policy.* Canberra: Australian Labor Party.

Huddleston, Mark W. 1988 "To the Threshold of Reform: The SES and America's Search for a Higher Civil Service." Presented at the Annual Meeting of the American Political Science Association, Washington, D.C.

Ingraham, Patricia W., and Carolyn Ban. 1988. "Politics and Merit: Can They Meet in a Public Service Model?" *Review of Public Personnel Administration* 8 (2):7–19.

Kelleher, S. R. 1989. "Departmental Secretary Appointments Observed." *Canberra Bulletin of Public Administration* 58:9, 11.

Nethercote, J. R. 1984. "Public Service Reform: Its Course and Nature." In *Australian Commonwealth Administration 1983: Essays in Review,* ed. Alexander Kouzmin, J. R. Nethercote, and Roger Wettenhall, 16–42. Canberra: CCAE/RAIPA.

———. 1988. "Changing Climate of Public Service." In *Hawke's Second Government: Australian Commonwealth Administration 1984–1987* ed. Roger Wettenhall and J. R. Nethercote, 1–126. Canberra: CCAE/RAIPA.

Newlands, Chester A. 1988. "The American Senior Executive Service: Old Ideals and New Realities." *International Review of Administrative Sciences* 54 (4):625–60.

Public Service Board, Commonwealth of Australia. 1986. *Annual Report 1985–86.* Canberra: Australian Government Publishing Service.

Public Service Commission, Commonwealth of Australia, 1989. *The State of the Australian Public Service.* Canberra: Occasional Paper 4 (July).

Pusey, Michael. 1988. "Our Top Canberra Public Servants Under Hawke." *Australian Quarterly* 60 (1):109–22.

RCAGA (Royal Commission on Australian Government Administration). 1976. *Report.* Canberra: Australian Government Publishing Service. Chairman: H. C. Coombs).

Scarrow, Howard A. 1957. *The Higher Public Service of the Commonwealth of Australia.* Durham, N.C.: Duke University Press.

Sherwood, Frank P. 1986. "Senior Management Systems." *Bureaucrat* (Fall):25–30.

Smith, Bruce L. R., ed. 1984. *The Higher Civil Service in Europe and Canada: Lessons for the United States.* Washington, D.C.: Brookings.

Spann, R. N. 1979. *Government Administration in Australia.* Sydney: Allen and Unwin.

Thompson, Elaine. 1989. "The Boyer Committee on Public Service Recruitment in Retrospect." *Australian Journal of Public Administration* 48 (2):146–54.

Uhr, John. 1987. "Rethinking the Senior Executive Service: Executive Development as Political Education." *Australian Journal of Public Administration* 46 (1):20–36.

Walter, James. 1986. *The Ministers' Minders: Personal Advisers in National Government.* Melbourne: Oxford University Press.

Wettenhall, Roger. 1989. "Recent Restructuring in Canberra: A Report on Machinery-of-Government Changes in Australia." *Governance* 2:95–106.

Wheeler, F. H. 1964. "The Responsibilities of the Administrator in the Public Service." *Public Administration* (Sydney) 23:293–94.

Wilenski, Peter. 1980. "Has the Career Service a Future?" In *State Servants and the Public in the 1980s,* ed. R. M. Alley, 27–28. Wellington: New Zealand Institute of Public Administration.

Wilenski, Peter, and Di Yerbury. 1983. "Reconstructing Bureaucracy: Towards a Vehicle for Social Change." In *Labor Essays 1983,* ed. John Reeves and Kelvin Thomson, 154–80. Melbourne: Drummond.

———. 1986. *Public Power and Public Administration.* Sydney: Hale and Iremonger.

14. Watch What We Pass
A Brief Legislative History of Civil Service Reform

Paul C. Light

Autumn 1978 was a very busy time for Congress. With the midterm elections only weeks away, members of Congress disposed of one bill after another in the typical mad rush to adjournment. Jimmy Carter's CETA job training program passed one day, strip mining protection the next, a $19 billion tax cut the next. Debate was often cursory, and knowledge of legislative specifics narrow. It was a normal end of session.

As Congress worked through the backlog, it also dispatched its good government bills, including Carter's Civil Service Reform Act (CSRA). Originally introduced as two bills—a reorganization plan and a reform bill—the Senate finally passed a combined measure on 4 October by voice vote; the House followed suit with a 365 to 8 vote two days later.

The bill promised a new era in public service. Flexibility and responsiveness were to be the code words, with merit pay, performance appraisal, bonuses, sabbaticals, and demonstration projects the opportunities, all led by an elite senior executive service (SES), the new motivators with support from the president's own Office of Personnel Management (OPM).

Weighing in at 128 pages, the CSRA had a provision for just about every political and administrative philosophy. Presidents won new authority, albeit slight, to remove incompetent employees. Unions finally earned the statutory right to organize. Conservatives secured a three-year cap on federal employment, liberals a strong section on prohibited personnel practices. Whistleblowers achieved a measure of respect through new protections against reprisals. Senior career employees gained the chance to compete for substantial bonuses. Veterans retained lifetime preferential treatment in the federal hiring process.

Agency personnelists even won a modicum of delegation. In short, it was a normal legislative process, replete with all the horse trades, compromises, pet projects, and occasional dogfights (particularly over Carter's proposed elimination of veterans' preference) that mark the passage of complex bills.

As with any bill 128 pages long, the CSRA also became a vehicle for an odd issue here and there. Congress could not resist, for example, restricting the SES bonus provision to an employee who "contributes to the efficiency, economy, or other improvement of Government operations or achieves a significant reduction in paperwork," thereby sending a typically confusing signal about the true intent of the provision.[1] Senior executives could easily ask whether this bill was about paperwork reduction or civil service reform. The likely answer, of course, was both. In this one provision Congress seemed to be conveying its own doubts about the true contributions of the civil service. Two years later, Congress would pass the 1980 Paperwork Reduction Act, formally codifying its growing concerns about the amount of needless paperwork imposed by unaccountable bureaucrats on the rest of humankind.

Despite such devil's compromises, however, the bill contained the first comprehensive civil service reform in nearly one hundred years. Alas, after four OPM directors and a phalanx of political appointees, the promise is far from realized, in large measure because of a host of decisions made and not made during that autumn of 1978. Although the CSRA produced improvements in many areas, the list of unfinished business remains long, in part because so much of the reform was left to the discretion of the implementers:

• The close defeat of reforms in veterans' hiring preference, for example, amplified the growing challenge in recruiting women and minorities into the federal work force.

• The failure to address pay equity in clear legislative terms, even to the extent of authorizing a simple study of gender segregation in the federal work force, intensified the growing sense of unfairness among women in government.

• The failure to cap total noncareer SES appointments and schedule C personal and confidential assistants produced crowding out at the very top of government, including persistent politicization at the OPM itself.

• The failure to decide which jobs should be career and political generated continued confusion about the proper role of each.

• The failure to decouple congressional, executive, and judicial pay doomed the SES to a decade-long struggle against the growing pay gap between public and private jobs.

• The failure to fund the basic components of civil service reform, particularly merit pay and sabbaticals, violated the underlying incentives for enhanced performance.

Without the dollars for full implementation, of course, the CSRA has come to represent a new generation of rules and regulations, a new wave of presidential appointees, pay freezes, grade creep, overlayering, and unfulfilled promises—more harm than good. Those in the civil service who believed that the 1978 legislative trade-offs were warranted by the promised incentives could not help but conclude they had been betrayed. Even though few could have predicted the outright hostility toward the civil service that Ronald Reagan's first OPM director, Don Devine, would bring to the job, CSRA gave him the tools to systematically weaken the career work force in government.

More to the point of this brief history, the success or failure of the 1978 CSRA cannot be understood as a problem of one bill alone. As noted above, Congress was very busy that muggy September and crisp October, passing and defeating a series of measures of direct relevance to civil service reform.

In fact, there were at least three other bills considered that fall that stand as metaphors for a broad philosophy of government that has often worked in contradiction to the new freedoms and responsibility of the CSRA. After reviewing these three bills in brief, this chapter will consider three questions that must be answered before CSRA or its successor can succeed.

Three Bills

Buried in the roughly one hundred public and private bills awaiting Carter's signature at the end of the 1978 session were two items that would fundamentally alter the management of the executive branch: the 1978 Inspector General Act and the 1978 Ethics in Government Act. And missing from the stack was one bill that would have fundamentally changed Congress: the Federal Regulation of Lobbying Act.

Although many other bills passed during the period that also changed the course of the public service, these three measures illustrate just how confused Carter and Congress were about the goals of reform.

In passing the CSRA, for example, Congress had accepted the notion that the public service could be reclaimed. All criticism of incompetent employees notwithstanding, Congress was willing to bet that performance could improve; that the civil service was worth supporting. As he had explained in announcing his proposal in March 1978, Carter was to be the great liberator, sweeping clean a bureaucratic maze "which neglects merit, tolerates poor performance, permits abuse of legitimate employee rights and mires every personnel action in red tape, delay and confusion" (Carter 1978).

Yet, at virtually the same moment, both Carter and Congress expressed continued concern about big government, corrupt appointees, and fraud, waste, and abuse. All celebrations of human potential aside, the Inspector General Act and Ethics in Government Act were highly prescriptive in tone, establishing new surveillance entities to keep the newly freed bureaucrats in check, even as Congress refused to bring itself into the new limelight through tighter regulation of its sprawling lobbying community.

This is not to argue that either the Inspector General Act or the Ethics in Government Act were somehow flawed. Both had noble aims. Rather, the two bills reflected the general ambivalence of the period. Ultimately, Congress was not willing to bet that civil servants would do the right thing at all, bracketing the CSRA with a host of new statutes limiting discretion. So, too, for Carter and his successors, Reagan and George Bush, who tightened their central oversight, whether through new regulatory review systems at the Office of Management and Budget (OMB) or politicization of the career layers of government.

The 1978 Inspector General Act

The day before Carter put his pen to the CSRA, he signed the Inspector General Act. The measure was anything but a presidential priority, however, having originated deep within the House of Representatives' Government Operations Committee staff.[2]

Nevertheless, the bill was significant enough to warrant discussion at two cabinet meetings—7 November 1977, and 10 April 1978—in which Carter expressed his concerns about his appointing authority. Under the original legislation, the inspectors general (IGs) could be removed by the president only if the reasons were communicated to Congress. Carter and his attorney general were troubled by this tepid limitation on the president's prerogative, and eventually convinced the House to allow removal without reporting, only to find the clause fully restored by the Senate in the final legislation. The original bill, introduced on 1 February 1977, was relatively simple. Only eighteen pages long, it would have created inspector generalships in eleven departments and agencies—Agriculture, Commerce, Housing and Urban Development, Interior, Labor, Transportation, Energy Research and Development Administration, Environmental Protection Agency, NASA, and the Veterans Administration.

By the end of the process two years later, the Community Services Administration and the Small Business Administration had been added and the new departments of Energy and Education had been covered under separate reorganization bills, while Heath and Human Services retained the IG created under a separate measure in 1976. By the end of the Reagan administration, ten years later, virtually every federal department and agency had been brought under the act, including the departments of Defense, State, Justice, and Treasury, the Central Intelligence Agency, Nuclear Regulatory Commission, and thirty-three small agencies, from the Government Printing Office to the Office of Personnel Management.

Even a cursory inspection of the basic statute reveals the legislative intent:

Sec. 2. In order to create independent and objective units—
(1) to conduct and supervise audits and investigations relating to programs and operations of the [establishment];
(2) to provide leadership and coordination and recommend policies for activities designed (A) to promote economy, efficiency, and effectiveness in the administration of, and (B) to prevent and detect fraud and abuse in, such programs and operations; and
(3) to provide a means for keeping the head of the establishment fully and currently informed about problems and deficiencies relating to the administration of such programs and operations and the necessity for and progress of correction action;
thereby is hereby established in each of such establishments an office of Inspector General. (P.L. 95-452)

Although the organizational thrust of the act was to consolidate audit and investigation units into single, quasi-independent units, passage involved far more than a thirst for accountability. Congress could have easily assuaged its concern about a lack of attention to fraud, waste, and abuse without the dual reporting relationship contained in Sec. 5 (b):

Semiannual reports of each Inspector General shall be furnished to the head of the establishment involved not later than April 30 and October 31 each year and shall be transmitted by such to the appropriate committees or sub-committees of the Congress within thirty days after receipt of the report, to-gether with a report by the head of the establishment containing any comments such head deems appropriate. (ibid.)

In adding this reporting chain to the inspector general concept, Congress was clearly moving from retail into wholesale, augmenting its own oversight through what has now become a 10,000-employee work force in offices of inspector general (OIGs) all across government.[3] Indeed, the first version of the House bill actually contained a provision requiring the inspector general to provide "such additional information or documents as may be requested by either House of Congress or, with respect to matters within their jurisdiction, by any committee or subcommittee thereof," while also mandating that these reports, information, and documents be transmitted to Congress or its committees or subcommittees *"without further clearance or approval."*[4] Although this broad authority was eventually dropped in negotiations with the Senate and the Carter White House, the provision sheds light on at least one secondary intent of the law: to provide greater congressional access to executive information.

This is not the place to review the success or failure of the Inspector General Act over the past decade—suffice it to say that the IGs have been extraordinarily effective in ferreting out fraud, waste, and abuse as measured by prosecutions and dollars saved. Whether their agencies are working better as a result is an entirely different issue, one that is best left to more rigorous analysis, (see Light 1992). Rather, it may be enough to simply note the enormous investment Congress and the president initially made in supporting the inspector general concept during its first years—years in which CSRA and the IGs were both competing for scarce resources. This investment is easily measured in table 18 by comparing the staffing of the OIGs themselves.

As table 18 suggests, the OIGs did very well during those first six years, largely through support from OMB and Congress. Admittedly, the OIG growth involved relatively small numbers in the grand scheme

Table 18. Percentage Changes in Employment of Civilians and Appointees, Office of Inspector General, 1980–1986

Department	IG Staff Employment	Total Agency Civilian Employment	Senior Executive Service Career	Senior Executive Service Noncareer	Schedule C Positions
Agriculture	\−9	\−12	\−11	37	40
Commerce	20	\−29	\−12	6	\−3
Defense[a]	15	1	19	23	7
Education	\−4	\−38	\−20	25	82
Energy	42	\−23	\−26	\−31	27
EPA	83	\−5	\−7	\−17	27
General Services Admin.	\−32	\−39	\−9	166[b]	283
Health and Human Services	41	\−14	\−11	\−24	\−20
HUD	\−2	\−30	\−14	29	\−1
Interior	53	\−4	1	\−15	33
Labor	28	\−25	\−17	21	3
NASA	\−2	\−6	\−6	—[c]	\−100
Small Business Admin.	\−3	\−16	\−7	7	27
State	46	8	80	33	29
Transportation	2	\−15	11	17	42
Veterans Administration	17	5	—[d]	\−54	50
Total (average)	23	1	\−5	13	13

SOURCES: The figures on SES and Schedule C appointments are drawn from GAO, 1987.
a. Defense OIG created in 1982.
b. GSA noncareer SES increased from 6 to 16 during this period; GSA Schedule C from 6 to 23.
c. NASA noncareer SES moved from zero to 8 during the period.
d. The VA does not have a career SES, per se.

of government—2,000 or so new full-time-equivalent slots. Nevertheless, the growth ran counter to the downsizing in most other career offices of government. Moreover, even in agencies where the OIGs lost staff, the decline was always less than the rest of the work force. In addition, noncareer members of the SES and Schedule C appointees also prospered during the first six years of the CSRA implementation, perhaps sending the overall message that those involved in oversight or political management were exempt from the deep cuts under way in most corners of the government.

The 1978 Ethics in Government Act

At the same time Congress took action to gain a greater information foothold in the executive branch, it passed comprehensive legislation to regulate presidential appointments. One might add, parenthetically, that the Ethics in Government Act passed its final hurdle on 12

October, one day before the House and four days before the Senate declined to press further investigations of the Koreagate lobbying probe that had involved members of both chambers. The staff of *Congressional Quarterly* described the conclusion of the House investigation as "a bang of hyperbole, a whimper of opprobrium and a mass of uncertainties about the future of the House ethics process."[5]

Whatever the outcome of Koreagate, Congress was firm regarding new financial disclosure requirements for its own members, passed in separate ethics codes at the opening of the Ninety-fifth Congress in 1976, as well as for presidential appointees, passed in the final Ethics in Government Act. The key difference, perhaps, was that violations by members of Congress were addressed only through internal disciplinary action by the respective chamber, while violations by presidential and judicial appointees were subject to civil penalties.

Like the CSRA and Inspector General Act, the Ethics in Government Act consisted of a new set of rules for behavior and an enforcement body. As summarized by G. Calvin Mackenzie, the law had its greatest impact on presidential appointees in "the requirement that all high-ranking and noncareer federal officials make annual public disclosure of their personal finances, the limitations placed on the activities of former federal officials after they leave the government, and the creation of an Office of Government Ethics to supervise compliance" (1987:81).

Alongside the financial disclosure, conflict of interest, and postemployment provisions, Congress also used the bill to create an independent counsel mechanism providing for judicial appointment of a special prosecutor to investigate criminal allegations against high-level appointees. As Mackenzie concludes, "recent efforts to raise the standards of ethical conduct in government have resulted in a web of legalisms in which public financial disclosure is the most prominent strand. These have been designed to enshrine fairness, and the appearance of fairness, as the highest standard of public choice. Americans have relied on the law for this purpose because they have not felt free to place a full measure of trust in the personal integrity of their public servants" (ibid.: 82–83).

Again, this is not the appropriate place to review the success or failure of the Ethics in Government Act. Rather, it may be enough to note that the act made the process of recruiting any leadership for the civil service, whether competent or not, much more difficult, which has resulted in the indiscriminate and unintentional decapitation of many federal units. As I have noted elsewhere, vacancies can leave the career civil service directionless:

Vacancies that are left open short-circuit the policy process, and departments cannot fight cuts without top leadership. With unfilled slots at the assistant secretaryships and below, newly appointed secretaries have little access to the kinds of information and expertise they need to win budget battles. In short, the political-career connection can be easily severed by simply leaving the bottom band of appointments unfilled. Whether the strategy is deliberate or simply the product of the sheer number of positions to be filled, the result is a lack of leadership. (Light 1987:163)

Unfortunately, the single most visible impact of the Ethics in Government Act may be the creation of a seemingly endless stream of vacancies across government. Its virtuous goals notwithstanding, the act created a time-consuming, highly public process that is often intimidating to the very best candidates. As Mackenzie concludes,

The more rigorous financial disclosure and conflict of interest requirements of the past decade are an important new hurdle in the recruiting process. They are confusing, frightening, and often costly. They raise a widespread specter of public embarrassment and give pause to people who might otherwise willingly endure financial and personal sacrifices to serve their country. No one familiar with the presidential appointments process could possibly argue that the laws have no effect on recruiting. (Mackenzie 1987:89)

According to data collected by the National Academy of Public Administration under Mackenzie's direction, two-thirds of the presidential appointees selected between 1978 and 1984 reported having to take action to comply with the new rules, even as the amount of presidential appointee scandal appeared to grow unabated. Thus, the cost of the Ethics Act may be in creating a disincentive to serve among large numbers of highly qualified individuals who will not stand for public disclosure or the considerable time and accounting cost of filing, while doing little to deter those whose primary motives for service are fraud, greed, and theft.

More importantly, not only are presidential appointees arriving in place later and later in the term, they are staying for a shorter and shorter time in the same position. The incentive for presidential appointees, whose average time in-position has declined over the past three decades to twenty-two months in Reagan's first term, is clear: make a quick hit and get out.

Given an explosion in the number of jobs now subject to presidential appointment—up from 71 cabinet and 200 subcabinet and non-career SES-equivalent positions under Franklin Roosevelt to 290 cabinet and 2,500 subcabinet and SES slots in 1985—the greater challenge for presidents lies in merely reducing the number of vacancies in a department or agency, and, in doing so, maintaining open lines of communication both upward and downward.

In that regard, both Reagan and Bush fared poorly, each setting a new record for lateness in filling the top jobs. The average time involved in filling a presidential, Senate-confirmed post has steadily risen from 2.4 months under John F. Kennedy to 5.3 months under Reagan and 8.1 months under Bush (Mackenzie 1990:30). To be fair, the Ethics in Government Act is only one part of a complex problem. Following eight years of a like-minded Republican regime, Bush may have simply run out of available appointees. Caveat noted, the Ethics in Government Act opened a new era in the inspection of presidential appointees, which, in turn, reflected deeply felt congressional and public cynicism toward the very individuals about to be chosen to lead a revitalized civil service.

The Public Disclosure of Lobbying Act

As in any Congress, many more bills were defeated or buried in committee than passed and signed into law. All totaled, over 19,000 bills were introduced in the House and Senate during the Ninety-fifth Congress, 1977–1978, while only 633 passed (Ornstein, Mann, and Malbin: 154–55, 160).

Lost in the final frenzy of the session were dozens of bills that might have changed the prospects for civil service reform. One involved Carter's proposal for hospital cost containment, which might have constrained the rapid growth in federal employee health insurance expenditures. Another would have placed a sunset on any federal spending program not specifically reauthorized by Congress every eighteenth year. Still another bill would have created the first equal opportunity protection for Senate employees, who, to this day, are still not governed by the prohibited practices covering the civil service. Still another would have established public financing of congressional campaigns. However, no bill was more potentially supportive of a new public service than H.R. 8494, a bill to completely revamp the 1946 Federal Regulation of Lobbying Act. By refusing to tackle the growing influence of special interest groups on Capitol Hill, Congress may have condemned itself, and the nation, to the budget crisis that crippled funding of civil service reform.

The initial bill as reported by the House Judiciary Committee was relatively simple: registered lobbyists would have to report quarterly to the comptroller general regarding their legislative and executive branch activities. By the time the bill left the floor, however, two amendments had been added, one to require reports on grass-roots lobbying expenditures, the other to require disclosure of groups that contributed more than $3,000 to their organizations.[6] Despite considerable debate about freedom of speech and the chilling effect of such stringent reporting, the bill survived a series of amendments offered by Republican Tom Kindness of Ohio (that would have provided a new definition of killing with kindness) and passed 26 April 1978, on what usually passes for a reasonably close vote in the House, 259 to 140. Immediately following passage, Carter expressed his strong support: "This bill will enable the American people to understand and see more clearly how the legislative process is being affected by organizations that engage in significant lobbying activities" (Carter 1978).

At a very minimum, the reporting requirements would have enabled members of Congress, ably assisted no doubt by public interest groups, to determine whether a particular lobbying effort was real or manufactured. And it would have established clear trails of influence from lobbyists to subcommittees and committees. With penalties of up to $10,000 and two years imprisonment per violation, the bill clearly meant business.

Given the natural tendency of Congress to respond to issues on the basis of mail tonnage, the Public Disclosure of Lobbying Act might well have altered some of the normal politics leading to the bureaucrat bashing that the National Commission on the Public Service (Volcker Commission) and so many others have criticized.

Moreover, the bill might have blunted the rising tide of entrepreneurism on Capitol Hill, well chronicled by Burdette Loomis in his work on *The New American Politician* (1988). Ambition and entrepreneurship have changed the face of political life. With huge expansions in staff support and no limits on access to information from a host of sources, each member of Congress has become a separate enterprise, unaccountable to all but the voters back home and, even then, not without enormous incumbency advantages that virtually assure re-election every time out.

Ultimately, the entrepreneurship that so characterizes the contemporary Congress may work against the kind of stable leadership that might support a revitalized public service. As Loomis suggests, "The very fragmentation of the Congress allows ambitious politicians to strive, almost continually, for one new position or another. Like builders enterprises or seeking publicity, moving up, even incrementally, offers politicians the sense that they are accomplishing something, in the absence of more concrete evidence. Again, the entrepreneurial style often invites talented politicians to turn away from substantive accomplishment in pursuit of more accessible goals" (ibid.: 232). In such a world, public disclosure of lobbying might have brought somewhat greater exposure to the often invisible linkage between members of Congress and special interest groups and, therefore, somewhat lesser incentives for the free-wheeling entrepreneurship described above.

Alas, it was not to be. Although Senate Governmental Affairs Committee Chairman Abraham Ribicoff, a Connecticut Democrat, had introduced an even tougher measure, covering more groups and more grass-roots activity, it was amended, refined, and redrafted into such a weak alternative to the House that Ribicoff refused to manage the now-tepid bill if it ever reached the Senate floor. It died unceremoniously with thousands of other bills at the close of the Congress.

Three Questions

Nothing in this brief legislative history is meant to suggest that presidents and Congress get confused only about civil service reform. They are often capable of setting course one moment only to change the very next. Witness the recent flip-flops on catastrophic health insurance and tax increases.

Rather, the confusion about whether to free the civil service or imprison it reflects a lingering doubt about just what course to set in the first place. Although everyone seemed to agree reform was in order, no one appeared to know the answers to many of the basic questions that might have shaped reform. Consider three simple questions as examples. How many political appointees is too many? What are the baselines against which to measure the success or failure of reform? Just how much does pay matter anyway? Lacking answers to these and other queries, the president and Congress could feel quite comfortable passing a reform measure one day and new constraints the very next. And they continue to do so to this day.

How Many Political Appointees Is Too Many?

Few questions have haunted civil service reform as thoroughly as the proper balance between political and career appointees. There is simply no way of knowing how many is too many, creating a new round of confusion every time a new agency is established or a new commission is formed to address the state of the public service.

Consider the Volcker Commission as but one example. Composed in 1987 to address the perceived crisis in the public service, the thirty-six commissioners clearly agreed that there were too many appointees in government. Indeed, few of the commission's conclusions were as strongly supported. "Presidents today are further away from the top career layers of government with 3,000 appointees," argued the final report, "than was Franklin Roosevelt 50 years ago with barely 200" (National Commission on the Public Service 1989:17).

Yet, when it came time to recommend a specific lower number, the commission could find no calculus for reduction.[7] The best the commission could do was recommend that the growth of presidential appointees be curtailed: "Although a reduction in the total number of presidential appointees must be based on a position-by-position assessment, the Commission is confident that a substantial cut is possible, and believes that a cut from the current 3,000 to no more than 2,000 is a reasonable target" (ibid.:18).

The commission was hardly the first to encounter the difficulty of setting an appropriate target, however. To this date, no one knows how much politicization is too much. What is known is that the number of political appointees has grown steadily since passage of the CSRA, while the number of senior career slots has declined. Table 19

Table 19. Growth in Career and Noncareer Appointees, 1980–1990

Type of Appointee	1980		1990		Percentage Change, 1980–1990
	Number	Percentage of Total	Number	Percentage of Total	
Presidential appointee	488	5.5	557	6.1	14
Noncareer SES	582	6.5	675	7.4	16
Schedule C appointment	1,456	16.4	1,700	18.6	17
Career SES	6,379	71.6	6,190	67.9	−03

SOURCE: 1990 figures are drawn from monthly OPM reports.

supports the overall conclusion, showing the numbers of presidential executive schedule appointees, career and noncareer senior executives, and schedule C personal and confidential assistants from the first full year of the CSRA, fiscal year 1980, with the tenth year.

Some readers will note that the number of political executives in table 19 differs somewhat from the data presented by Kirke Harper in chapter 12. The explanation is quite simple. Harper's data are from September 1989, still in the first year of the Bush administration, and would be expected to be low given the long start-up of the president's personnel operation. By summer 1990, most of the Bush noncareer positions had been filled.

Beyond sorting out the respective numbers—filled versus allocated positions career versus noncareer—the question becomes one of degree. In the grand scheme of a 2.2-million-employee federal government, what difference could a few more political appointees make? A first answer depends upon the unit of analysis. If the unit is the federal government, then surely a few hundred political appointees will not matter, an argument made by many in the Reagan White House and OPM. If, however, the unit is the secretary's conference room, not the department parking lot, a few hundred appointees can make a very great difference, crowding out career appointees from critical policy debates and ultimately depriving the president of a needed long-term perspective.

Moreover, as noted in the opening pages of this chapter, the remarkably high level of politicization at OPM itself sends powerful signals to career civil servants. From 1980 to 1983, the years in which Don Devine made his mark as OPM director, the number of presidential executive schedule appointees remained at three, while the number of noncareer SES increased from five to eleven and the number of Schedule C positions jumped from seven to twenty-two, even as total OPM employment fell from 8,280 to 6,369.

Alas, in an era of high turnover of political appointees and growing distrust among career and political appointees, some careerists may see a conflict of interest in a highly politicized agency like OPM setting basic federal personnel policy. Although there was some downward adjustment in Schedule C positions over the next seven years, OPM remains an agency led by a high number of political appointees of one kind or another.[8]

A second answer depends on the value of politicization itself. For many civil servants, politicization is the longest dirty word in the dictionary, but as Terry Moe argues, supporters of a strong institutional presidency may simply be overreacting: "Politicization is deplored for its destructive effects on institutional memory, expertise, professionalism, objectivity, communications, continuity, and other bases of organization competence. Centralization is disparaged for its circumvention of established institutions and its ineffective reliance on an already overburdened White House" (1985:235).

Yet, as Moe argues, the institutional defense ignores the changing structure of incentives in the presidency:

It ignores the potential contributions and centralization to responsiveness, innovation, and other components of presidential leadership. It ignores their demonstrated compatibility with presidential incentives—a crucial property that is the Achilles' heel of standard reform proposals. It ignores the role of institutional memory in transmitting "ephemeral, politicized" structures—for example, for appointments and congressional liaison from one administration to the next. It ignores the necessary trade-offs that presidents are forced to make in seeking a working balance between responsiveness and organization competence. And it ignores the very real threats to presidential leadership capacity that entrenched interests and established organizational routines represent. (Ibid.:269)

Having listened to this very debate for six months at the Volcker Commission, I can attest that politicization remains a puzzle among some of the strongest supporters of the career senior service. None disagrees with the president's right to form a government. This admiration for strong leadership notwithstanding, the heart of the politicization question involves each president's obligation to the next. While the politicization and centralization pressures may be great, each president owes the next a reasonable chance for success. Much as every president may wish to respond to the latest short-term incentives, there is a fragile balance to be maintained.

Unfortunately, no one knows quite where the balance rests. As table 19 suggests, it may be very difficult indeed to tell where politicization begins, particularly given the vast federal enterprise on which this relatively small number of political and career executives sits.

What Are the Baselines Against Which to Measure Reform?

The unresolved debate about political appointees parallels a more general lack of agreement on the baselines against which to judge the success or failure of the CSRA. Consider the range of studies done over the past years as an example of the confusion over how to measure the changing quality of the work force:

- Employee satisfaction surveys
- Analysis of the stated reasons for leaving government among separated employees
- Perceptions of government among Federal Executive Institute alumni and *Government Executive* magazine readers
- Supervisor rankings of employee performance
- Personnel officer assessments of OPM technical assistance and leadership
- Opinions of the public service from graduate school deans, professional headhunters, incoming college students, and student honor society inductees
- Attitudes toward federal service among presidential management interns

As might be expected from such an eclectic blend of research, no one general conclusion emerges regarding the general quality of the civil service, nor of its performance. For a field that can be said to be preoccupied with questions of work force quality, there is a surprising dearth of high-quality research. As the General Accounting Office concluded after looking at work force data at Air Force, EPA, HHS, Interior, Justice, NASA, Navy, and Veterans Affairs:

Review of data now kept at eight agencies showed that information on indicators of workforce quality is limited in comprehensiveness, accessibility, and recency. A few measures of education are maintained in central computer files, but these are not consistently updated. Other indicators of education or work experience are available only on paper records in employees' official personnel folders, which are kept at decentralized personnel offices. Nothing on attitudes or job-skill match appeared consistently or in accessible form. The bulk of data that are accessible and up-to-date pertain to pay and benefits, which do not match the items needed for the [GAO] proposed definition of workforce quality. (U.S. GAO 1988:38)

Lacking such data, supporters of civil service reform have little choice but to turn to the broad cross-agency studies cited above. Unfortunately, few of these surveys meet even the minimum criteria for scientific research. Few have random samples, fewer still ever mention error rates. Indeed, for every carefully designed survey by GAO or the

Merit Systems Protection Board, there appear to be six others so rife with bias that the results cannot be interpreted, let alone added to an existing data base of opinion.

More to the point of this chapter, even assuming the field could agree on methodology, it would still face serious arguments about which questions to ask. Here, too, the measures are in chaos. Thus, on top of the confusion over whom to ask about quality, consider the range of indicators of the state of the civil service:

• Intention to quit; intention to stay
• Perceived delays in hiring and promoting
• Perceived declines in quality and performance
• Perceived unfairness in merit and performance appraisal systems
• Overall employee satisfaction with work
• Amount of challenge in work; fit of skills to the job
• Chance to accomplish something worthwhile
• Willingness to recommend a job in government to friends, children, colleagues, and graduating college students; willingness to "do it again"
• Political appointee satisfaction with careerists; careerist satisfaction with politicals

Not surprisingly, this plethora of questions yields widely varying conclusions on the state of the public service. Even a simple variable like intention to quit, for example, can produce a confused portrait, particularly since intention to quit may commingle with a host of other variables, such as age, to blunt its usefulness as an indicator of dissatisfaction.

In addition, dissatisfaction is not always the exact inverse of satisfaction. Just as individual voters may be Democrats on some issues and Republicans on others, so can civil servants be extremely satisfied with their jobs yet be on the verge of retirement at the first available opportunity. The theoretical challenge, of course, is to specify which indicators matter and when.

Some of the indicators listed above have little or no linkage to actual civil service behavior at all. One's willingness to recommend a job in government to one's children, for example, simply does not translate into any meaningful interpretation of quality, particularly since there is absolutely no agreed upon baseline against which to measure the answers. Should all civil servants recommend the same careers to their children? Would it make any difference if they did? (The very fact that my father pushed me toward law school, for example, was a sure predictor that I would not go.)

The lack of agreement on baseline measurement affects the course of civil service reform in at least three ways. At a first level, it reflects continued confusion about the purpose of reform. It is not altogether clear, for instance, that the reformers intended the CSRA to have any impact on employee satisfaction at all. Instead, the legislative record is replete with a performance orientation. Employee satisfaction and morale were rarely mentioned as goals, while increased productivity and removal of incompetent employees certainly were.

Second, the lack of agreement has produced an almost complete absence of reliable longitudinal data. Without strong research support from OPM itself, scholars are drawn to the topic for one-shot research, often taking important snapshots of the civil service at a given point in time only to move on to other research venues for their next projects. As a result, even the most rigorous one-shot design takes on an almost anecdotal quality, rarely followed up with second and third waves of research. Although there are important exceptions to this rule—including Joel Aberbach and Bert Rockman's longitudinal study of senior executives and James Perry's work on merit pay[9]—the absence of a sustained research focus has left the president and Congress to interpret and reinterpret each succeeding study out of context.

Third, the lack of agreement makes further refinement of the CSRA extremely difficult. How frequent, for example, is the challenge to demonstrate a link between work force morale and actual outcomes? How often do we hear the call for proof that politicization matters in some objective sense? Without stable measures showing such linkage, calls for funding the full promise of the CSRA will fall on a disinterested Congress. Further, without convincing research on quit rates, low rates of civil service turnover will be read as prima facie evidence of employee satisfaction.

Just How Important Is Pay, Anyway?

Ultimately, those who struggled for civil service reform believed that there was more to job motivation than just pay. Civil servants were seen as having the same needs for job enrichment, feedback, performance incentives, and time for reflection as other professionals. In many ways, the CSRA gave senior executives many of the same privileges as tenured academics, including sabbaticals.

To be fair to the legislative drafters, few could have predicted the hyperinflation that came with the oil embargo at the end of the 1970s. Nor could most have foreseen the growing pay gap between public and private jobs—after all, the gap was virtually nonexistent in 1977. Furthermore, under the Federal Salary Reform Act of 1962 and the Federal Pay Comparability Act of 1970, the president already had the power to recommend comparable pay increases if so desired. Surely reformers could not be blamed for failing to foresee twelve straight years of sub-comparable increases, and even freezes, driving a growing wedge between public and private salaries.

This is not to say that federal pay was so outlandish at the time that no one worried about the future. Rather, it was clear from the outset that the CSRA was to be a low-cost, high-return initiative. Facing increasing pressure from Carter to hold down a growing budget deficit (then running a relatively few billion dollars a year), reformers had little money to spend. While there was very little rhetoric regarding overpaid, underworked employees, there was considerable agreement on the need to get more for less.

Looking back to 1978 with perfect hindsight, it seems that supporters of civil service reform might have been better off reserving their political capital for the decade-long fight over pay, reductions in force, and politicization. Instead, they have been forced to fight one skirmish after another defending the particulars of the CSRA along a broad front of attack. Whether, for example, merit pay was worth defending is in some doubt, given Perry's assessment earlier in this volume. Whether bonuses have made much difference is also in doubt.

In contrast, it appears that pay itself matters very much indeed. The decade-long deterioration in federal purchasing power has clearly affected the health of the civil service in at least three ways.

First, pay has a profound effect on the overall climate of federal recruitment and retention. In only the latest in a long series of excellent studies led by Rosalyn Kleeman, director of Federal Workforce Future Issues, the GAO reported that low federal pay was the factor most agency personnel officials report as the reason why employees leave the federal government and why applicants decide not to join. Unfortunately, as the GAO concluded in an all-too-familiar refrain,

The agencies seldom kept systematic records documenting how recruitment and retention difficulties affected their operations. However, respondents commonly said they believed that these difficulties had caused reductions in service delivery and productivity losses. They also described numerous examples of increased training; recruiting; over-time; and, to a lesser extent, contracting costs caused by these difficulties. Thus, while restoring federal pay rates to competitive levels will be costly at first, GAO believes the cost will be offset to some degree by savings and improvements in government operations. GAO also believes those costs are preferable to the further deterioration of government services. (GAO 1990:3)

Second, pay has affected work force confidence in the performance appraisal system. Again, the linkage between pay and perceived unfairness in the system is difficult to document, but exists nonetheless. As the system moved toward zero-sum conflict with clear winners and losers, the failure to provide an adequate pay floor made the meager merit and bonus dollars all the more valuable and the resulting bitterness among the losers more persistent.

Third, pay has clearly altered the very structure of government. By rejecting one pay increase after another, those who railed against top-heavy bureaucracy on the floor of the House and Senate ensured that the structure of government would grow ever taller as managers built new layers for promoting their employees into higher salaries. Alas, the growing height of government has now become an obstacle to recruitment of entry-level employees, who worry that there is no room for advancement. As America's brightest young graduates look upon agencies with thirty or more career steps to the top, who could blame them for concluding that there is no room for advancement? Even here, however, the GAO suggests that better pay might resolve the problem:

Federal pay also helps to explain why federal career advancement opportunities, while viewed as a reason to join government, were also viewed as a significant reason to leave. In those federal jobs where opportunities for advancement beyond the journeyman level are limited (e.g., attorneys and police), employees who are dissatisfied with their pay reportedly leave for equivalent but better paying nonfederal positions. The responses suggest that if the federal/nonfederal pay disparity were eliminated, training and career advancement might properly be featured as virtues of federal employment. (ibid:73)

Many of these pay problems may have been addressed in the recent enactment of locality pay, which allows for differentials based on local cost-of-living measures. Would that the CSRA had contained a locality measure before the twelve-year drought!

A Legislative Epitaph

Overall, the lack of answers to these and other questions had to affect congressional sentiments toward the CSRA when it passed and toward civil service reform today. Perhaps supporters would have taken a different path; perhaps Congress would have reconsidered passage of the Inspector General, Ethics in Government, or Public Disclosure of Lobbying acts. Again, it is not enough to merely focus on the debate within the boundaries of Carter's proposal. What Congress did and did not pass during the 1978 session, indeed during the two decades preceding and following the CSRA, is equally revealing.

It is not that Congress suddenly discovered the executive branch in 1978. Congress was always interested in the details of administration. Rather, facing growing budget constraints by the mid-1970s, Congress began to keep a closer watch on the administrative state, using a host of new legislative devices to ensure executive responsiveness.

Alongside passage of traditional management bills like the Paperwork Reduction Act, which set year-by-year tonnage reduction targets, and the Federal Managers Financial Integrity Act, which required detailed assessments of internal control systems, Congress pioneered the legislative veto as a monitoring device, eventually placing approval or disapproval vetoes in over two hundred statutes. By the early 1980s, Congress had also discovered the merit of deadlines and action-forcing devices. These included dozens of so-called hammers buried in environmental legislation like the Resource Recovery and Conservation Act and citizen activators like the citizen action provisions in the False Claims Act amendments of 1986. After the legislative veto was declared unconstitutional, Congress innovated again, turning to report-and-wait provisions hidden in appropriations bills—my favorite being the requirement that the Veterans Administration report to Congress any reorganization affecting more than 10 percent of the employees in any unit of the agency employing more than twenty-five full-time employees, even though the total work force was almost 250,000 strong.

This is not to forgive the president either, for Reagan brought a new level of inspection and central clearance to virtually every feature of the administrative presidency, from his cradle-to-grave regulatory

review process to the single-minded review of *every* political appointment throughout the executive branch. Rather, the point is that
neither Congress nor the president was willing to release the civil service to fulfill its new freedoms under the CSRA. If the liberation ever
occurred, it was quickly overturned.

NOTES

1. The provision can be found in Title 5, USC, Sec. 4503 (1).

2. For an excellent short history of the Inspector General Act, see Gates and
Knowles (1985).

3. The phrase "from retail into wholesale" comes from one of the key staffers
involved in drafting the legislation, as quoted by Light (forthcoming).

4. These provisions are contained in Sec. 4 (d) and (e), H.R. 2819, introduced
1 February 1977. This bill was subsequently replaced by H.R. 8588, which was
passed into law as the Inspector General Act of 1978.

5. "Congress Ends 'Koreagate' Lobbying Probe," *CQ Almanac*, 1978, p. 803.

6. This summary is drawn from "Senate Inaction Kills Lobby Reform Bill," *CQ
Almanac*, 1978, pp. 782–87.

7. I was appointed senior advisor to the commission upon the untimely death
of the original deputy director, Charles Levine, and was ultimately responsible for
the commission's final draft report.

8. In contrast, agencies like NASA, the Bureau of Prisons, Census Bureau, Bureau of Labor Statistics, and the armed services make do with remarkably low
numbers of political appointees.

9. See, for example, Aberbach and Rockman (1988); see also chapter 9 in
this volume.

SOURCES

Aberbach, Joel, and Bert Rockman. 1988. "Mandates or Mandarins: Control and
Discretion in the Modern Administrative State." *Public Administration Review*
48 (March/April): 606–12.

Aberbach, Joel, and Bert Rockman. 1990. *Recruitment and Retention: Inadequate
Pay Cited as Primary Problem by Agency Officials*. GAO/GGD-90-117.

Carter, Jimmy. 1978. In *Weekly Compilation of Presidential Documents* 14. 2 March.

Gates, Margaret J., and Marjorie Fine Knowles. 1985. "The Inspector General Act
in the Federal Government: A New Approach to Accountability." *Alabama
Law Review* 36 (Winter): 473–514.

Light, Paul. 1987. "When Worlds Collide: The Political-Career Nexus." In *The In-
and-Outers: Presidential Appointees and Transient Government in Washington*.
Baltimore: Johns Hopkins University Press.

————. Forthcoming. *Monitoring Government: The Inspectors General and the Search
for Accountability*. Washington, D.C.: The Governance Institute/Brookings.

Loomis, Burdette, 1988. *The New American Politician: Ambition, Entrepreneurship, and the Changing Face of Political Life*. New York: Basic Books.

Mackenzie, G. Calvin. 1987. " 'If You Want to Play, You've Got to Pay': Ethics Regulation and the Presidential Appointments System, 1964–1984."
In *The In-and-Outers: Presidential Appointees and Transient Government in Washington*. Baltimore: Johns Hopkins University Press.

———. 1990. "Appointing Mr. (or Ms.) Right." *Government Executive* 22 (April).

Moe, Terry. 1985. "The Politicized Presidency." In *New Directions in American Politics*, ed. J. Chubb and P. Peterson. Washington, D.C.: Brookings.

National Commission on the Public Service (Volcker Commission). 1989. *Leadership for America*. Washington, D.C.

Ornstein, Norman, Thomas Mann, and Michael Malbin. 1990. *Vital Statistics on Congress 1989–1990*. Washington, D.C.: American Enterprise Institute, Congressional Quarterly Press.

U.S. GAO (General Accounting Office). 1987. *Federal Employees: Trends in Career and Noncareer Employee Appointments in the Executive Branch*. Washington, D.C.

———. 1988. *Federal Workforce: A Framework for Studying Its Quality Over Time*. GAO/PEMD-88-27.

Notes on Contributors

Carolyn Ban is Associate Professor of Public Administration and Policy, Rockefeller College, the State University of New York, Albany. She has written extensively on issues relating to civil service reform and is coeditor of *Public Personnel Management: Current Concerns, Future Challenges.*

John Halligan is Director of the Centre for Research in Public Sector Management and Senior Lecturer in Public Administration at the University of Canberra. He is Convenor of the Master of Public Administration Program and Review Editor for the *Australian Journal of Public Administration.* He has co-edited *Local Government Systems of Australia, Australian Urban Politics, Hawke's Third Government: Essays in Commonwealth Administration 1987–1990;* and co-authored *Political Management in the 1990s,* and *Leadership in an Age of Constraint: The Australian Experience.*

Kirke Harper is Deputy Director of the Human Resources Development Group at the U.S. Office of Personnel Management, where his responsibilities include overseeing the Senior Executive Service, establishing governmentwide policy on personnel training and development, and supervising implementation of the Intergovernmental Personnel Act. He previously served with the Bureau of the Budget and the Office of Management of Budget, the Environmental Protection Agency, and the Consumer Product Safety Commission.

Mark W. Huddleston is Associate Professor of Political Science at the University of Delaware. He is the author of *Comparative Public Administration* and *The Public Administration Workbook,* and has written extensively on the Senior Executive Service. He is currently working on a book on the history of the U.S. higher civil service.

Patricia Wallace Ingraham is Professor of Public Administration and Political Science at the Maxwell School of Citizenship and Public Affairs, Syracuse University. As Project Director of the Task Force of Recruitment and Retention for the National Commission on the Public Service (the Volcker Commission), she wrote the Task Force's Report. She was a member of the National Academy of Science Committee on Performance Appraisal for Merit Pay and of the Office of Personnel Management Task Forces on Education and Training of the Federal Workforce and Quality of the Federal Workforce. She was book review editor for the *Public Administration Review* and serves on the editorial board of several journals. She co-edited *Legislating Bureaucratic Change: The Civil Service Reform Act of 1978* and *An Agenda for Excellence: The American Public Service.*

J. Edward Kellough is Assistant Professor of Political Science at the University of Georgia, where he teaches in the graduate programs in public administration. His research interests are primarily in the field of public personnel management and he has published articles in *Public Administration Review*, the *American Review of Public Administration, Social Science Quarterly,* and the *Review of Public Personnel Administration*. He is the author of *Federal Equal Employment Opportunity Policy and Numerical Goals and Timetables* (1989).

Larry M. Lane is currently Assistant Professor of Management at the American University. He was recently an adjunct professor of public administration at Virginia Tech and at Troy State University. He was a charter member of the federal Senior Executive Service and was Deputy Director of Personnel for the Department of the Interior. He writes frequently on public service issues and is co-author, with James F. Wolf, of *The Human Resource Crisis in the Public Sector: Rebuilding the Capacity to Govern.*

Paul C. Light is Professor of Public Affairs and Planning at the Humphrey Institute at the University of Minnesota. He has taught government and public policy at the University of Virginia, was an American Political Science Association Congressional Fellow in 1982–1983, a guest scholar at the Brookings Institution, and director of studies at the National Academy of Public Administration. From 1987 to 1989 he was special advisor to the Senate Governmental Affairs Committee. He is the author of *The President's Agenda: Domestic Policy Choice from Kennedy to Carter* (1982, rev. 1991); *Vice Presidential Power: Advice and Influence in the White House* (1983); *Artful Work: the Politics of Social Security Reform* (1985); *Baby Boomers: A Political and Social Reappraisal* (1988); *Forging Legislation* (1992); and *Monitoring Government* (1993).

Chester A. Newland is Professor of Public Administration, University of Southern California, Sacramento and Washington, D.C. He managed the Labor-Management Relations Task Force that worked on the Civil Service Reform Act of 1978 and was twice director of the Federal Executive Institute. He was editor of the *Public Administration Review*. He is a past president of the American Society for Public Administration, a member of the National Academy of Public Administration, and an honorary member of the International City Management Association. He received the Stockberger Award of the International Personnel Management Association and the Elmer Staats Award of the National Association of Schools of Public Affairs and Administration.

James Perry is Professor of Public and Environmental Affairs and Political Science at Indiana University, Bloomington. He has published work on public management and personnel administration in the *Academy of Management Journal, Academy of Management Review, Administrative Science Quarterly, American Political Science Review,* and *Public Administration Review*. He has coauthored or edited four books, including the *Handbook of Public Administration* (1989).

He received the Yoder-Heneman Award for innovative research from the American Society for Personnel Administration and the Charles H. Levine Award for Excellence in Public Administration from the American Society for Public Administration and the National Association of Schools of Public Affairs and Administration.

Beryl A. Radin is Professor of Public Administration at the Washington Public Affairs Center of the University of Southern California. Her major research and teaching interests focus on the implementation of national policies in a complex, federal system. She has published many books and articles dealing with education policy, human services policy and administration, federal management, and advice giving. Professor Radin has been a consultant to a number of federal agencies, including the Office of Management and Budget, NASA, the Social Security Administration and the Office of the Assistant Secretary for Planning and Evaluation in the Department of Health and Human Services.

John A. Rohr is Professor of Public Administration at Virginia Polytechnic Institute. His principal areas of interest are questions of ethics and of constitutionalism in public administration. His books include *To Run A Constitution: The Legitimacy of the Administrative State* (1986); *Ethics for Bureaucrats: An Essay on Law and Values,* 2d ed. (1989); *The President and the Public Administration* (1989).

David H. Rosenbloom is Distinguished Professor of Public Administration in the School of Public Affairs at American University. His research focuses on the politics, law, personnel, and intellectual history of public administration. Professor Rosenbloom is currently Editor-in-Chief of *Public Administration Review.* In 1992, he received the Distinguished Research Award of the National Association of Schools of Public Affairs and Administration and the American Society for Public Administration. Among his books are *Federal Service and the Constitution* (1971); *Federal Equal Employment Opportunity* (1977); *Public Administration and Law* (1983); and *Public Administration: Understanding Management, Politics, and Law in the Public Sector,* 2d ed. (1989).

Robert Vaughn is an Allen King Scholar and Professor of Law at the Washington College of Law at American University. His books include *The Merit Systems Protection Board: Rights and Remedies.* He has also published many articles on various public employment law topics, including protection of whistleblowers, the right of public employees to disobey illegal orders, disciplinary procedures, preferences in public employment, ethics regulation, and comparisons with public employment law in other countries. In addition, Professor Vaughn has published widely on public information law and policy. Until recently, he was a member of the American Bar Association's Special Committee on Lawyers in Government.

The Impact of Policy Analysis
James M. Rogers

Iran and the United States: A Cold War Case Study
Richard W. Cottam

Japanese Prefectures and Policymaking
Steven R. Reed

Making Regulatory Policy
Keith Hawkins and John M. Thomas, Editors

Managing the Presidency: Carter, Reagan, and the Search for Executive Harmony
Colin Campbell, S.J.

The Moral Dimensions of Public Policy Choice: Beyond the Market Paradigm
John Martin Gillroy and Maurice Wade, Editors

Native Americans and Public Policy
Fremont J. Lyden and Lyman H. Legters, Editors

Organizing Governance, Governing Organizations
Colin Campbell, S.J., and B. Guy Peters, Editors

Party Organizations in American Politics
Cornelius P. Cotter et al.

Perceptions and Behavior in Soviet Foreign Policy
Richard K. Herrmann

Pesticides and Politics: The Life Cycle of a Public Issue
Christopher J. Bosso

Policy Analysis by Design
Davis B. Bobrow and John S. Dryzek

The Political Failure of Employment Policy, 1945–1982
Gary Mucciaroni

Political Leadership: A Source Book
Barbara Kellerman, Editor

Tage Erlander: Serving the Welfare State, 1946–1969
Olof Ruin

Traffic Safety Reform in the United States and Great Britain
Jerome S. Legge, Jr.

Urban Alternatives: Public and Private Markets in the Provision of Local Services
Robert M. Stein

The U.S. Experiment in Social Medicine: The Community Health Center Program, 1965–1986
Alice Sardell